Other books on Africa by the same author

REPORT ON SOUTHERN AFRICA

THE AFRICAN AWAKENING

THE LOST CITIES OF AFRICA

THE AFRICAN PAST

The African Slave Trade

PRECOLONIAL HISTORY 1450-1850

THE AFRICAN SLAVE TRADE

Precolonial History 1450-1850

BASIL DAVIDSON

Published in the hardcover edition as BLACK MOTHER

an atlantic monthly press book
little, brown and company
boston / toronto

COPYRIGHT © 1961 BY BASIL DAVIDSON

ALL RIGHTS RESERVED. NO PART OF THIS BOOK MAY BE REPRODUCED IN ANY FORM OR BY ANY ELECTRONIC OR MECHANICAL MEANS INCLUDING INFORMATION STORAGE AND RETRIEVAL SYSTEMS WITHOUT PERMISSION IN WRITING FROM THE PUBLISHER, EXCEPT BY A REVIEWER WHO MAY QUOTE BRIEF PASSAGES IN A REVIEW.

LIBRARY OF CONGRESS CATALOG CARD NO. 61-13894

0401905 E2

L

ATLANTIC–LITTLE, BROWN BOOKS
ARE PUBLISHED BY
LITTLE, BROWN AND COMPANY
IN ASSOCIATION WITH
THE ATLANTIC MONTHLY PRESS

BP

PRINTED IN THE UNITED STATES OF AMERICA

To the Memory of
WILLIAM ADLINGTON CADBURY
February 17, 1867 — July 8, 1957

Only the wholly other can inspire the deepest love and the profoundest desire to learn.

JOSEPH NEEDHAM

Author's Note

AFRICAN INDEPENDENCE IS ONE OF THE GREAT FACTS OF THE MODern world. Yet Africa was also independent in the past. African states had many and varied links of alliance and commercial partnership with Europe for several hundred years before the colonial period began.

This book is about the course and consequences of this long African-European connection that endured from the fifteenth century to the nineteenth. It makes an answer to three vital questions: What kind of contact was this with Europe and America? How did the experience affect Africa? Why did it end in colonial invasion and conquest?

As with its predecessor, *The Lost Cities of Africa*, the aim of this book is to reassess the past of Africa, and thus contribute to a fuller understanding of the independent Africa of today.

Introduction

Black Mother

NEARLY FIVE HUNDRED YEARS HAVE PASSED SINCE EUROPE AND AFrica — continental Africa, the land of the blacks — first made acquaintance and began their trading intercourse.

After this early discovery of one another, Africans and Europeans knew four centuries of varied friendship and hostility, good and evil, profit and loss; and the fortunes of Africa and Europe, through all these years, were caught and woven ever more tightly together. Then came the onset of European conquest and now, in our own day, an end to the colonial system and the rise of independent Africa. And so the cycle is rounded and complete. The relations of equality and self-respect that were known in the early years of this long connection are reforged or are once again in the making.

But why did history take this course? Why was European conquest so much delayed; and why, after that delay and the often lengthy experience of one another, did so large a part of Africa collapse into rapid and unrelieved subjection to Europe? We know that the Spanish occupied Central America; the Portuguese seized Brazil; the French and British spread across the seaboard lands of North America; and all of them flew conquering flags in the Eastern world. Yet Africa, except for small footholds here and there, remained inviolate until the nineteenth century. Then, almost from one decade to the next, wide areas of Africa became colonies of Europe.

One can ask the question in other ways. Why did Europe tremendously expand and grow in power and wealth, while Africa failed to do the same? How was it that early European captains

Introduction

and their backers could treat Africans with the respect that was due to equals, and yet a later world, setting this aside or else forgetting it altogether, could regard Africans as naturally inferior?

Some of the answers lie in purely European history. They can be found in a thousand books, telling the story of commercial growth, industrial revolution, empire, and expansion. But other answers lie in Africa. And of these, I think, the most potent and illuminating are provided by the curious tale of Europe's dealings with Africa, and Africa's with Europe, in the period between the middle of the fifteenth and the middle of the nineteenth centuries — between, let us say, 1450 and 1850.

This book is therefore an attempt to explain the nature of the European-African connection in precolonial times, and its peculiar and special impact on Africa. No such attempt can hope to be definitive at this early stage in the recovery and rediscovery of African history; nor could it ever be comprehensive within the limits of one short book. Yet something useful can be done, it seems to me, even within these limits. So I have taken three important areas of Africa — those of the old Congo kingdoms, of the city-states of the East Coast, and of some of the strong societies of the Guinea Coast — and examined these against a general background of their time and circumstance.

Inevitably, this means a fresh look at the oversea slave trade, the steady year-by-year export of African labor to the West Indies and the Americas that marked the greatest and most fateful migration — forced migration — in the history of man. Many writers have investigated the European and American side of the slaving experience, but little or nothing has been written on the consequences of the slave trade for Africa itself. Yet slaving rapidly engulfed the whole connection. Its influence bore heavily, perhaps decisively, on the destiny of many African societies. Nothing in their history during these centuries can be understood without a cool appraisal of

Introduction

the slaving impact. What I have tried to offer here, accordingly, is an unsentimental inquiry into some characteristic aspects of African history in several regions where slaving was of major importance.

One comes up at once against a difficulty. The records are copious, but mainly they are European records and they are colored indelibly by the myth and prejudice which the trade itself did so much to promote. Through long years the "Black Mother" of Africa would populate the Americas with millions of her sons and daughters, and Europe would pile up libraries of comment on the nature of these victims and of the Africa that could yield them. But where in the multitude of these opinions — philanthropic or cynical, sincere, self-interested, or merely superstitious — can one safely draw the line between illusion and reality? Perhaps it is only now, when the bitter memories of slaving are assuaged by time, when the old servitudes of Africa are dispelled by a new freedom, and when there is no longer any point in the beating of breasts or the apportioning of blame, that one can usefully look for the truth of those astounding years.

But to set the scene and indicate its special flavor — so vigorous and obstinately hopeful in spite of all its misery and death — let us begin with some contrasts.

There was misery, unending misery. There was so much death in the Americas that whole slave populations had to be renewed every few years. The records are eloquent enough. . . .

In 1829 an Englishman called Walsh took passage from Brazil in a British frigate, the *North Star*. Somewhere in the South Atlantic they chased and stopped a slaver. Walsh went on board and afterwards described what he saw — the familiar horrors of the Middle Passage. The slaving ship's cargo was of five hundred and five men and women — the crew had thrown fifty-five overboard during their seventeen days at sea — and these slaves "were all enclosed under grated hatchways, between decks. The space was so low that they sat between each others' legs, and stowed so close together, that there was no possibility of lying down, or at all changing their position, by night or by day. As they belonged to, and were shipped on account of different individuals, they were all branded like sheep, with the owners' marks of different forms. These were impressed under their breasts, or on their arms, and, as the mate informed me with perfect indifference, burnt with a red hot iron. . . ."

Many of these branded chattels, Walsh found, had no more than one square foot of sitting space, with no chance of standing up, and all suffered from a deadly shortage of water. Walsh was shocked, but his naval companions, "who had passed so long a time on the coast of Africa, and visited so many ships" in the course of their antislaving patrols, said that this slaver was "one of the best they had seen." Headroom for slaves was as much as three feet three inches, whereas sometimes, Walsh was told, headroom was no more than eighteen inches; and slaves were generally chained, as these were not, by the neck and legs during their crossing of the Atlantic.

Such scenes were frequent. They had occurred month after month for nearly three hundred years by the time that Walsh took passage from Brazil. This was the physical degradation of the trade.

There was also a moral degradation — both of the slaves and of the slavers. Through enslaving Africans, Europeans abused their own humanity as well. They came to believe that Africa was indeed cast away in savage chaos, that Africans had never known any reasonable social order of their own, and that African slaves deserved no better than they got. The slavers justified their work by such beliefs.

Introduction

"Africans being the most lascivious of all human beings," declared a Liverpool pamphlet of 1792, "may it not be imagined, that the cries they let forth at being torn from their wives, proceed from the dread that they will never have the opportunity of indulging their passions in the country to which they are embarking?"

Often the arguments were less coarse and brutal. Sometimes they verged on the "scientific." Writing of the Guinea Coast in the late eighteenth century, a German named Soemmering observed that the people there "are more insensible than others towards pain and natural evils, as well as toward injurious and unjust treatment. In short, there are none so well adapted to be the slaves of others, and who therefore have been armed with so much passive obedience."

What could be the value of such captive trash? The spirit of the times awarded them no value; even the achievements of their toil and sweat were denied them. African slaves had fertilized great regions of the New World by the nineteenth century, but their part in all this was ignored or forgotten. "Before the West Indies could grow a pumpkin for any Negro," Thomas Carlyle was declaring, and without irony, in 1849, "how much European heroism had to spend itself in obscure battle; to sink, in mortal agony, before the jungles, the putrescences and waste savageries could become arable, and the Devils be in some measure chained up!" Thus was history stood upon its head.

There was another side to the story: surprisingly, one of hope and courage and survival. Here too the records are eloquent.

Consider the epic, or such as is known of it, of Jacintha de Siqueira, a woman of Brazil. Brief but intriguing fragments of her biography were collected by Luis Pinto, a diligent clerk of the inland province of Minas Gerais. Gilberto Freyre has presented them

Introduction

in his famous book about Brazilian beginnings, *The Masters and the Slaves*.

Pinto was an obscure archivist whose task was the ordering and arrangement of official papers in a small Brazilian town. Yet Pinto was also something of a local historian. He enlivened his daily round by collecting facts about the early settlers of his province; and these facts were anything but dull and dreary, for the province of Minas had lately been — indeed, still was — the wild *sertão*, the lawless badlands of the far interior that settlers along the Brazilian coast held cautiously in awe. Even today the men and women who trekked inland to the conquest and settlement of the *sertão* are famous in memory as bold heroes, flaming and flamboyant in their grip on life, turbulent and reckless, enterprising and ambitious.

These pioneers pressed inland from the coast in small companies, *bandeiras*, that were soon legendary in the seaports and plantations for their courage and endurance. They climbed to the unknown hills with their pack-mules and pack-horses wending up behind them — perhaps a dozen or twenty men and women in leather jerkins and trousers or long cotton gowns and wide-brimmed hats of straw, with red and blue and yellow blankets rolled tight at their saddles or wound upon their shoulders against the upland wind, flourishing their whips, the muzzles of their strange old guns like clumsy banners prodding the South American sky. It was they who took the challenge of this new country and opened up the mineral-rich interior.

Few saw them go, for among these *bandeirantes* were many on the run from slave plantations. Once clear of the coast-long tyranny, they made their own law, as other pioneers would do on other frontiers. This unwritten law was as strong as armed daring could enforce or care to enforce. Some of it had to do with the taking of the land and the enslavement of Indians. Some of it was concerned with the staking out of mining claims or the establishment of tented camps. However much they might prey on one another, these *bandeirantes* were not bandits but intending settlers.

Their aim was to build a new life for themselves beyond the reach of colonial law, and to search for the gold and silver, diamonds and emeralds that were said to lie in this fabulous but utterly unknown *sertão*; and to these ambitions they brought, each of them, whatever skills and knowledge they might have. When they were fortunate, they built their camps into towns; some of these towns are the cities of modern Brazil. They married or took mistresses and begat as many children as might be, brown and black and white and all the shades between; among these children were many who became the active makers of the Brazil we know today.

So it was that the memoirs gathered by Luis Pinto or others like him, and put together by their inquisitive forgotten hands, were the tales of a frontier folk of unusual daring and accomplishment. They were the gossip of a thousand meetings and disputes, squalid or amazing, which come about when a land is settled and a nation is born.

Somewhere around the year 1700, records Pinto, a company of pioneers of this sort departed on the inland trail from the port of Bahia — Bahia of All the Saints, greatest of the ports of old Brazil — and made their way into the remote wilderness that would one day be the province of Minas Gerais. They were, says Pinto, "various *bandeirantes*." Among them was Jacintha de Siqueira.

Jacintha became famous. To her "is due the credit for the discovery of gold in the Quatro Vintens ravine and the founding of the settlement of Villa Nova do Principe in 1714." To her, as well, is due the credit of founding not one family, but many families. Women were few and the land cried out for settlement. "The fathers of all the sons of Jacintha de Siqueira were rich and important individuals," says the record, "and many of them were prominent in the government."

Introduction

What manner of woman was Jacintha, this founding mother of the richest of all the provinces of Brazil? Pinto offers one fundamental fact: he calls her "the celebrated African woman." Jacintha, that is to say, was a woman either brought in slavery from Africa or born into slavery in Brazil. She would have had her origins somewhere on the Guinea Coast or in Angola — a woman, one may well imagine, of large and splendid frame, strong and confident, tough in mind and morals — just such a woman as any traveler will meet today, without much searching, in the villages and towns of western Africa.

This Jacintha, founder of Villa Nova do Principe, was typical, in being an African, of many of the *bandeirantes* who settled the interior. It is because of this that the settlement of inland Brazil (as of some other parts of Central and South America) has left a unique and often astonishing body of evidence on the kind of men and women these African slaves really were, and on the nature of the African cultures from which they came.

Here in their regained freedom these Negroes applied the skills and knowledge they had brought from their homeland. Already, as workers in the coast-long plantations, they had made a success of cultivation under climatic conditions that were new to their European masters, but not to them. Now in the interior they applied their arts of cattle-breeding, learned in the African savannahs, and their old skills in mining for metal and in smelting ore and in forging tools. Strange though it may seem, it was the Africans — whether bond or free — who often led the way.

In 1818, a Swedish engineer, von Eschwege, lately returned from service in Brazil, published a book of memoirs. "The Captaincy of Minas Gerais," he observes, "seems to have been the last in which the usability of iron ore and the extraction of iron was learnt from African negro slaves." The equipment used by these Africans in-

Introduction

cluded the small furnace and the hand-blown bellows that were the traditional equipment of Africa.

"The search for gold in the Brazilian highlands," comments Lowrie, "depended largely upon Negro labour, and the mineral industries of colonial Colombia would have been impossible without Negro slaves." Roberto Simonsen, in a standard work, has estimated the total number of Negroes employed in Brazilian mining throughout the eighteenth century as not fewer than six hundred thousand men. Even as late as 1856, Ewbank could note in Rio de Janeiro that "the modes of working copper are very similar to ours. . . . In one shop twenty blacks were at work, and not a white face among the blacks." Yet for the most part these skills had not been learned from Europeans; they had come with the slaving ships from Africa.

One could multiply the evidence. What went for metals was also true for precious stones. The very folk customs of the country proved it. "When a Negro is so fortunate as to find a diamond of the weight of an octavo (17½ carats), much ceremony takes place; he is crowned with a wreath of flowers and carried in procession to the administrator, who gives him his freedom, by paying his owner for it. He also receives a present of new clothes, and is permitted to work on his own account. . . ."

Negroes were thus the "technological element" in early Brazilian society. "I have now seen," Ewbank wrote in the middle of the nineteenth century, "slaves working as carpenters, masons, pavers, printers, sign and ornamental painters, carriage and cabinet workers, fabricators of military ornaments, lamp-makers, silversmiths, jewellers and lithographers." No fewer than a million African slaves labored in the Brazilian sugar plantations toward the end of the eighteenth century; but as well as providing field work, Negroes also provided the arts and crafts and the foundations of Brazilian industry. They tilled and bred cattle and mined and gathered wealth for others if not for themselves. Far from showing "passive obedience," they rebelled time and again. They built free republics of their own. They added their own culture to the cultures of Europe and of aboriginal South America, for along with their strength and experience they had brought with them their songs and superstitions and their gods. They were, Freyre says, "an active, creative and, one might almost add, a noble element in the colonisation of Brazil."

An astounding contrast . . . that glimpse of human cattle in the slaving ships compared with this other scene of bold and skillful pioneering. But it is also, I hope, a useful introduction to what follows here, for it suggests how widely the reputation of peoples can stand apart from their true ability.

Many African peoples escaped the oversea slave trade and even the overland slave trade. Anthropologists and historians are able to give an increasingly clear account of them, since much of their traditional culture survived into recent years. But many other African peoples failed to escape the trade, and some were overwhelmed by it. Even for those who were able to fight off its worst effects the trade grew often into a dominant influence on their life and development or failure of development. And it is precisely of these populations, coastal and near-coastal for the larger part, that the Europeans' records mainly tell; slaving became the main regulator of their lives. But slaving also became, as a matter of fact or a matter of myth, the great conditioning factor of most European ideas about Africa; and this is where myth and fact about Africans have become most confounded.

Modern research has made it possible to distinguish more closely between illusion and reality. The trade now dwindles to its true proportions and may be seen for what it was, an episode in African

Introduction

history, though a major episode that was huge in its consequences. This remains a complicated story. But the plan of this book, at any rate, is simple. To place the European-African connection in its historical perspective, it is first of all necessary, even at the risk of being briefly tedious, to consider how matters stood in Africa before the trade got into its stride, and how far the structure of leading states in Africa differed from that of contemporary states in Europe. This is the aim of Part One.

Then what were the course and growth of the trade, why did it rely so enormously on slaving, and how did it end? That is the subject of Part Two, "The Years of Trial." Part Three fills in this outline with some of the vivid and densely personal experience of the old trading partnership, its manners and morals, attitudes, customs, and ambitions.

But how did all this affect Africa? Here is the main question of my book. In answering it, Parts Four, Five, and Six are concerned with three regions that were renowned during the trade, and where the coming of Europe had profound and often decisive influence on Africans, on the way they lived, and on what they believed or hoped of the outside world. Part Seven, finally, offers some general thoughts and conclusions on this epoch in African history.

Contents

Introduction	BLACK MOTHER	xiii
ONE	FACT AND FABLE	1
	1 *Before the Trade Began*	3
	2 *The Old States of Africa*	8
	3 *Similarities*	11
	4 *Slaves and Slaving*	21
	5 *Differences*	25
TWO	THE YEARS OF TRIAL	31
	1 *At First a Trickle*	33
	2 *Gold and Elephants' Teeth*	40
	3 *And Then a Flood*	45
	4 *Battle for the Coast*	53
	5 *The Trade Pays Off*	60
	6 *Abolition*	68
THREE	MANNER OF THE TRADE	77
	1 *How Many?*	79
	2 *The System Installed*	81
	3 *Rules and Customs*	87

Contents

    4 *Attitudes and Opinions*   96
    5 *Where Did They Come From?*   102
    6 *Three Regions*   108

FOUR   MANI-CONGO   115

    1 *Discovery*   117
    2 *Royal Brothers*   120
    3 *Congo, Ngola, Matamba*   129
    4 *Law and Order*   135
    5 *From Alliance to Invasion*   144
    6 *Root of the Evil*   153

FIVE   EAST COAST FORTUNES   163

    1 *A Riddle at Kilwa*   165
    2 *Cities of the Seaboard*   168
    3 *The Vital Contrast*   179
    4 *In the Wake of the Storm*   185
    5 *When You Pipe at Zanzibar . . .*   191

SIX   FRONTIER OF OPPORTUNITY   197

    1 *Like Nothing Else . . .*   199
    2 *The People of the Salt Water*   205
    3 *"Children of God"*   210
    4 *Partners in Trade*   214
    5 *Behind the Coast*   224
    6 *Disaster at Benin*   229
    7 *One Gun: One Slave*   238
    8 *Ashanti: The New Battle for the Coast*   246
    9 *The Partnership Cracks*   255
   10 *Men like Ja Ja: The Last Phase*   260

Contents

SEVEN	FOUR CENTURIES: A SUMMING-UP	271
	An End and a Beginning	273
Acknowledgments		291
Bibliography		293
Index		305

one

Fact and Fable

Lang heff I maed of ladyes quhytt,
  Nou of ane blak I will indytt,
That landet furth of the last schippis;
  Quhou fain wald I descryve perfytt,
My ladye with the mekle lippis.
                    William Dunbar

1 Before the Trade Began

EUROPEAN IDEAS ABOUT AFRICA, BEFORE THE YEARS OF DISCOVERY, varied remarkably with time and place. In southern Europe, face to face with North African power and commerce, there was beginning to be a good deal of solid information by the year 1500. Some knowledge of the scope and wealth of the lands beyond the Sahara was getting through to influential men. Yet even the well-informed ports of the Mediterranean could yield extraordinary fluctuations of judgment; and the facts they had to go on were encased, all too often, in a lavish covering of superstitious legend.

Much of this legend was learned from the Moors — Berbers and Arabs of the Moorish states of North Africa. Seldom could Christians penetrate the African interior, and only a handful of those who did have left any trace in the records. The earliest known European traveler's memoir from "inner Africa" — and it would stand alone for many years to come — dates from 1447, and was written by an Italian called Antonio Malfante in Tuat, an oasis of the northern Sahara. Tuat in those days was an important staging-post for trans-Saharan caravans which had come from the south with African slaves, whether as victims or as porters, since times beyond recall.

Malfante picked up the caravan gossip of Tuat, and already it was rich with strange misunderstandings. He explains to a friend in Genoa that to the south of Tuat and the Great Desert there are black peoples who have "innumerable great cities and territories." But these peoples of the south "are in carnal acts like the beasts: the father has knowledge of his daughter, the son of his sister. They breed greatly, for a woman bears up to five at a birth. Nor can it be doubted that they are eaters of human flesh." Already the image of Black Africa is beginning to be the image of Caliban.

Elsewhere in Europe, especially in northern Europe, where the trade with Africa was virtually unknown, opinions could be interestingly different. Northern Europe might understand Africa no more than Africa understood northern Europe: "Scotland," an Andalusian Arab writer had declared in 1154, "has neither dwellings, nor towns, nor villages." Yet even in remote Scotland a little was beginning to be known and thought of Africa by late medieval times; and the Scots, by the early years of the sixteenth century, had even welcomed a few visitors from Africa. Such rare "travelers" were evidently men and women taken out of Portuguese slaving ships by Scottish privateers. One or two of these visitors from the far south became famous in Edinburgh society, and not the least of these was that "black lady with the fulsome lips" of whom, in about 1460, the poet Dunbar wrote some memorable verses.

This black lady had her moment of fame. The occasion was a royal jousting at Edinburgh in 1508 or perhaps 1509 — "the justing of the wild knycht for the black ladye." Fourteen men, it is recorded, carried her from Edinburgh Castle, where she was lodged, to the "barres and syne to the Abbey." The "wild knight" who was the challenger seems to have been a Frenchman; but it was the king himself, brawny James IV, who carried off the day and the prize. It was just as well for James that he acquitted himself well because the award for valor was as enviable as the penalty for cowardice was not. At least, according to Dunbar:

> Quhai for hir saik, with speir and scheld,
> Preiffis maist mychtele in the feld
>   Sall kiss, and withe her go to grippis;
> And fra thyne furth his luff sall weld
>   My ladye with the mekle lippis.

Before the Trade Began

The gallant who stained his knightly name had less to hope for:

> And quhai in feld receawes schame,
> And tynis thair his knychtlie name,
> Sall cum behind and kiss her hippis,
> And neivir to other comfort claime:
> My ladye with the mekle lippis.

The times were broad, but at any rate they were not condescending.

And if European attitudes toward Africans in those early times displayed a wide range of contrast, they were generally uniform in one important respect. They supposed no natural inferiority in Africans, no inherent failure to develop and mature. That was to be the great myth of later years: the central myth of European expansion that first took shape on the deck of a slaving ship. Race contempt crept in when free men could justify their material interests by the scorn they had for slaves — for men, that is, to whom an unnatural inferiority had given every appearance of a natural inferiority. How otherwise would so intelligent a man as Thomas Jefferson have reached the conclusions that he did?

"Comparing them [Negroes in North America] by their faculties of memory, reason and imagination," Jefferson was writing after more than a century of intensive slaving had passed by, "it appears to me that in memory they are equal to the whites; in reason much inferior, as I think one could scarcely be found capable of tracing and comprehending the investigations of Euclid; and that in imagination they are dull, tasteless, and anomalous."

An American contemporary, as it happened, gave the answer to Jefferson. "Now I beg to know," wrote Imlay White in reply, "what can be more uncertain and false than estimating and comparing the intellect and talents of two descriptions of men: one enslaved, degraded and fettered in all their acts of volition . . .

the other free, independent and with the advantage of appropriating the reason and science which have been the result of the study and labours of the philosophers and sensible men for centuries back?"

Was the charge of inferiority altogether a myth? To be treated as an inferior is often to become an inferior, and it is precisely because the judgments of Europe were applied, so persistently and repeatedly, to Africans who were slaves that the writing of African history for this period must involve an analysis of the European state of mind as well as of the African condition. If we keep that in view, we shall still not arrive at any final truth because history is not an exact science, susceptible of clear and completely objective categorization, but a more or less fallible means of explaining the present in terms of the past. It will be better or worse history according to the supply and use of fact. Propaganda, one may note, aims at just the opposite, explaining the past in terms of the present; a great deal of historical writing is propaganda. But Africa stands in dire need, not of propaganda, but of historical explanation.

And here one may take good heart, for in the matter of African history the supply of fact has immensely broadened and improved over recent years. Yet the task of coming to grips with this exciting and elusive theme will nonetheless remain a problem — and race contempt and its reactions define the reasons why — of coming to grips with oneself and with the limits of one's own development.

In the early days of discovery, men in Europe believed they had found partners and allies and equals in Africa. "Let them go and do business with the King of Timbuktu and Mali," Ramusio, secretary to the rulers in Venice, was urging the merchants of Italy in 1563, "and there is no doubt they will be well received there with their ships and their goods, and treated well, and granted the favours that they ask. . . ."

Before the Trade Began

Four hundred years afterwards, other men in Europe were sure that Africans had never so much as known the rudiments of political organization, let alone the means of building powerful states and operating central governments; Africans, it would be commonly said, simply lacked the faculty for growing up. "Their inherent mental inferiority, almost more marked than their physical characters," Professor Keane was writing with assured Victorian complacency in 1896, "depends on physiological causes. . . ." Once an African grew beyond childhood, Richard Burton had decided a little earlier, "his mental development is arrested, and thenceforth he grows backwards instead of forwards."

If earlier Europeans had been closer to the truth, though having less information, they too were astray in their judgment. They avoided the crass absurdity of opinions such as those of Keane and Burton. They were right in thinking that their captains and caravels were discovering powerful states and potent commercial partners. But they were wrong in imagining that this Africa of lord and vassal and willing merchant was passing through the same political development as the states of Europe.

Looking back now, we can see that appearances were double-faced. On the one side, it was true that the "cultural gap" between the European discoverers and the Africans they found was narrow and was often felt to be nonexistent. On the other side, it was false that these appearances reflected a similar experience and potential of society in Africa and Europe. For the African states, evolving their governments and empires in lands remotely muffled from the heat and clash of European or Mediterranean competition, had reached a phase of relative stability. They could and would continue at much the same level of power and organization for a long time to come. But the states of Europe were anything but stable. On the contrary, they were about to trip the springs of all those piled-up tensions and turbulent contradictions that a restless and much-invaded past had compressed in their inheritance. Unlike the states of Africa, they were about to enter a time of fast and furious growth and change.

It was in these peculiar circumstances of great likeness and unlikeness that the African-European connection began. It was out of this equivocation that the confusion and misunderstanding of later years would grow.

2 The Old States of Africa

ONE OUTSTANDING FACT ABOUT THE OLD STATES OF AFRICA, WELL understood in earlier times but afterwards forgotten, is that they were seldom or never conquered from outside the continent. They resisted invasion. They remained inviolate. Only here and there along the coast could European men-at-arms gain a foothold even when they tried to win more. The Moorish states of northern Africa had little luck with their overland invasions of the south, and were in the end frustrated and forced to withdraw.

Writers of the colonial period have sometimes explained this fact of successful African resistance by reference to the climate and the mosquito. Certainly, malaria and the sun were grim discouragers of foreign invasion. Yet the early records indicate another and more persuasive safeguard against conquest. They point to the striking-power of African armies. They show that it was the military factor, time and again, which proved decisive.

Even in the fifteenth century the Portuguese, then feeling their way around the long western coast, were vaguely aware of powers and principalities beyond the shoreward skyline whose alliance was desirable. "The King," wrote Barros, "began cautiously to send agents with messages to the important chiefs, and to involve himself as a close and powerful friend in their affairs and their wars." In the last quarter of the fifteenth century he sent "Pedro de Evora and Gonsalo Eannes to the Prince of Tekrur" — inland from the coast of Senegal — "and to the lord of Timbuktu." From further to the southward, the Portuguese also dispatched a mission up the Gambia River "to Mansa Mundi, one of the most powerful chiefs of the province of the Mandingo."

In 1481 they built their first fort on the Gold Coast, at a place they named Elmina, "the mine," believing that from here they could best tap the sources of African gold. Yet they built this fort by agreement with the chief of the people of the region, and not after conquest. At the close of a long plea by Diogo d'Azambuja, who commanded the Portuguese expedition, the chief in question consented to the building of a fort, but only on condition that "peace and truth must be kept." And one of the earliest actions that followed on the building of the castle at Elmina was not a military expedition to "the mines" of the interior, but a diplomatic mission of friendship and alliance. Messengers had come from Mamadu, lord of Mali. King John of Portugal ordered that these messengers should be accompanied back to their country by eight Portuguese emissaries, including two knights of the royal court, "with gifts of horses and mules and arms and other things prized in that country."

Elmina was no disappointment. It delivered the gold of Africa, and in large quantity through many years. But neither the Portuguese nor the Dutch nor any other European power ever secured access to the "land of gold" until the British fought their way into Ashanti in the nineteenth century. Forts were built, but they were never secure. Garrisons were placed in them and repeatedly replenished from Europe; time and again they were besieged and

FACT AND FABLE

overwhelmed. Governors were installed; yet they were obliged to live in close agreement with African neighbors or else lose their power.

Opinion in Europe nonetheless grew common that European power held sway over the interior. "There is no small number of men in Europe," a Dutch factor on the Gold Coast wrote back to his employers in the year 1700, "who believe that the gold mines are in our power; that we . . . have no more to do but to work them by our slaves: though you perfectly know we have no manner of access to these treasures." By this time men in Europe were accustomed to seeing Africans only as men in chains, slaves without power, and they transferred their impressions to Africa and the states from which these slaves had come. The belief in African inferiority was already in full bloom.

Those who traveled in Africa knew better. "With nauseating presumption," complained Father Cavazzi of the states of the Congo in 1687, "these nations think themselves the foremost men in the world, and nothing will persuade them to the contrary. They imagine that Africa is not only the greatest part of the world, but also the happiest and most agreeable." The lords of Congo, he found, were even more arrogant. "Similar opinions are held by the king himself, but in a manner still more remarkable. For he is persuaded that there is no other monarch in the world who is his equal, or exceeds him in power or the abundance of wealth. . . ."

The reasons for this African self-confidence were not really obscure. They were the same reasons as those that had enabled Africans to resist invasion: the steady growth of Iron Age concentrations of power, the evolution of central government, the raising of armies, the swearing-in of vassals, or the elimination of rivals that had accompanied much of African social development for the previous thousand years. They were, in short, the reasons that had enabled African types of feudal rule to emerge and grow strong.

3 Similarities

IT WOULD BE AN ILLUSION TO SEE THE FEUDALISM OF AFRICA AS being the same as the feudalism of Europe in these opening years of discovery. But the similarities were often strikingly close. They are worth dwelling on because nothing but powerful feudal organization can properly explain the military strength of many African states that were found by Europe in the fifteenth and sixteenth centuries, and respected by Europe (at any rate in the beginning) as allies and partners and equals.

To get at the true position, one must look at the nature of society as it had evolved in the maturity of Africa's Iron Age. A useful approach, especially in the light of what was to come, is from the standpoint of who was bond and who was free. In Western Europe during the Dark Ages, the formative period of feudalism, there had come a gradual transformation of slave into serf; and this change was accelerated in feudal times until "old slave" and "old freeman" were little by little merged together into "new vassal." In Africa, meanwhile, wherever strong states and empires shook and changed the old framework of tribal equality, there emerged the new phenomenon of mass subjugation of one people by another. This was not slavery as Europe understood the word — chattel slavery, the stripping from a man of all his rights and property — but serfdom, vassalship, "domestic slavery." Degrees of servility and obligation would immensely vary with time and place, as they would elsewhere; but this vassalship in Africa would become essentially the same as that of Europe.

An arresting parallel may be seen in land rights. "The Ashanti, under certain conditions not unlike those that existed in England at the time of the Norman conquest, seem to have evolved an almost exactly similar land code." This parallel of Rattray's can be greatly extended. Thus the titles and the rights of great lords, the obligations of the common people, the customs of trade and tribute, the swearing of fealty, the manners of war — all these and a hundred other manifestations have seemed to speak the same identical language of feudalism.

Not much more than a hundred years ago the little army of Amadou Hammadi, founder of the Fulani empire in the Macina grasslands of the Middle Niger, faced their much more powerful assailants in a battle for survival. They took the field in doubt and great anxiety. Amadou gave the command of his army to his henchman Usman and bestowed on him the title of Amirou Mangal, "great chief." Then tradition makes Amadou say to Usman: "Great chief, raise your eyes and look about you and tell me what signs you see." Amirou Mangal does as he is bidden and replies: "Verily, I see on every hand the signs of our victory. I see that God is with us." At this point there enters the herald of the "invincible" king of Segu. He rides up with his entourage in a grand flurry of horses and banners and demands that Amadou Hammadi should at once surrender, admit homage to the king of Segu, pay tribute, and be gone. "For otherwise the vultures shall tear your flesh."

Calm of heart, Amadou answers with a mocking smile and says to the herald: "A messenger can meet no evil. Be welcome here, bold herald, and you shall have refreshment." As for submitting to the king of Segu, "let him know that my submission is already to God and will be made to no man."

Similarities

That is one example among many, and completely African. Yet King Henry V before the Battle of Agincourt said nothing different to the herald of King Louis of France, although he may have said it, thanks to Shakespeare, somewhat better:

> There's for thy labour, Mountjoy.
> Go, bid thy master well advise himself:
> If we may pass, we will; if we be hinder'd,
> We shall your tawny ground with your red blood
> Discolour: and so, Mountjoy, fare you well.

The medieval states of the Western Sudan repeatedly show how closely the condition of subjugated peoples — commonly referred to, alike by Arabs and Europeans, as "slaves" — resembled that of feudal vassals. In the Songhay Kingdom of the fifteenth century along the Middle Niger, "slaves" from the non-Muslim peoples of the forest verge were extensively used in agriculture. They were settled on the land and tied to it. In return for this livelihood they paid tribute to their masters both in crops and in personal services. Their bondage was relative: time and custom gave them new liberties. Yet being generally restricted by feudal rule in the varieties of work they might undertake and the peoples among whom they might seek wives, these "slaves" tended to form occupational castes. They became blacksmiths, boat-builders, stablemen, makers of songs, bodyguards of their sovereign lord. Along with the "free peasants," whose social condition was really little different, these "vassal peasants" and "vassal artisans" formed the great bulk of the population.

Contrasts in status between the freeman who belonged to a conquering people and the "slave" who came of a conquered people would grow narrower as time went by and the system grew stronger; and in this too, there was a broad parallel with medieval Europe. Caste and even class divisions might emerge and

FACT AND FABLE

sharpen among the mass of "commoners"; the dominant factor in society increasingly became the difference in power which separated prince and lords from the people, from all the people. This stratification occurred among the strong nations of the forest belt, behind the coast, just as it appeared among the Muslim peoples of the northern plains. It was narrowly limited by the nature of West Africa's feudal economy which remained largely one of subsistence and barter. It was greatly modified by the electoral principle of chiefdom and the checks and balances of customary rule. But the lord-and-vassal stratification nonetheless grew sharper among the groups who held power. There are many examples.

Early in the nineteenth century the old Hausa states of northern Nigeria were taken over by an invading army of Fulani. All the captains and leaders under Usman dan Fodio, the great Fulani leader, were then endowed with large landholdings seized from the defeated Hausa lords (except where these, as occasionally happened, had thrown in their lot with the new regime). The old Hausa royal title of *Sarki* was perpetuated, and the whole titular structure was bound directly to the newly created fiefs and regions of command. And this oligarchy came with time to exercise rights of life and death over the common people, and could call on them for labor in the fields or the building of houses or the maintenance of roads and river fords.

The case is especially instructive, since the origins of this Fulani invasion had lain in revolt against a gross social inequality. Explaining "the reasons for our holy war with the Hausa Sultans," a contemporary Fulani document, written some four years before Europe heard news of the Battle of Waterloo, says that in the beginning Usman dan Fodio "did not address himself to the kings. After a time his people grew and became famous, till they were known in Hausaland as '*The People*.' Men kept leaving their countries and coming to them. Of the ruling classes some repented" — for Usman preached a puritanical Islam, calling on the rich to abandon their wealth and calling on the poor to put their trust in God — "and came to him with all they possessed, leaving their [Hausa] Sultans. Then the Sultans became angry, till there ensued between them and their chiefs the war we remember."

Yet in freeing the people of the Hausa states from their old bondage, the Fulani reformers soon found themselves binding on a new one. However egalitarian Usman dan Fodio might be, his henchmen were ambitious men whose reforming zeal was tempered by a healthy territorial ambition. Besides, they were rulers of their time. They soon found they must either forfeit their new-found power and wealth or else revert to those very methods of bureaucratic government that they had set themselves to overthrow. And little by little, there being in any event no alternative but abdication, the new Fulani feudalism came to resemble the old Hausa system; except for a tightening of Islamic discipline, little was altered but the men at the top.

Usman himself resisted the trend toward feudal centralism. Many vivid stories tell of his shrewd prevarications when faced with the urgent pleas of his commanders. One day they came to him and said they must be allowed to sell land, as the Hausa lords had done before them, for otherwise they could not discipline the people. Usman had always laid it down that the land belonged to God and was not for anyone to sell. Now, faced with this new demand, he asked for a cupful of earth and sent it to the market place for sale; after a few days he inquired of his servants whether anyone had bid for it. They replied that none had made an offer. Whereupon Usman, calling his commanders together, declared that there could be no sense in giving them the right to sell land, since none desired to buy.

FACT AND FABLE

But the feudal bonds grew tighter. The early reforming vows were forgotten. The ruling emirs claimed more and more power. And in this increasingly stratified society, just as earlier in medieval Europe, the dividing line between bond and free among the common people became ever more hard to trace. The degree of freedom or unfreedom that distinguished the "free peasants" (*talakawa*) from the "serfs" (*cucenawa*) narrowed to the vanishing point: all were embraced as subjects, and perhaps the most that one can say about their difference in status was that some were more subjected than others.

Naturally, the process varied with circumstances. In nineteenth century Bornu, heir to the ancient state of Kanem in the region of Lake Chad, custom generally recognized three social groups beneath the noble families: the *kambe*, who were freemen drawn from the ranks of freed slaves and the children of freemen married to slaves; the *kalia*, who were slaves, whether foreigners or men and women captured in war; and the *zusanna*, the descendants of slaves, who were also the rank-and-file footsloggers of the army of Bornu. Yet the differences between the *kambe* and the *kalia* and the *zusanna* were undoubtedly less important, so far as the distribution of social power was concerned, than the differences between all these three on one hand and the nobles on the other. Here, once again, was a system recognizably feudal — a system, moreover, which had grown with Iron Age development from the earliest beginnings of the old pastoral empire of Kanem, forerunner of Bornu, during a period that was contemporary with the growth of European feudalism.

Such systems continued into modern times. One other example may be useful from another part of Africa, the kingdom of Ruanda, lying in a small country of tall mountains between the Congo and the East African lands of Uganda and Tanganyika. Ruanda possessed a close-knit social order that persists in large

Similarities

measure even today, so that anthropologists have been able to make direct reports about it.

This society is divided into three kinds of people. Foremost are the Watutsi — of late years much photographed for their splendid dancing — who may number about one-tenth of the population. They, says Maquet, "do no manual work and have leisure to cultivate eloquence, poetry, refined manners." Beneath them are the Bahutu, who "do not enjoy such gracious living," because "they have to produce for themselves and for the Watutsi." And beneath the Bahutu, in the third rank, are the Batwa — "so low in the social hierachy and . . . considered so irresponsible, that they have had a greater independence of action."

In Ruanda, accordingly, nobody is "free" in the modern sense of the word, for even the Watutsi are wedded to their laborers by a formal code of interwoven duties. Moreover, it is better for a Mututsi (that is to say, one Watutsi) to become the vassal of a strong man than to remain on his own. "We desire," Maquet's Watutsi informants told him, "to become the vassals of great chiefs, or even of the king, because we are then under the protection of somebody very important, we get more cows, and that allows us to have more 'clients' " — that is, more Bahutu workers who will labor in their turn so as to gain "protection."

Compare this "ladder of duty-and-obligation" with that of feudal Europe. Many European slaves were liberated — "manumitted" in the language of the times — but few were then able or desired to remain on their own. They found it better and safer to bind themselves to a master, and they chose the most powerful lord they could find. "The manumitter," Bloch has written of medieval France, "even if he agreed to give up a slave, wished to conserve a dependent. The manumitted himself, not daring to live without a protector, thus found the protection he desired." In Europe as in Africa, like causes produce like effects.

FACT AND FABLE

Next to Ruanda, in the neighboring Ugandan kingdom of Ankole, there was (and to some extent there still is) much the same system of rulers and ruled: Bahima nobles, in this case, and Bairu vassals. Such as were chattel slaves — genuine slaves without rights or claims — consisted, Oberg reports, "entirely of Bairu captured in raids made upon neighbouring kingdoms, [but] there is nothing to indicate that slaves were sold or exchanged, although chiefs gave each other slaves as presents . . . [and] from all accounts, slavery was restricted to the very wealthy, and slaves were restricted in numbers."

This was the broad type of centralized social organization in Africa that would prove, time and again in the coastal regions, too strong for challenge from outside. Along the seaboard of the Guinea Coast there emerged states and empires — Oyo, Benin, Denkyira, Akwamu, and many others — that European venturers would respect. And here, too, society had become increasingly divided into rulers and ruled, base and noble, bond and free, with weaker clans or even whole tribes reduced to this or that productive position in the social system of the stronger peoples.

Europeans of a somewhat later day often misunderstood the essentially vassal nature of this African subjection. Such slavery, argued the defenders of the slave trade, was no different from any other. This argument they used repeatedly in their eighteenth century battles against those who wished to abolish the trade. Do not prevent us from taking these poor savages away from Africa, the slavers urged, for otherwise you will condemn them to a fate much worse. Confirm us in our right to carry them off to America, and you will encourage "a great accession of happiness to Africa." The British Privy Council of Enquiry into the slave trade, which sat in 1788, was doubtfully impressed. One may note that other men would afterwards urge a continuance of the colonial system with much the same argument. Do not ask us to abandon our

Similarities

responsibilities for governing Africans, for you must otherwise confirm these peoples in a savage fate. . . . Support us in our powers of dominion, and you will ensure rich benefits for Africa. . . .

Yet the "slave" peoples of the coastal regions, like those of the Sudanese grasslands, were in truth serfs and vassals, often with valued individual rights. Their status was altogether different from the human cattle of the slave ships and the American plantations. Early European traders on the coast, though freely misusing the word "slave," repeatedly drew attention to this. "Those who come from the inward part of the country to traffick with us," Bosman reports of the Guinea Coast around the year 1700, "are chiefly slaves: one of which, on whom the master reposes the greatest trust, is appointed the chief of the caravan. But when he comes to us he is not treated as a slave, but as a very great merchant whom we take all possible care to oblige. . . . Indeed, I have observed that some of these slaves have more authority than their masters; for having long exercised command over their masters' dependents, by their own trading they are become possessors of some slaves themselves, and in process of time are grown so powerful, that their patrons are obliged to see with their eyes only. . . ."

One could multiply such observations, and for every part of Africa where the outside world had contact. Sometimes they were casual and inconclusive, mere traders' gossip of strange people and exotic countries. Now and then they were more than that. An early American Negro explorer of southern Nigeria, Martin Delany, spoke in sharper tones. "It is simply preposterous to talk about slavery, as that term is understood, either being legalised or existing in this part of Africa," he wrote. "It is nonsense. The system is a patriarchal one, there being no actual difference, socially, between slaves (called by their protector sons or daughters) and the children of the person with whom they live. Such persons intermarry and frequently become the heads of state. . . . And were this not the case, it either arises from some innovation among them or those exceptional cases of despotism to be found in every country. . . ."*

What was true of southern Nigeria was true of other "forest" peoples. In Ashanti, Rattray found "a slave might marry; own property; himself own a slave; swear an oath; be a competent witness; and ultimately become heir to his master. . . . Such briefly were the rights of an Ashanti slave. They seemed in many cases practically the ordinary privileges of an Ashanti free man. . . . An Ashanti slave, in nine cases out of ten, possibly became an adopted member of the family, and in time his descendants so merged and intermarried with the owner's kinsmen that only a few would know their origin. . . ." Captives, that is to say, became vassals; vassals became free men; free men became chiefs.

Set this highly mobile social order alongside the slave system of the United States, and the vital and enormous difference becomes immediately clear. There the slaves were entirely a class apart, labeled by their color, doomed to accept an absolute servitude; in Tannenbaum's words, "the mere fact of being a Negro was presumptive of a slave status." And slave status was forever. Manumission became increasingly difficult; often it became impossible. An early law of Maryland, dating from 1663, declared: "All Negroes or other slaves within the province, all Negroes to be hereafter imported, shall serve *durante vita*"; but their children were to serve likewise. A few free Negroes there might be; yet they were tolerated with the utmost difficulty. A South Carolina law of 1740 provided that any free Negro should

* I am indebted for this quotation to Dr. George Shepperson; it comes from the official report of the Niger Valley Exploring Party, published in New York, 1861, p. 40. Delany was a serious observer who traveled in West Africa between July, 1859, and August, 1860.

be sold at public auction if he had harbored a runaway slave or was charged "with any criminal matter." A Negro or mulatto in Mississippi could be sold as a slave unless he was able to prove himself a free man. As late as 1801 a Georgia law imposed a fine of two hundred dollars on any master who freed a slave without previous consent of the legislature. Seventeen years later the lawmakers of Georgia went even further. They imposed a fine of one thousand dollars on anyone who gave effect to a last will and testament freeing a slave or allowing him to work on his own account.

This is not to suggest that the life of an African vassal was one of unalloyed bliss, but that the condition he suffered was in no way the same as plantation or mining slavery in the Americas. His condition often was comparable to that of the bulk of the men and women in Western Europe throughout medieval times. In this respect Africa and Europe, at the beginning of their connection, traded and met as equals. And it was this acceptance of equality, based on the strength and flexibility of feudal systems of state organization, that long continued to govern relations between Africa and Europe. Even in the matter of slaving their attitudes were much the same.

4 Slaves and Slaving

WHEN THE TRADERS OF EUROPE FIRST BEGAN THEIR TRAFFIC WITH the empire of Benin, not far from the coast of Nigeria, they found that captives could be purchased there without much difficulty.

"The trade one can conduct here," Pacheco was writing in about 1505, some thirty years after Portugal's earliest contact with

FACT AND FABLE

Benin, "is the trade in slaves . . . and in elephants' tusks." But the traders also found that objection was taken at Benin to the enslavement of the natives of the country — of men and women, that is, who were within the protection of the Oba of Benin, a monarch whose power derived from God. By custom and by moral law, slaves ought to be men and women captured from neighboring peoples. They ought to be "outsiders," "unbelievers." This rule was often broken; but it was universally admitted.

Turning to the European records, one finds the leaders of Christianity busy endeavoring to apply precisely the same rule — and with about as much success. Slaves being a highly perishable commodity, the supply was always running short. Where possible, the European merchants who dealt in chattel slaves were accustomed to buy infidels or Jews; otherwise, they simply did as the Benin traders would do in somewhat later times. They bought "believers." They sold their "fellow-natives." Papal records show the Vatican repeatedly inveighing against this practice.

All the great city-states of medieval Italy appear to have dealt in Christian slaves. The Venetians and the Genoese were deep in the trade as early as the tenth and eleventh centuries. They continued in it, together with the Pisans and the Florentines and the merchants and mariners of ports as far apart as Lucca and Amalfi, until as late as the middle of the fifteenth century. Throughout the thirteenth century, European slaves were being carried in European ships to the Sultanate of Egypt despite all ecclesiastical rebukes and threats. "The excesses of the traders," Scelle records, "were such that Pope Clement V excommunicated the Venetians and authorised all Christian people to reduce them in turn to slavery."

Little more than half a century before the launching of the oversea slave trade from Africa, Pope Martin V published a bull of excommunication against the Genoese merchants of Caffa,

Slaves and Slaving

Genoese city-state on the Black Sea, for their persistence in buying and selling Christians. This was as ineffectual as the earlier excommunication of the Venetians, and in 1441 the laws of Gazaria (as the Genoese called their little trading "empire" on the Black Sea coast) expressly provided for the sale and purchase of Christian as well as Muslim slaves.

Another aspect of this early equality between Europe and Africa, in respect to slaves and slaving, lies in the treatment of those who were captured. In Africa, as we have seen, slaves could almost at once begin climbing the ladder of liberation from their rightless condition. And it was not much different for the captives who were brought from Africa into fifteenth century Portugal and Spain. The many Negro slaves of Andalusia enjoyed a special code of law awarded by royal authority; and their principal judge, who was one of their own folk and represented them, was known as the "Negro count." With the passing of the years they mingled with their free neighbors and lost their ethnic identity.

Or consider the attitude of the fifteenth century Portuguese to the Negroes who were beginning to arrive in the earliest slaving ships. Zurara has described this in his famous chronicle of 1453. Finding these captives prepared to become Christians and "not hardened in the belief of the other Moors" — the Muslims of North Africa — the Portuguese "made no difference between them and their free servants, born in our own country. But those they took while still young, they caused to be instructed in the mechanical arts. But those whom they saw fitted for managing property, they set free and married to women who were natives of the land — making with them a division of their property, as if they had been bestowed on those who married them by the will of their own fathers. . . .

"Yes, and some widows of good family who bought some of these female slaves, either adopted them or left them a portion of their estate by will; so that in the future they married right well; treating them as entirely free. . . ." Portugal in the time of its greatness would thus anticipate Brazil.

As in Africa, so in Europe: the medieval slave, in one as in the other, was a captive who could soon win access to the system of mutual duty and obligation that bound noble and commoner together. And what went for the manners of society went for the morals of the merchants too — whether in Europe or Africa. European traders sold their fellow-countrymen to the oversea states of Egypt and North Africa. The lords of Africa would sell their own folk to the mariners who came from Europe.

It is important to establish this point. For it was the ground of departure on which the whole relationship between Europe and Africa was firmly set. Out of this common acceptance of bondage in a feudal situation there would flow, in postmedieval times, a common acceptance of the slave trade between the two continents. Thus the African notion that Europe altogether imposed the slave trade on Africa is without any foundation in history. This idea is as baseless as the comparable European notion that institutions of bondage were in some way peculiar to Africa.

Africa and Europe were jointly involved. Yet it is also true that Europe dominated the connection, shaped and promoted the slave trade, and continually turned it to European advantage and to African loss. And when one begins to examine why this was so, one sees how the similarities between European and African feudalism concealed differences that were more important — and were decisive.

5 Differences

MUCH HAS REMAINED OBSCURE ABOUT THE EARLY YEARS OF CONtact between Europe and Africa. One of the certainties, however, is that it was only from the north that discovery came. The little ships of that heroic enterprise came always from the ports of Western Europe, from Lisbon and Seville, Nantes and Boulogne and Plymouth, and never from the harbors of the Guinea Coast. Why was this? If leading peoples in Africa and Europe alike lived under systems of feudal rule, why was the initiative always European?

The answer has nothing to do with innate capacity, racial talent, intellectual or cultural potential, nor with any kind of natural superiority or inferiority. It lies in the profound difference in social content of these feudal systems — a difference that was the product of deep contrasts in environment and circumstance. These systems in Africa and Europe might often appear the same. At several points, as we have seen, they might actually be the same. Yet their formative backgrounds were altogether diverse. The similarities between them concealed an equivocation.

By the period of oversea discovery, Africa had reached a social equilibrium and evolved a society that was largely balanced in itself, any "overflow of discontent" being allowed to disperse across the endless lands. Yet Europe was anything but stable. Europe had already jumped from feudal equilibrium into the tumult of social progress through acquisitive advance. Spinning on its money-driven axis, heir to the peculiar pressures of its past, and impelled by a marvelous curiosity and will to know, Europe now moved across the threshold of a new age. Within eighteen years of the Portuguese arrival at Benin, Columbus had found land across the Atlantic. Within another seven years, Vasco da Gama had reached the golden East.

FACT AND FABLE

In this comparison of Africa and Europe in the fifteenth century, the equivocation between appearance and reality was the fruit of complex differences. The old system of society in Iron Age Europe had worked on the basis of a chattel slavery wherein men and women who were slaves had enjoyed no rights and held no property. This was the slavery of the Ancient World, of Greece and Rome and the empires of the Near East before them. It was a vital part of the social foundation of all those Iron Age concentrations of wealth and power that had given Europe its high civilizations of antiquity.

Then "tribal Europe" intervened. The nomad peoples of the north conquered Rome, assumed Roman civilization, were in turn absorbed in it, and yet destroyed the old and clear distinction between freeman and slave. And men in Europe, notably in Western Europe, became fused increasingly into a unified society, but a society in which the old divisions reappeared in another and more strictly hierarchical form. The feudal idea was enthroned.

Gradually, the chattel slaves of Roman Europe disappeared. The liberation, of course, was relative. Chattel slaves were transformed into tied laborers whose rights were few; even their old name, *servi*, being perpetuated in their new name, serfs. And as the slaves came up a little, so the freemen also went down, until the two classes came gradually to occupy positions that were not essentially different. However imperfectly, feudalism may thus be said to have enclosed Western Europe in a framework of social service, ideal of the medieval world. Only when the system broke down, as the cities grew and the barons and princes ruined each other in endless wars, was the way cleared for another unification — this time in terms of social equality, ideal of a later world.

The point here is that the system did break down. It broke down throughout medieval times, continuously if erratically, and

Differences

gave way little by little, confusedly, obscurely, to the capitalism that would dominate the future of Europe. And it may well be — extending a parallel of Needham's — that the key component in this tortuous and onward-shifting machinery of social movement lay precisely in the industrial slavery of Roman Europe.* For it was this mass slavery — acid solvent of the old relations of "tribal equality" — which first "detribalized" large numbers of Europeans, concentrated wealth in the hands of a few men who were not necessarily kings and rulers, enabled these men to discover new ways of using and accumulating money, and created the mass of "masterless wights" who increasingly found a new life in towns and cities. And it was these cities and towns that were the makers of commerce, the gatherers of capital, the champions of individual liberty, the promoters of inquiry, the sources of new thought, and the powerful levers that switched the whole of Europe into new directions. It was here that the banker and merchant and entrepreneur were born and had their being and rose to power.

This explanation telescopes much history. Yet it may contain a good part of the reason why Africa and Europe, at the time of their early confrontation, were both living under systems that were recognizably feudal in character, and yet had reached sharply different stages of social growth.

There were towns in Black Africa before the coming of Europe, even large towns, but they were only another type of settlement for men who continued, for the most part, to live by the old rules of tribal loyalty and custom. Their inhabitants were seldom or never opposed to their feudal princes in the way that London was opposed to the barons, or the cities of the Holy Roman Empire

---

* J. Needham, "Science and Society in Ancient China," a paper prepared for the Conway Memorial Lecture Committee of the South Place Ethical Society.

FACT AND FABLE

to their kings and emperors. They were not the refuge of large numbers of men who sought to fashion a new society out of a new concept of freedom. They were powerless to impel Africa into new directions.

Exceptions to this there undoubtedly were, notably in the Western Sudan and along the East Coast, Djenné and Timbuktu, Malindi and Kilwa; but these exceptional cities were of marginal importance to the situation in continental Africa as a whole. The capitalist techniques they began to evolve — banking, lending, the use of currency — had little impact outside the relatively narrow limits of their mercantile connections across the Sahara and the Indian Ocean.

Why this contrast with Europe? There was, to begin with, the absence in Black Africa of any direct and steady influence from the high civilizations of the Mediterranean and the Middle East. Beyond its seas of sand and salt water, continental Africa was left to work out its own destiny. In fact, Africa worked out many destinies. Some African societies, their contact with the outside world muffled by immense forests and daunting plains, carried their ancient tribalism into very recent times. Even today, after half a century of incessant pressure for change, the loyalties and attitudes of ancient custom and morality often remain powerful and even decisive, and give life there a special accent and appearance.

Other African societies embarked on a process of social and economic change which brought them to forms of feudal unification. They passed from the Stone Age into a Metal Age (northern Nigeria, for example, began using iron for tools and weapons only a few centuries after northern Europe) and evolved new cultures, fashioned systems of centralized government, developed hierarchies of power, and extended their rule by imperial conquest. Islam, here and there, infused something of the same leveling and centralizing force that Christianity supplied in Europe.

Yet the "key component" was missing. There lay in the heritage of these feudal systems in Africa no great period of chattel slavery, no far-reaching process of "detribalization." That is why, I suggest, this Africa feudalism may reasonably be called "tribal feudalism," a system of centralized government that was almost always qualified by the precedents of "tribal equality." It was in some important ways nearer, not having arisen from a society which rested on slave labor, to the quasi-feudalism of pre-Roman Gaul or perhaps to the early feudalism of Anglo-Saxon England. When the Portuguese arrived in West Africa in times of European autocracy, they thought they found there the same stiff hierarchies of rule and precedence as those they knew at home. They hastened to interpret Africa in terms of fifteenth century Portugal. Vercingetorix and Boadicea, chiefs in Gaul and Britain long before, might have understood the situation better. The thegns and ealdormen of Alfred's England would certainly have done so.

Another explanation of why the kings and emperors of medieval Africa never developed the same autocracy and tyranny as their contemporaries in Europe may be found in the balance of weapon power. The European knight in steel from head to foot, riding a great horse, was immensely more powerful than the mass of freemen and serfs, at least until the coming of the longbow and later the gun. But the lords of medieval Africa were seldom much better armed or mounted than the plebes; even when they tried to behave as autocrats — and no doubt they often tried — their superiority in weapons could rarely allow them to succeed for long.

A third reason why African feudalism remained closely tied to its tribal past may lie in the far-ranging movement of African

FACT AND FABLE

peoples. This was the ever-freshened impulse of migration that took them across the continent from northward to southward throughout the centuries of an Iron Age which began, for Africa, at about the same time as Europe knew the decline of Greece and the rise of the Roman Republic. There is scarcely a modern African people without a more or less vivid tradition that speaks of movement from another place. Younger sons of paramount chiefs would hive off with their followers, and become paramount themselves in a new land. Stronger peoples would conquer those who were weaker, marry their women, merge with them, weave yet another strand in the fabric of Negro life.

But this wandering of peoples clearly acted as a powerful preserver of the old system of tribal-feudal relationships, for it gave play to an elasticity and tolerance that could absorb and eliminate strains and stresses which must otherwise have forced a social crisis. Hence, to a large extent, the enduring stability of the general pattern of society in Iron Age Africa. Hence its appearance of immobility. For this continual making and weaving of new threads and strands strengthened rather than weakened the total fabric.

When Europeans first entered on their trading and political missions in Africa, here and there along the coast, it seemed for a time that their coming must provide the break and change whereby African society would move into a new form, mercantile and capitalist. The outcome was different. There were many shifts of power and many innovations; yet African society generally failed to undergo any radical and basic change of structure. What happened instead was a tremendous change in the African-European balance of power. And it was slaving that now occupied the center of the picture. It had stood there, indeed, from the very first. But then the cloud had been no bigger than a man's hand.

two

The Years of Trial

Car, comme ont dict les vieux proverbiaux,
Tousjours Aphrique apporte cas nouveaux.

Jean Temporal

1 At First a Trickle

IN THE YEAR 1441, JUST HALF A CENTURY BEFORE CHRISTOPHER Columbus crossed the Atlantic, there sailed from Portugal "a little ship" under the command of one Antam Gonçalvez. The orders of this "very young man," as he was called by Zurara, the Portuguese chronicler, were to steer southward along the western shore of Africa as other captains had done for several years before him. He was not yet to try for new discoveries but to prove his worth by shipping a cargo of skins and the oil of those "sea wolves" — sea lions — whose acquaintance the Portuguese had lately made on the Atlantic coast of Africa.

Gonçalvez and his crew took their cockleshell as far as the southern seaboard of what is now Morocco or the Spanish colony of Río de Oro. This was a considerable achievement, for it was only seven years since the long-feared Cape Bojador had been doubled by a Portuguese ship which had then managed to return in safety. In this southward sailing it was not the going beyond Bojador that was difficult but the returning: on that coast the winds blow always from the northward. Only with their recent adaptation of the lateen sail of the eastern Mediterranean were the Portuguese capable of sailing close enough to the wind to enable them to count on getting safely back again.

Having persevered southward for as far as he judged it wise or useful to the winning of a reputation, the youthful Gonçalvez conceived the idea of pleasing his royal master, Prince Henry of Portugal, by capturing some of the inhabitants of this unknown southern land. "O how fair a thing it would be," Zurara makes him say to his crew, "if we, who have come to this land for a cargo of such petty merchandise, were to meet with the good luck to bring the first captives before the face of our Prince."

THE YEARS OF TRIAL

On the following night Gonçalvez went ashore with nine of his men. "When they were about a league distant from the sea they came on a path which they kept, thinking some man or woman might come by there whom they could capture; but it happened otherwise." They pushed on for another three leagues, and there they "found the footmarks of men and youths, the number of whom, according to their estimate, would be from forty to fifty, and these led the opposite way from where our men were going."

Should they persist or go back? Heat, fatigue, and thirst discouraged the raiders. They decided to give up. But while returning over the sand-warm dunes to the sea, "they saw a naked man following a camel, with two assegais in his hand, and as our men pursued him there was not one who felt aught of his great fatigue. But though he was only one, and saw the others that they were many, yet [this African] had a mind to prove those arms of his right worthily and began to defend himself as best he could, shewing a bolder front than his strength warranted.

"But Affonso Goterres wounded him with a javelin, and this put the Moor in such fear that he threw down his arms like a beaten man." The Portuguese took him prisoner; then, "as they were going on their way, they saw a Black Mooress come along," and so they seized her too.

Spear to spear — such is the first recorded skirmish of Europeans and Africans south of the Sahara. The Moor was probably a Berber of the Sanhaja Tawreg of the far western desert, while the woman may have been a Negro slave in Sanhaja keeping. And this capture was otherwise no different from countless other episodes of the time, except that it was made by men from Europe, since the first thought of such raiders was to seize prisoners who might tell them the nature of the land and its people.

This need for information merged in Europe, as in Africa, with

At First a Trickle

the commercial and social advantages of capturing people who could be sold as slaves. Portugal was full of Moorish captives, but the market was still a good one. The taking of prisoners for information led to kidnaping for profit. Luck had it that another Portuguese venturer, Nuño Tristão, was also on the coast. Tristão joined the little ship of Gonçalvez and, thanks again to Zurara, we have an almost direct and altogether dramatic record of what these raiders did together. The newcomer, "a youthful knight very valiant and ardent," was captain of an armed caravel with orders both to explore the coast and to take captives "as best he could." The two captains decided on a joint enterprise.

"And so it chanced that in the night" — after their landing together — "they came to where the natives lay scattered in two encampments. . . . And when our men had come nigh to them, they attacked [the natives] very lustily, shouting at the tops of their voices 'Portugal' and 'Santiago,' the fright of which so abashed the enemy that it threw them all into disorder.

"And so, all in confusion, [the natives] began to fly without any order or carefulness. Except indeed that the men made some show of defending themselves with their assegais (for they knew not the use of any other weapon), especially one of them who fought face to face with Nuño Tristão, defending himself till he received his death. And besides this one, whom Nuño Tristão slew by himself, the others killed three and took ten prisoners, what of men women and boys. And it is not to be doubted that they would have slain and taken many more, if they had all fallen on together at the first onslaught."

These twelve captives they carried back with them to Lisbon, and one of the Africans, a man who claimed to be of chiefly birth, explained to the Portuguese what manner of land he had come from. Much encouraged, Prince Henry thereupon sent a special embassy to the Pope, explaining his plans for further raid and

THE YEARS OF TRIAL

even conquest; and the Pope, welcoming this new crusade, granted "to all of those who shall be engaged in the said war, complete forgiveness of all their sins."

The prisoner of chiefly birth "greatly desired to be free, and often asked Gonçalvez to take him back to his country, where he declared he would give for himself five or six Black Moors." In the end he had his way. Gonçalvez sailed once more to the southward and ransomed this prisoner and another for "ten blacks, male and female, from various countries" — Negro slaves, that is, of the Sanhaja Berbers of Mauretania; and these in turn he brought back to Lisbon.

So far, the score was only twenty. Now it rose by leaps and bounds. In 1443-1444 Nuño Tristão, again far down the western coast, reached the island of Arguim, soon to become famous in Portuguese slaving annals, and seized twenty-nine men and women from canoes in which they were paddling near the shore. And now the critics at home were confounded. Many had blamed Prince Henry for incurring the expense of sending ships where nothing seemed more likely than their total loss. "And the worst of it was that besides what the vulgar said among themselves, people of more importance talked about it in a mocking manner, declaring that no profit would result from all this toil and expense.

"But when they saw the first Moorish captives brought home" from the African coast, "and the second cargo that followed these, they became already somewhat doubtful about the opinion they had at first expressed; and altogether renounced it when they saw the third consignment that Nuño Tristão brought home, captured in so short a time, and with so little trouble. . . ."

Such was the effect that so small a cargo as twenty-nine slaves could have on medieval Lisbon. The critics changed their tune, "and their covetousness now began to wax greater. And as they saw the houses of others full to overflowing of male and female

At First a Trickle

slaves, and their property increasing, they thought about the whole matter and began to talk among themselves." The outcome of their talking was financial support for a large expedition of six ships under Lançarote and Gil Eannes (he who had first passed southward beyond Cape Bojador in 1434), and a small-scale war on the western coast in which one hundred and sixty-five men, women, and children were taken captive "besides those that perished and were killed."

Beating northward, Lançarote and Eannes looked for still more captives. Fifteen Portuguese were ordered to "march along the land, and look if they could see any Moors, or find any trace of them." The ships stood off from the flat coastline while boats were launched to row along the shore within sight of the marching men. "And on their way they saw the Moors flying as fast as they could; for they had already caught sight of [the Portuguese]; and at once all our men leaped on shore and began to run after them. But as yet they could not overtake the Moor men, but only the women and little children, not able to run so fast, of whom they caught seventeen or eighteen." The whole expedition reached Lagos in southern Portugal with two hundred and thirty-five captives. With this pathetic triumph the oversea slave trade may really be said to have begun.

It spread with the daunting speed of a plague. As proof of that, there are the memoirs of another early voyager from Europe, a Venetian in Portuguese service called Ca' da Mosto, who sailed in 1456 as far as the estuary of the Gambia River, where the great western bulge of Africa begins to bend eastward. Already the early raiding of Tristão and Lançarote, a dozen years before, had given way to regular trading.

"Note that before this traffic was organised," Ca' da Mosto wrote, "the Portuguese caravels — sometimes four, sometimes more — were wont to come armed to the Gulf of Arguim, and descend-

THE YEARS OF TRIAL

ing on the land at night would assail the fisher villages and so ravage the land. Thus they took of these Arabs [they were not Arabs, of course, but Berbers and Negroes] both men and women, and carried them to Portugal for sale: behaving in a like manner along all the rest of the coast. . . . But for some time past all have been at peace and engaged in trade."

The chiefs of the Sanhaja Berbers and of neighboring peoples had in fact quickly shown the Portuguese that slaving was easier by trade than by war. Hitherto the slaving chieftains of the southern Sahara had acted only as intermediaries in the overland slave trade from the Negro lands to the Mediterranean and Europe. Now they began to sell slaves directly to Europe; and Arguim became an important market. The Portuguese had thus triumphed in one of their main objectives. They had broken the monopoly on African trade that the Muslim states of Mediterranean Africa had possessed for many centuries. They had turned the Muslim flank at last.

"These Arabs," observed Ca' da Mosto (but once again he meant the Berber chieftains of the southern Sahara and the fringes of the Sudanese savannah), "have many Berber horses, which they trade and take to the land of the Blacks, exchanging them with the rulers for slaves. Ten or fifteen slaves are usually given [by the rulers of the Blacks] for one of these horses, according to their quality." These rulers of the Blacks would have been tributaries, for the most part, of great Negro states such as Mali and Songhay. Their need of horses, which they found difficult to breed efficiently for themselves, had previously been met from North Africa.

Other luxury goods were also in demand at Negro courts. "The Arabs likewise take articles of Moorish silk, made in Granada" — in southern Spain — "and in Tunis of Barbary, silver and other goods, obtaining in exchange any number of slaves and some gold. These slaves are brought to the market and town of Hoden:

At First a Trickle

there they are divided. Some go to the mountains of Barcha and thence to Sicily, [others to Tunis, . . . and others again are sold to the Portuguese leaseholders of Arguim]. As a result, every year the Portuguese carry away from Arguim a thousand slaves."

The trade prospered, though still on a tiny scale compared with what was to come. From the first it was essentially a royal trade. A year after Ca' da Mosto's voyage to the Gambia the records show Diogo Gomes taking ten horses to Arguim, and finding there another Portuguese called Gonçalo Ferreira, as well as a Genoese in Portugal's service, Antonio da Noli. Both were in the business of trading horses for slaves. But Gomes, having the king's commission, took their horses from these other two at the rate of seven slaves each, while he obtained from the African dealers as many as fourteen or fifteen slaves for a horse. In this early incident one may see at work the principle of royal monopoly that would later on prove fatal to the whole Portuguese trading venture in Africa, India, and beyond.

Another encounter on this same voyage of Gomes casts light on the mind and temper of the times. Gomes came up with a caravel commanded by a fellow-countryman called Prado, went aboard and found that Prado was carrying arms for the Moorish enemies of Portugal and Christendom. Prado was handed over to royal punishment. "The King ordered that they should martyrise him in a cart, and that they should make a furnace of fire and throw him into it with his sword and his gold."

Under the eager influence of the court at Lisbon, slaving was pushed on southward along the African coast. By about 1506, Duarte Pacheco Pereira is writing that the goods exchanged at Arguim and elsewhere consist of gold, black slaves, oryx leather for shields, and other items, against Portuguese red and blue stuffs and various textiles, both of poor and good quality, as well as horses. More than fifty years had passed since Lançarote had brought back that first great cargo of slaves to an astonished Portugal, and the trade by now was extended far to the south.

"When trade was good here," Pereira could report of the estuary of the Senegal River, "as many as four hundred slaves could be had in this river . . . in exchange for horses and other merchandise." For the whole trade from the estuary of Senegal "on the frontier of the kingdom of the Joloffs, where are the first Negroes," as far as Sierra Leone on the Guinea Coast, Pereira's estimate was that "when the trade of the country was well ordered, it yielded 3,500 slaves and more, many tusks of ivory, gold, fine cotton cloths and much other merchandise." The European slave trade from Africa had trebled in size during its first fifty years.

2 *Gold and Elephants' Teeth*

RAPIDLY THOUGH SLAVING GREW, IT STILL REMAINED WITHIN THE bounds of a trading system in which other goods were valued and were often more important. Thus far, the trade of the Portuguese differed little from the trans-Saharan trade of the Moors or the transocean trade between East Africa and the lands of India and beyond. Iron Age Africa, whether east or west, had much to offer Europe and Asia — gold, wrought iron, ivory, tortoise shell, even textiles — while there was much that the states of Africa (or at any rate their chiefs and notables) desired to buy in exchange. Slaving was merely a part of the trade from Africa, just as it was merely a part of the trade from Europe.

With the advent of the Portuguese, slaving undoubtedly became a larger part of the whole trade, since slaves were increasingly important for the Portuguese economy; but men in Lisbon

Gold and Elephants' Teeth

were even more interested in gold, and gold soon became the lodestar of their enterprise. Gradually, too, their ships began to act as maritime carriers for African states along the coast. "Our people who are sent out by the Most Serene King in his ships," Pereira reported, "buy slaves two hundred leagues beyond the Castle [of Elmina in modern Ghana] by a river where there is a very large city called Beny [Benin] . . . and from there the slaves are brought to the castle of São Jorge da Mina [Elmina] where they are sold for gold."

Portuguese and Spanish demand for slaves was limited; other European countries had no demand at all. In the sixteenth century neither France nor England had any significant interest in slaves. Neither possessed the large slave reserves which Christian reconquest had conserved in Portugal and Spain. Both were moving into a mercantile economy which would soon give them primacy through the western world. Their early expeditions to the Guinea Coast accordingly concentrated on gold and ivory and pepper.

Thus the first English voyage to West Africa, that of William Hawkins in 1530, yielded a cargo of ivory; and the next, that of John Landye, a captain in Hawkins's service, did the same ten years later. Its bill of lading shows "one dozen elephants' teeth weighing one cwt." Thirteen years later Thomas Windham sailed from Plymouth to the Gold Coast and Benin, where he bargained successfully for gold and ivory and pepper but showed no interest in slaves. Lok followed with still greater success. While Windham's voyage had yielded 150 pounds of gold, Lok came home with more than twice as much.

"They brought with them," says a contemporary account, "foure hundred pound weight and odde of gold, of two and twentie carats and one graine in finenesse: also sixe and thirtie buts of pepper graines, and about 250 elephants' teeth of all quantities. . . ." Lok also returned with "certaine blacke slaves, whereof

THE YEARS OF TRIAL

some were tall and strong"; but it appears that these captives, actually five in number, were acquired more or less haphazardly, and somewhat later they were taken home again.

Rules for trading were already firmly established. These merchants of the Guinea Coast, runs the account of Lok's voyage, "are very wary people in their bargaining, and will not lose one sparke of golde of any value. They use weights and measures, and are very circumspect in occupying the same. They that shall have trade with them must use them gently: for they will not traffique or bring in any wares if they be evill used." When an English sailor stole "a muske cat," the Africans in that place brought all trading to a stop until restitution was made.

And so it continued for a time. Towerson made three voyages between 1555 and 1557, returning with various goods but no slaves. Rutter did the same in 1562. Even as late as 1623 an English captain called Jobson could describe how he was offered slaves on the coast but refused them. A Mandingo trader "showed unto me certain young black women who were standing by themselves . . . which he told me were slaves, brought for me to buy. I made answer, We were a people who did not deal in any such commodities, neither did we buy or sell one another, or any that had our own shapes."

Besides, the profit on other goods was more than satisfactory. Lok's voyage of 1554 is thought to have shown a return amounting to about ten times the capital that was risked. True enough, Lok's was a more than averagely successful voyage, but others could always hope to copy it. Towerson's voyages proved that a copper basin on the Guinea Coast could be exchanged for gold worth some thirty pounds in the sterling of the time — a fabulous return. By 1561, if not before, Queen Elizabeth had taken a leaf out of the king of Portugal's book and engaged royal money in the Guinea trade. Her share in the voyage of 1561 was £1,000 in the

Gold and Elephants' Teeth

money of the time, or about a third of the total investment, and the profits were about 60 per cent.* The next year's expedition, that of 1563, had to fight the Portuguese; but in spite of this both ships, the *Minion* and the *Primrose* with Lok in command, came home with 155 tusks and 22 butts of pepper, commodities of great value; and an undated document which may refer to this voyage says that it also yielded three hundredweights of gold.

If the profits were great, so also were the risks. In the expedition of 1564, Williamson writes, the *Minion* "was reported lost, but she was an ill ship to beat. At midsummer, 1564, an Englishman coming from the Azores declared that he had seen her there, her victuals finished, most of her crew dead, and the few survivors refitting for the voyage home." Again she was given up for lost. Again she fooled the prophets. On July 5 that summer, she "came into the Thames, with a great haul of gold, ivory, and other wares."

French crews and captains had much the same experience and ambitions; and their country, unlike England, specifically condemned the trade in slaves. A royal declaration of 1571 had declared that "France, mother of liberty, permits no slaves"; and a famous legal dictum of 1607 confirmed this with the words: "All persons are free in this kingdom: as soon as a slave has reached these frontiers, and become baptised, he is free." Not for another century and a half would any judgment in England echo sentiments of that kind.

Up to this point, then, the picture is one of a profitable and developing exchange between the thriving maritime nations of Western Europe and some of the coastal states of western Africa. Neither the French nor the English (nor the Dutch, hard on their heels) engaged in slaving, while the Portuguese and Spanish were interested in slaving only to the limited extent of their domestic

---

* These profits were paid over to the Treasurer of the Navy for the use of his department.

THE YEARS OF TRIAL

slave markets. Had matters continued in this way, the slave trade to Portugal and Spain must have dwindled to an insignificant size and finally ceased altogether as the economies of Spain and Portugal merged with the mercantile system then expanding throughout Europe. The history of the oversea slave trade would have remained as little more than a relatively small if painful incident in the enlarging connection between Africa and Europe. The coastal states of Africa would have found themselves pressed and stimulated to deliver not more slaves but more pepper and palm oil, gold and ivory. There might then have arisen on the West African coast the same commercial civilization in trade with Europe as had already developed on the East African coast in trade with Asia. The old equality of status might have broadened into a new equality.

It turned out differently. No more than twenty years after the first Portuguese landing in the Bight of Benin — that of Ruy de Siqueira in 1472 — Columbus had sighted the West Indies. Another eight years, and Pedro Álvares Cabral had made a landfall on Brazil while steering far west of Guinea during a voyage to India. Another thirteen, and Balboa had climbed his peak in Darien and seen the Pacific. The course of history was abruptly changed — for Europe and America, but also for Africa.

Up to this time the trade may have delivered to Europe a few tens of thousands of slaves. But from then until late into the nineteenth century, a period of nearly four hundred years, millions upon millions of captives would suffer transportation in the ships of Portugal and Spain, and afterwards in those of England, France, Holland, Prussia, Denmark, Sweden, Brazil, and the United States of America. The early nature of the African-European connection would be utterly deformed.

3 And Then a Flood

THE SLAVE TRADE TO THE AMERICAS BEGAN, AT LEAST IN RUDIMENtary form, with the earliest ships that crossed the Atlantic; but it was not at first a specially African trade. Domestic hands were needed, and these could also be found in Europe.

Yet the demand for labor in the West Indies and the mines of Central America grew with frantic speed. The conquerors began by enslaving the populations they had found, the "Indians," but death robbed them of these. Next they turned back again to Europe and attempted to fill the ranks with "indentured" or near-slave workers from home. When this would not suffice, they applied to Africa; and there at last they saw their problem solved.

By as early as 1501, only nine years after the first voyage of Columbus, the Spanish throne had issued its initial proclamation on laws for the export of slaves to America — mainly, as yet, to Hispaniola (Haiti and the Dominican Republic today). These slaves were white — whether from Spain or North Africa — more often than black; for the black slaves, it was early found, were turbulent and hard to tame. How poorly grounded in fact was the old legend of "African docility" may be seen from the events of 1503. In that year the Spanish governor of Hispaniola, Ovando, complained to the Spanish Court that fugitive Negro slaves among the Indians were teaching disobedience, and that it was impossible to re-capture them. Ovando asked for an end to the export of Negro slaves, and Queen Isabella consented. She seems to have decided to allow the export to the Indies only of white slaves, although her motive was no doubt different from Ovando's: she hoped that Christian slaves would help in the work of converting the heathen, not knowing, of course, that most of the heathen would soon be dead.

THE YEARS OF TRIAL

Export of Christian slaves continued, though in small numbers, until the end of the seventeenth century; generally they were women, and they were for use but not for sale. Thus in 1526 a license was granted to a certain Bartolomeo Conejo for the opening of a brothel at Puerto Rico, and to Sanchez Sarmento for the establishment of another in Santo Domingo; and white girls were needed for these. A few years later the Spanish governor of Peru secured a license through his brother Fernando Pizarro for the import from Spain of four girls who, the license stipulated, "must be born in Castile and Christians baptized before the age of ten" — not, that is to say, converted Moorish or Negro women. This early white-slave traffic dwindled after the middle of the sixteenth century; yet as late as 1692 there is record of a permit issued for the export of four girls to Veracruz in Mexico.

The trade in Negro captives became important as early as 1510. Before that, there had been sporadic shipments whenever the need for labor was especially acute. Ovando, in Hispaniola, had soon been forced to change his mind about suppression of the Negro trade; already in 1505, thirteen years after Columbus had made his crossing, the Spanish archives mention a caravel sailing from Seville with seventeen Negro slaves and some mining equipment. Soon Ovando was asking for many more Negro workers. And in 1510 there came the beginning of the African slave trade in its massive and special form: royal orders were given for the transport first of fifty and then of two hundred slaves for *sale* in the Indies. Throughout the years that followed it was to be the searing brand of this trade that it would consider its victims, not as servants or domestic slaves who deserved respect in spite of their servile condition, but as chattel slaves, commodities that could and should be sold at whim or will.

From its earliest growth this trade bore the marks of an exceptional cruelty and waste. Yet these were not peculiar to the

And Then a Flood

Negro trade. European slaves and near-slaves were treated little or no better. Irish and other prisoners transported to the West Indies in Cromwellian and later times — all those, in the slang of the period, who were "barbadoe'd" — suffering appalling conditions. A petition to Parliament in 1659 described how seventy-two unfortunates from England had been locked up below deck during the whole passage of five and a half weeks, "amongst horses, that their souls through heat and steam under the tropic, fainted in them."

Transport conditions for slaves from Africa were generally worse: witness a well-known letter of the Spanish king to a certain Sampier, in Hispaniola, in the year 1511, in which the king complains that "I cannot understand why so many Negroes die." Yet the intolerable and special aspect of Negro slavery was its very permanence; even though manumission of slaves was always less resisted in the Catholic Indies and South America than in the Protestant states of North America, Negroes were everywhere intended to occupy the lowest ranks of society and to stay there.

This the Negro slaves resisted. They escaped when they could. They rose in bloody rebellion. They fought for their lives. The first notable Negro slave revolt in Hispaniola broke out as early as 1522. Five years later there was another in Puerto Rico. A third at Santa Marta in 1529. A fourth in Panama in 1531. By 1532 the Spanish had established a special police for chasing fugitive slaves.

Yet nothing could stop the trade. There was too much money in it for the courts of Europe. The Spanish king was probably in receipt of cash from slaving taxes even before 1510, the date of the first big "license" for Negro slaves. In 1513 a royal tax was promulgated which made every license cost two ducats, a license being understood as the permit for shipping a single slave; on top of this there was an export tax. These taxes immediately provoked smuggling; and it appears that the earliest African slaves shipped

THE YEARS OF TRIAL

from Portugal to the Indies were sent out clandestinely by tax-evaders.

In 1515 there came the first Spanish shipment of slave-grown West Indian sugar and in 1518, as though by the sheer logic of the thing, the first cargo of African slaves directly from Africa to the West Indies. Royal authority was given for transporting four thousand black slaves. These were to be obtained directly from the Guinea Coast to obviate any danger that North African captivity might have tainted them with Muslim loyalties; but it is quite clear, of course, that so large a number could not possibly have been gotten from anywhere except the Guinea Coast. The "Black Mother" had already shown how fertile she could be, and how blind to the consequences.

After 1518 the trade became increasingly an institution, a part of the Spanish economy, an absolutely essential aspect of the whole Spanish-American adventure. The kings of Spain lived off the trade. Even the licenses they authorized and sold became, with time, salable property in themselves — shares in the great process of colonial pilfering and pillage that were exchanged in the money markets of Spain just as government stock is bought and sold today.

As with other economic enterprises, the right to collect and deal in slaves remained a royal property. The kings themselves took no direct part in the business, but farmed it out to wealthy merchants and mariners. This method of farming out the right to buy slaves in Africa and sell them in the Americas was that of the assiento, in essence a royal permit carrying strict conditions of time and price. So far as slaving was concerned, the assiento system applied only to Guinea slaves, since Christianity forbade the sale (though not the use) of Christian slaves, and discouraged the export of North African slaves because they were Muslims and might make anti-Christian propaganda.

And Then a Flood

There were assientos for every branch of business that royalty could lay its hands on, but the slaving assiento topped them all. The system really began to show its value in 1592. Before that, the king had granted licenses for small numbers of captives and on few occasions. But in 1592, trying to meet a demand for slaves that was rendered practically inexhaustible by the holocausts of those who died, the court spewed up a monster of an assiento. No longer was it a question of delivering a few hundred African captives to the Americas; the new license was for the transport of 38,250 slaves. Gomes Reynal, who bought this license, was to deliver his captives over a period of nine years at the rate of 4,250 a year; of these, it was stipulated, at least 3,500 a year must be landed alive. Reynal had to pay nearly a million ducats for this concession and agreed to forfeit ten ducats for every slave short of 3,500 a year. The captives were to be fresh from the Guinea Coast and were to include "no mulattoes, nor mestizos, nor Turks, nor Moors." (They would have included many Negro Muslims, of course, but nobody in Spain would have known this, and perhaps nobody would much have cared.)

The profits of slaving came from many regions. A report of 1520 shows that Portuguese planters were already producing sugar by slave labor in the South Atlantic island of São Tomé, off the coast of Angola. Yet the main profits were always in the Americas. By 1540 the annual rate of direct shipment from Africa to the other side of the Atlantic was already running at several thousand captives, although fewer than fifty years had passed since the discovery of America.

Other maritime nations watched with gathering interest. Though formally debarred from any part in this promising enterprise, English and French interlopers soon took a hand. Nothing more clearly shows how things were moving than the contrast between most of the early English and French voyages to the

THE YEARS OF TRIAL

Guinea Coast, whose object was gold and pepper and ivory, and the slaving ventures of John Hawkins at about the same time.

Son of that old William Hawkins of Plymouth in whose service Landye had sailed to Guinea many years before, John Hawkins began his oversea trading with the Canaries. "There," says the record, "by his good and upright dealing being growen in love and favour with the people, he informed himselfe amongst them by diligent inquisition, of the state of the West India. . . . And being amongst other particulars assured, that Negroes were very good merchandise in Hispaniola, and that store of Negroes might easily bee had upon the coast of Guinea, resolved with himselfe to make triall thereof. . . ."

Merchants in London liked the scheme and backed Hawkins with "three good ships," the *Salomon*, the *Swallow*, and the *Jonas*. With crews totaling a hundred, Hawkins "put off and departed from the coast of England in the moneth of October 1562 and . . . passed to the coast of Guinea . . . where he stayed some time and got into his possession, partly by the sword and partly by other meanes, to the number of three hundred Negroes at the least. . . ." This is all that the English documents have to say; but the Portuguese, who suffered from Hawkins's large-handed piracy, add something to the tale. Their records complain that Hawkins seized a Portuguese slaver with 200 Negroes aboard, three other vessels with 70 apiece, and a fifth with 500. But these numbers seem exaggerated, for Hawkins's ships were small.

"With this praye," whatever its true dimensions, Hawkins "sayled over the ocean sea unto the iland of Hispaniola . . . and there hee had reasonable utterance of his English commodities, as also of some part of his Negroes. . . ." Thence he went on from port to port, "standing alwaies upon his guard," and finally disposed of all his cargoes. For these he received "such quantities

And Then a Flood

of merchandise, that hee did not onely lade his owne three shippes with hides, ginger, sugars, and some quantities of pearles, but he fraighted also two other hulkes with hides and the like commodities, which hee sent into Spain." (Why he should have sent goods to Spain remains obscure; they were seized on arrival, along with the crews of the ships that carried them, and Hawkins estimated his loss at £20,000 in the money of the time.)

Thus began the "Great Circuit" trade that was to dominate much of the commerce of the western world for many years thereafter. This circuit consisted in the export of cheap manufactured goods from Europe to Africa; the purchase or seizure of slaves on the Guinea Coast and their transportation across the Atlantic; the exchange of these slaves for minerals and foodstuffs in the West Indies and Americas; and, lastly, the sale of these raw materials and foods in Europe.

By this triangular system three separate profits were taken, all high and all in Europe: the first profit was that of selling consumer goods to the slavers; the second derived from selling slaves to the planters and mine-owners of the Americas; while the third (and biggest) was realized on the sale of American and West Indian cargoes in Europe. It was largely on the steady and often stupendous profits of this circuitous enterprise that France and England would ground their commercial supremacy.

Hawkins sailed again in 1564 and a third time in 1567; on both occasions he went mainly for slaves, and with like success. He financed at least one other slaving voyage on which he did not sail himself, that of Lovell in 1566. The king of Spain was furious but as yet unprepared to act — not for another twenty years would the Armada sail for England. Meanwhile, Queen Elizabeth returned soft, misleading answers to the protests of Guzman de Silva, Philip's ambassador at the Court of St. James; and so did Cecil, her principal minister.

THE YEARS OF TRIAL

"I have spoken to the queen about the six ships that are being fitted out for Hawkins," de Silva wrote to his master on the eve of the third voyage. "She says she has had the merchants" — the London backers of the venture — "into her presence and made them swear that they are not going to any place prohibited by your Majesty. . . . Cecil also says they are not going to your Majesty's dominions but still I am doubtful, because what they seek in Guinea most are slaves to take to the West Indies. I will use all efforts to prevent their going, but the greed of these people is great and they are not only merchants who have shares in these adventures but secretly many of the queen's Council. . . ." Philip might grieve for his slaving taxes. So much the worse for him. The gentlemen of England wanted their share as well.

Yet the slave trade of the sixteenth century, despite these occasional raids from the north, was essentially a Spanish-Portuguese monopoly. The French and English, early on the Guinea Coast in the wake of the Portuguese and Spanish, sometimes worked together against a common enemy, and sometimes fell out and fought. Their interest in any case was not in slaving. Towerson, on his second voyage, that of 1566-1567, both worked with the French and came to blows with them; his dramatic story illustrates the ruthless competition that would accompany the Guinea trade to the very threshold of the twentieth century.

Returning westward, Towerson says, "we had sight of a shippe in the weather of us, which was a Frenchman of ninety tunne who came with us as stoutly and as desperately as might be, and coming neere us, perceived that we had bene upon a long voyage, and judging us to be weake, as indeed we were, came neerer to us and thought to have layed us aboard.

"And there stept up some of his men in armour and commanded us to strike saile; whereupon we sent them some of our stuffe, crosse-barres and chainshot and arrowes, so thick that it made the upper worke of their shippe flie about their eares, and we spoiled him with all his men, and toare his shippe miserably with our great ordinance, and then he began to fall asterne of us, and to packe on his sailes, and get away.

"And we, seeing that, gave him four or five good pieces more for his farewell; and thus we were rid of this Frenchman, who did us no harme at all. We had aboord us a Frenchman, a trumpetter, who, being sicke and lying in his bed, tooke his trumpet notwithstanding, and sounded till he could sound no more, and so died. . . ."

Out of these grim rivalries, in small ships and with small crews, attacked by fevers and the furies of the sea, wrecked and ruined by one another in sudden battles from the coast of Senegal to the Bight of Benin and far beyond, there nonetheless emerged a pattern of commercial exchange and, gradually, a recognized order of behavior.

4 Battle for the Coast

NEW COMPETITORS APPEARED. THE FRENCH AND ENGLISH GREW bolder and were joined by Dutchmen and Danes and Swedes, and afterwards by Prussians. Tactics changed. The English and French had generally contented themselves with mere "interloping trade": their method was to anchor offshore, having slipped out of the way of large Portuguese fleets or fought their way through small Portugese fleets, and to stay just long enough to sell their goods and buy ivory and gold or — as now increasingly — their slaves. But the Dutch proceeded otherwise.

Commercially more efficient than the English or the French,

THE YEARS OF TRIAL

the Dutch in the early seventeenth century perceived that the key to a command of this rapidly developing trade was to copy the Portuguese example and establish permanent settlements and strong points on shore. They were helped on the Gold Coast by the exertions of a coastal people living near Komenda and known in the records as the Fetu. This people saw that Dutch wares would be preferable to Portuguese if only the Portuguese monopoly could be systematically broken, and not merely evaded from time to time. They accordingly rose against the Portuguese and drove them from all their settlements on the Gold Coast except Axim and Elmina, which the Dutch had already, though unsuccessfully, assaulted.

Taking advantage of this, the Dutch built a base of their own at Mowree (or Mouri) in 1611 or 1612, and named it Fort Nassau. Five years later they obtained from its local ruler a small island lying within the lee of Cape Verde, called Goree. There they built two forts; and opposite Goree, on the mainland at Rio Fresco (Rufisque), they ran up storehouses and established a "factory" — which meant a trading post, of course, and not a place where goods were manufactured. Finally they seized Elmina Castle from the Portuguese in 1637, one hundred and fifty-five years after its construction, and put an end to Portuguese presence on the Gold Coast by taking their last remaining fort of Axim in 1642.

Whether Dutch or not, these enterprises were set in train partly by the European governments concerned and partly by wealthy merchants. The usual procedure was for a government or king in Europe to grant a national monopoly of trade with the Guinea Coast to a company of merchants. Such ventures were among the earliest experiments in company formation. Thus the first genuine incorporation of English investors for the Guinea trade occurred in 1618, when James I gave a charter of monopoly to thirty London

Battle for the Coast

merchants, the Company of Adventurers of London Trading into Parts of Africa. Other companies followed, some successful and others not.

The Dutch were soon ahead of their rivals. They knew more about commerce and were unhampered by royal prerogatives. Their West India Company — joining trade to Guinea with settlement in the West Indies — was formed in 1621, only a few years after their first appearance in West Africa. This company prospered. It did so well that rival Dutch merchants found its monopolist claims intolerable and gave their backing in 1647 to a Swedish African Company, formed under Swedish royal patronage. On behalf of this Dutch-financed Swedish company, a Danish captain called Carloff founded four settlements on the Gold Coast. He then quarreled with his employers and transferred his service to the government and merchants of his own country. So Denmark appeared on the coast. Later in the same century the Danes were followed by the Germans of expanding Prussia.

Almost from the first, then, the coastal peoples were presented with the spectacle of intense and warring rivalry between these newcomers from oversea. They could not know exactly what the motives and methods of these European rivals might be, nor how the profits were realized and shared; but their own experience of trade was an old one, and they soon came to terms with the strangers. Between them these various and assorted partners worked out an intricate system of business habits, taxes, currencies, and trading jargon. This widely accepted system, one should note, had come into existence many years before slaving dominated the whole trade. The slave trade, in short, was grafted little by little into a living nexus of commercial needs and appetites and habits.

Many letters of the period throw light on the manners of this system. Rivalry was the great driving force. "The Dutch," writes

THE YEARS OF TRIAL

an English agent at the famous trading point of Cormantin on the Gold Coast in 1663, "give daily great presents to the King of Futton and the *cabesheers* [the African chief's trading agents] to exclude their honours [the English Royal African Company] from the trade, and to the King of Fantyn and his *cabesheers*, to make war on the English castle of Cormantin, saying that if they could but get that place never Englishman more should have trading upon that coast. . . ."

In the same year another English agent, Captain Stokes, at Ardra in modern Dahomey, is complaining: "The Dutch told the King of Ardra that they had conquered the Portugals, the potentest nation that ever was in those countries, and turned out the Dane and Swede, and in a short time should do the same to the English, and by these discourses hindered the Company's factors from trade. . . ."

Still in this same year of 1663, with English-Dutch rivalries coming to a peak, the English agent at Komenda on the Gold Coast, a Mr. Brett, reports how he "came to the place on the 21st [August], and the Dutch man-of-war told them they must not go ashore; in two days more the *Amsterdam* came from Castle de Myne [Elmina, then in Dutch hands], and sent two men on board to see if they belonged to the Royal Company, pretending if they had been interlopers that they [the Dutch] had power to take them. Next day the Dutch manned out three long boats, and continued firing at all canoes that would have traded with the English, and those canoes that were made fast to the English ship the Dutch cut from the ship's side, which one of the seamen endevouring to prevent, a Dutchman cut him in the leg. So the English boat weighed anchor, the long boat's men giving us such base language as was not to be endured. . . ."

These brawling manners on the Coast were to have their effect on the opinions about each other of Europeans and Africans. Both

Battle for the Coast

sides tended to generalize from their own experiences; and both reached some surprisingly odd conclusions.

It became common belief among Europeans that Africans habitually ate men from taste and preference. But it became just as common belief among Africans that Europeans did the same. "Among the many slaves we carry thence to America," an agent of the French Royal African Company, John Barbot, was noting around 1683, "there are many . . . who are positively prepossessed with the opinion that we transport them into our country in order to kill and eat them. . . ." Such reports were not rare. About fifty years later a British slaving ship's surgeon, John Atkins, warning of the risks of insurrection, remarked: "When we are slaved and out at sea, it is commonly imagined that the Negroes' Ignorance of Navigation will always be a safeguard; yet, as many of them think themselves bought to eat, and more, that Death will send them into their own country, there has not been wanting Examples of rising and killing a Ship's Company, distant from Land, though not so often as on the Coast." Nobody talked as yet of any "civilizing mission."

And as yet there was little talk of conquest, either. The coastal peoples were far too strong. European captains and traders went ashore, whether for trade or warlike expedition against rivals, in agreement with this or that coastal chief. More often than not, the two sides still dealt with each other as equals unless, as happened frequently, the Europeans sued for favors, bribed for preferences, bought the use of land for forts, or simply talked their way ashore. Gradually, as time went on and European striking power increased, this early equality would be altogether lost. Many of the smaller kings along the coast would become the clients or protected agents of this or that European fortress. Later again the bigger kings would be picked off one by one or else subjected by force of arms. But all that lay in the future. The nineteenth cen-

THE YEARS OF TRIAL

tury world that maritime Europe would dominate by war and conquest was still in the making.

That world was partly made by European penetration into the rich lands of the East. Yet penetration into the West Indies and the Americas was perhaps even more important. In the seventeenth century, when Portugal lost its command of the West African Coast, Spain also lost its primacy across the Atlantic. Spanish monopoly of the West Indies foundered and sank. The armed ships of England, France, Holland, and Denmark sailed there as they wished, went ashore and made new settlements, and entered the West Indian enterprise on their own account.

The English established themselves in the Bermudas in 1609, in St. Christopher in 1623, in Barbados in 1625, and thence onward to the Leeward Islands. The French came hard behind them, founding settlements on Guadeloupe in 1626, on Martinique in 1635, and elsewhere in following years. The Dutch, for their part, took the southern Caribbean islands of Curaçao, St. Eustatius, and Tobago during the 1630's. The Danes occupied St. Thomas in 1671.

The coastlands of North America saw the process of step-by-step settlement and occupation. By about the middle of the seventeenth century the French were firmly established along the valley of the St. Lawrence River and in Nova Scotia; the English were strong in New England, several hundred miles to the southward; and beyond that again there was the Dutch settlement of New Amsterdam, which would afterwards become New York. Continuing southward, there were the English settlements of Maryland and Virginia. Finally, in the extreme south, there was the Spanish colony of St. Augustine in Florida.

With this far-reaching spread of European settlement across the Atlantic, there came a fresh and potent encouragement to the Guinea slave trade. Up to now the "interloping nations" had seen

Battle for the Coast

their interest solely in conveying African slaves from West Africa to the Spanish possessions in the Caribbean or to Brazil. They continued to supply the Spanish colonies and Brazil. Cuba, for the West Indies, became their principal "point of exchange." But now they met with a new demand for slaves from their newly settled fellow-countrymen. This was not much of a demand at first, since these early colonists in the West Indies and North America could furnish their slave needs from the Cuba market. By about 1640, though, the settlements had grown and prospered to the point where an enormous extension in the slave trade became necessary. At this point the slaving tide became a flood.

The explanations were two: sugar and tobacco planting. Sugar had been rare in Europe. Now it became big business. For many European merchants the rest of the seventeenth century was almost literally "the century of sugar." Tobacco became important, and so did rum and West Indian coffee and cotton; but the grand consumer of slaves in the new lands across the Atlantic, and the great maker of profits for Europe, was "King Sugar."

Neither sugar nor tobacco could be grown without abundant field labor. Planters depended directly on the African slave trade. And they used their labor with such wasteful folly that whole slave populations had to be replenished time after time. A British eyewitness in the Dutch West Indian colony of Surinam at the end of the eighteenth century made an observation that applied to many other places. Plantation mortality was so high, he found, that "the whole race of healthy slaves, consisting of 50,000, are totally extinct once every twenty years."

France and England were the principal agents of this new commercial system. Sugar was introduced into the French West Indies in 1640. It soon rivaled tobacco as the main product and source of profit. Less than twenty-five years later France was importing so much West Indian raw sugar and had founded so many refineries that she was even able to sell processed sugar to the rest of Europe. And so consuming was the new need for slave labor that the French Government found itself obliged to break the slaving monopoly of the French West Indian Company. A royal order of 1670 threw open the slave trade to any Frenchman who wished to engage in it. The king's desire, declared this order, was to promote in every way possible "the trade in Negroes from Guinea to the Islands [of the Caribbean]. . . . There is nothing that does more to help the growth of those colonies . . . than the labour of Negroes."

The effects were immediate. Like its English counterpart, French slaving grew by leaps and bounds of furious enterprise. From 1670 to 1672, it would appear, French vessels carried slaves across the Atlantic at the rate of more than three thousand a year. This was far more than ever before. But it was still far fewer than during the years of tremendous commercial expansion that now began.

5 The Trade Pays Off

SPECULATION WAS THE PARTICULAR FURY OF THAT TIME. GREAT fortunes were made — and sometimes lost — in colonial enterprise. Money in Europe not only talked; perhaps for the first time on any massive scale, it was also seen to talk. Parliament and posts of influence and favor were repeatedly stormed and won by little men who climbed to power on the profits of sugar, tobacco, and slaves. "As wealthy as a West Indian" was the eighteenth century forerunner of phrases that would later celebrate the potent riches of oil barons and steel tycoons.

In those racketing years a man like William Miles could walk

The Trade Pays Off

into the port of Bristol with three ha'pence in his pocket and make a fortune. The story of Miles was certainly not unique. He worked as an unskilled laborer until he had saved fifteen pounds. Then he signed as ship's carpenter for a voyage to Jamaica, where he bought "a cask or two of sugar" with his savings and sailed back to Bristol, there selling his sugar at the usual fat profit. His next operation was fully in the old Bristol "circuit." Miles now bought a consignment of English manufactured goods, sold them against sugar in Jamaica, and resold the sugar in Bristol. After that, he simply repeated the operation until strong enough to launch out on his own. When his son died in 1848, the Miles estate was valued at more than half a million pounds.

Everyone was doing it. "Almost every man in Liverpool is a merchant," runs a description of that city in the 1790's, "and he who cannot send a bale will send a band-box." In 1720, England had imported just over half a million tons of sugar; by the end of the century, the average annual import was about five times as large. In Britain's rising accumulation of capital, the West Indies was now more important even than India. "There were comparatively few big merchants in Great Britain in 1761," Namier would comment in 1929, "who, in one connection or another, did not trade with the West Indies, and a considerable number of gentry families had interests in the Sugar Islands, just as vast numbers of Englishmen now hold shares in Asiatic rubber or tea plantations or oil fields."

The big men carried off the prizes. In 1753 the Cunliffes of Liverpool fitted out four ships for the transport from Africa to the West Indies of 1,210 slaves. These ships made two or three voyages a year on the regular circuit — England to West Africa, thence to the West Indies and North America, and so back again to England — and brought the Cunliffe family enough return on their investment to stock another dozen vessels in the Caribbean

THE YEARS OF TRIAL

with rum, sugar, and other articles for highly profitable sale in England. In 1719 the port of Liverpool had 18,371 tons of registered shipping. By 1792 this rose to 260,382 tons. And it was the "Great Circuit" trade in consumer goods, slaves, sugar, and tobacco and rum that commissioned most of the new tonnage.

Later imperial expansion would make people forget this early importance of the West Indies to the growing wealth of England and France. But no one forgot it then. They saw the fabulous mansions of the West Indies merchants, their glittering displays of wealth, their careless influence on affairs; and they drew appropriate conclusions. "Sugar, sugar, eh — all *that* sugar! How are the duties, eh, Pitt, how are the duties?" Such was the King of England's disgruntled comment to his Prime Minister when confronted with the lavish spectacle of a West Indies merchant in the pleasure resort of Weymouth, driving in state with liveried outriders and every sign of gilded wealth, towards the end of the eighteenth century.

By that time the value of British incomes derived from trade with the West Indies was said to be four times greater than the value of British incomes derived from trade with the rest of the world. And this West Indian trade was in many respects the ideal colonial system. For unlike the trade with the East Indies, which required the export of bullion and threatened Europe with the import of cheap Eastern textiles, the trade with the West Indies consisted in simple exchange of cheap manufactured goods for African slaves; of African slaves for West Indian foodstuffs and tobacco; and of these products, once brought to Europe, for a high return in cash.

Out of this rapid economic expansion there flowed the circumstances that enabled England to achieve an industrial revolution. Among these, the stimulus of the Great Circuit trade was undoubtedly a main factor. It was not only that relatively small capital

The Trade Pays Off

investments in this trade could show big returns, for direct reinvestment by "West Indians" often went into mere consumption and display. More important, the trade brought an ever-growing demand for cheap manufactured goods to fill the slave ships on their outward journey. "What the building of ships for the transport of slaves did for eighteenth century Liverpool," notes Williams, "the manufacture of cotton goods for the purchase of slaves did for eighteenth century Manchester."

It was the same in France. To merchants in the Atlantic ports the Great Circuit trade was returning a regular profit of 300 per cent on their investment. "The founding of industries, private fortunes, public opulence, the rebuilding of towns, the social glories of a new class: great merchants eager for public office that should reflect their economic importance and impatient to be rid of what they called, with careless exaggeration, 'the shame of servitude'; such," writes Gaston-Martin, "were the sum of the essential consequences for eighteenth century France of the African slave trade."

On a different scale the East Indian trade was doing the same work. Import from the East of expensive consumer goods — silks, calicoes, china — stimulated the manufacture of cheaper copies in England and France; just as, later on, the East would take its revenge and would in turn manufacture still cheaper copies from European examples. Porcelain from China was expensive; but Josiah Wedgwood showed how glazed earthenware could offer a native substitute within reach of many pockets. Silks and calicoes were costly; but Lancashire led the way in spinning cottons that were not. These factory-made goods spread across the world. Lancashire textiles soon began to oust the home-made cottons of West Africa and elsewhere.

These were years of great industrial invention. More coal, for example, was needed for the new factories: "the demand for coal was so great," says Plumb, "that it is almost possible to speak of a coal rush." But the demand could be met only if better methods were devised for pumping water from ever-deepening mines. The solution was the steam pump. Newcomen and Savery found it as early as 1712. Watt went a step further in 1776. By 1803 Trevithick was building a steam locomotive to run on iron rails; and in 1830 Stephenson's "Rocket" pulled thirty passengers from Stockton to Darlington at thirty miles an hour.

Growth and innovation in the textile industry showed the same movement. In 1733 Kay invented a mechanical shuttle to displace the hand-thrown shuttle. Five years later, Paul came out with a means of spinning by rollers. In 1768 Hargreaves combined various inventions into his "spinning jenny." At first an operator could work eight spindles on the jenny; later, as many as eighty or more. Arkwright followed almost at once with the "throstle" for spinning by use of animal or water power. By 1774 there were 30,000 cotton workers in or near Manchester, and by 1811 Britain had more than 300,000 spindles working by Arkwright's principle.

These inventions were the work of craftsmen struggling to meet an apparently inexhaustible demand for cheap consumer goods. The mere export figures suggest what this demand did for the accumulation of capital in Britain: in 1701 the value of British exports of cotton goods and yarns stood at little more than £23,000; yet in 1800 the total was nearly £5,500,000. Industrialism was born, and it was the West African trade in all its ramifications that presided over the event.

For the vast majority of those involved, it was not a happy event. If the birth was bitter for Africans, it was scarcely less painful for the new workers of Britain. Slave labor on the one side, factory labor on the other — there was little in the manner of the times to distinguish one from the other. The old England of farming comfort and small merchant cities was hemmed around or swallowed

The Trade Pays Off

up entirely by a new land of huge and hungry manufacturing towns where poverty and squalor sank to depths not touched before. This was the England Shelley remembered: "Such starvation cannot be, as in England now we see."

At this time, whatever may have happened later, there was no social spreading within Britain of the wealth of industrialism. The pyramid of money was hard to climb and remained so. One of the greatest of the West Indies merchants, William Beckford, a Member of Parliament and Lord Mayor of London, declared in 1770 that his son's fortune would be "£40,000 a year, besides many thousands in cash." Another London merchant-politician, Sir Samuel Fludyer, amassed a fortune that was valued in 1767 at about £900,000. Labor was dirt cheap and income tax unheard-of· no one before had ever possessed such wealth in cash.

Rivalry for seats in Parliament — straight road to influence for the common man in a Britain still ruled by aristocracy — expressed the spirit of the times. For money could talk to better effect here than anywhere else in social life. The electorate was tiny, and purchase and intimidation were the order of the day. "Taking England as a whole," Namier observes of 1761, "probably not more than one in every twenty voters at county elections could freely exercise his statutory rights." Polling was a public affair; and votes were "usually even recorded in print in the so-called poll books."

Here was an open field for the self-made man, whether city merchant or planter returned from the islands. He and his kind lost no time in tilling it. The price of seats rose to fantastic levels. In 1761 as much as £2,000 in the money of the day had to be paid for a "pocket borough"; and the records swell with aristocratic complaint against West Indian and other merchants for pushing up the price. And although the actual number of oversea merchants who sat in these Parliaments was small — only twelve West Indians in that of 1761, two East Indian "nabobs," and nine or ten mer-

THE YEARS OF TRIAL

chants with Eastern interests — they represented a most puissant concentration of wealth.

A few bare facts are enough to show the central and indispensable part that was played in all this by the African trade, now almost exclusively a trade in slaves. From a casual bargain or "trading accident," the business of slaving had become a matter of colonial policy, an important affair of state. Gaston-Martin remarks of the French West African trade that after about 1715 it was involved primarily and overwhelmingly in slaving; the purchase of gold, ivory, and other goods had fallen to a secondary consideration of dwindling importance. The comment is true also for the trade of Britain and of other nations.

By the beginning of the eighteenth century the Dutch were falling behind. In 1702 the French Guinea Company acquired the Spanish assiento, and actually changed its name to the Assiento Company. Its contract called for the delivery of 38,000 Negro slaves to the Spanish colonies, or 48,000 if the war between France and England should meanwhile come to an end, over ten or twelve years. The slaving revenue of the Spanish king was fixed at 33⅓ silver crowns for each *pièce d'Inde*, a reckoning which might mean several slaves or only one, according to quality; and the company was required to pay the greater part of this in advance.

Britain got hold of the slaving assiento in 1713; and the trade to the Spanish colonies now became officially British. The terms were much the same as before: the British were to provide 144,000 slaves over thirty years, or an average of 4,800 a year. This monopoly they purchased from the Spanish king for 200,000 crowns and agreed to pay a duty of 33⅓ crowns for each slave landed alive. Of their trading profits the merchants were to pay the Spanish royal treasury one quarter, and the English royal treasury another quarter.

But slaving for the Spanish colonies was now only a small part

The Trade Pays Off

of the business. The British and the French (and the Dutch, to a much lesser extent) were also slaving for their own colonies. After 1713, for one reason or another, the business in slaves became increasingly valuable. The English slavers alone probably carried as many as 15,000 slaves a year in the period immediately after 1713, or three times the number required by their contract with Spain.

In England the ports of Liverpool, Bristol, and London led the way. Records for 1744, a typical midcentury year, show 104 ships as having cleared from those three ports, and a further 13 from Lancaster, Glasgow, Chester, and Plymouth. As the years passed and the new industrial and mercantile system gathered strength, slaving totals continued to swell and multiply. What appears to have been a reasonably reliable estimate for the years 1795-1804, when the trade was at its height, gave the following clearances of ships from the three main English ports:

Port	Slaves Allowed by Regulations	Number of Ships
Liverpool	323,770	1,099
London	46,505	155
Bristol	10,718	29

The profits of the slaving aspect of the circuit trade were seldom a major interest; and they do not seem, in themselves, to have founded great fortunes. The reason for this was that the risk of loss was always great with a cargo as perishable as sardine-packed slaves. But slaves were a vital factor in the system, which could not be worked without them; and large profits were undoubtedly extracted from "fortunate" voyages. Liverpool records for the years 1795-1804 suggest that such voyages were by no means rare. The *Lottery* took 305 slaves to Jamaica at a net profit of £11,039, or about £36 a head. The *Enterprize* took 392 slaves to Cuba at a net profit of £6,428, or about £16 a head. The *Fortune* made a net profit of £1,847 on 343 slaves, or about £5 9s. a head. For ten earlier years — 1783-1793 — a contemporary writer estimated that Liverpool slavers had made a profit of about £2,360,000 on the conveyance of about 303,000 slaves.

These few examples indicate the scale of the business. But to grasp it in its full significance one needs to remember that slaving engulfed the maritime effort of many European nations. Towards the end of the eighteenth century, the worst hundred years of slaving the world had ever known, it became the interest of a handful of Englishmen and Frenchmen to discover how great that effort really was. They did not find it easy to collect their facts. But they persevered with their inquiries, and they used their hardwon information to tremendous effect. They successfully challenged the whole existence of the trade.

6 Abolition

THE TIMES WERE RIPE FOR CHANGE. ENGLAND'S ECONOMY WAS NO longer that of a hundred years earlier. Then it had rested in its imperialist aspect on the import of raw sugar and cotton, rum and tobacco; and on the sale of these, whether processed or not, at regularly higher prices. Now it was based, more and more, on export of the finished products of a manufacturing industry that drew its strength from accumulated capital, from mechanical methods of work, and from England's fortunate command of large deposits of coal and iron ore.

These new industries, the fruit of new skills and new investment, needed raw materials and foreign markets — not slaves in the Caribbean. They had created their own labor force at home.

Abolition

They had brought into being their own native system of productive coercion. They were strong enough to stand on their own feet; and their owners, the new industrialists, felt themselves less and less dependent on the planters and merchants and slavers of the Great Circuit trade. West Indian interests might rail and rage; but their day was really over.

Early in the nineteenth century, Britain abolished the oversea slave trade by means of British ships and actively sought to prevent slaves being carried by any other ships. And the coercion of slave labor in the islands, as industrialism in Britain gathered force, was gradually transferred and tranformed to the new coercion of factory labor in Britain, just as, in later days, the same coercion would be once again transferred and extended to cheap mining and plantation labor in the African colonies. Today, looking back across the years, the process can be seen well enough; yet it remains a strange irony that early British industrialism, bitter curse to its victims, should thus have helped to bring about the abolition of the slave trade.

The full impact of the change still lay ahead. Growing demands for cheap raw materials and for security of foreign markets would eventually trace the outlines of territorial conquest, of the colonial system of the twentith century; and Africa, when this came about, would register the full consequences of the slave trade that had gone before. But it was the end of oversea slaving that now held all attention.

To say that economic changes underlay the abolition of the slave trade is not to deny the great work of the humanitarian abolitionists. They were brave and devoted men, and it was thanks to them that abolition came in the first years of the nineteenth century and not later — perhaps much later. It was they who mobilized opinion, attacked the slavers, exposed the horrors of the Middle Passage, spoke for the victims, and drew the whole

THE YEARS OF TRIAL

question of slavery into the train of liberal thought and political action. Even today there is no one, I imagine, or no one with a heart that beats, who can read the story of Thomas Clarkson riding into Bristol without a thrill of pride and admiration for a bold, unself-regarding man.

On that day, still many years before the parliamentary triumph of 1805, it was David challenging Goliath. Clarkson tells in his famous book how he first came within sight of Bristol, the second of the great slaving ports of Western Europe, on turning a corner of the road. "The weather was rather hazy, which occasioned Bristol to look of unusual dimensions. . . . I began now to tremble, for the first time, at the arduous task I had undertaken, of attempting to subvert one of the branches of the commerce of the great place which was before me. . . . I anticipated much persecution in it, also; and I questioned whether I should even get out of it alive. . . ."

But Clarkson did get out of it alive; and the noble work of subversion, thanks to his friends and himself, went boldly forward. Much that they did was important for the future of liberal protest in England: they pamphleteered, lobbied, pressured, stumped the country in speaking campaigns. They played on the hopes and ambitions of Members of Parliament as well as on their sense of humanity. They engineered debates, promoted commissions of inquiry, drew up "bodies of evidence." They sent men out to the West African coast to report the facts that really lay behind the smooth denials of the slaving interest. They tapped the gathering tide of humanitarian liberalism that flowed through those years.

The first sharp notes of criticism began to be heard in Europe. "Although Europeans have carried on a trade with the natives of the western coast of Africa for three centuries," wrote Dr. Thomas Winterbottom after a visit to the Guinea Coast in about 1796,

Abolition

"the latter have no cause to rejoice in the intercourse. Instead of introducing among [the Africans] what [the Europeans] pride themselves in possessing, the boasted arts of civilised life, to say nothing of the slave trade, the natural effects of which in degrading and brutalising the human character are sufficiently apparent, Europeans have brought them only the vices of their own countries." Such comments were grist to the mill of Clarkson and his friends.

For using such evidence and for daring to draw the obvious conclusions, the abolitionists were denounced, pilloried, and vilified by the slaving lobby, still powerful in Parliament and high places. They were accused of plotting the ruin of society and the state. Many respectable people found it utterly incomprehensible that honesty should drive other men to radical opinions; and, as usual in such cases, they also found it intolerable. When the ferments of the French Revolution blew their gusty challenge across the Channel, the fears of the respectable became witch-hunting hysteria.

Clarkson recalls of the year 1790 that the publication of Tom Paine's *Rights of Man*, and the new liberties proclaimed by the Jacobins in France, "had the effect of producing dissatisfaction among thousands; and this dissatisfaction was growing, so as to alarm a great number of persons of property in the kingdom [of Britain], as well as the government itself. . . ." The slaving lobby saw their chance and took it. "Their cry," says Clarkson, "succeeded. The very book of the abridgement of the evidence" — a condensation of evidence against the slave trade presented to Parliament by the abolitionists — "was considered by many Members as poisonous as that of the *Rights of Man*. It was too profane for many of them to touch; and they who discarded it, discarded the cause also. . . ." There began that great retreat from the revolutionary ideas of the end of the eighteenth century that

THE YEARS OF TRIAL

was eventually captained by the kings and emperors of the Holy Alliance, ruling Europe in the name of the past, and presiding in their crass charade of dignity over the long years of bitter reaction that were to follow.

Nevertheless, the abolitionists succeeded in Britain and soon afterwards in France. They had the new industrialism to help them, and another ally in the greedy foolishness of West Indian planters. These men cared little or nothing for any general future; their idea was to enrich themselves as quickly as they could, regardless of the consequences, and return to England, where they could build huge mansions and go into Parliament or rot away the remainder of their lives in careless splendor. But it happened that the French sugar islands, for a number of reasons, were better managed. By the middle of the eighteenth century, according to Williams, "the French were selling their sugar in the West Indies from thirty to forty per cent cheaper than the British planters."

Long before abolition, in other words, this French-produced sugar had begun to undersell the British product in Europe. When this continued, thoughtful investors in England saw that their immediate interest must lie in cutting down the supply of slave labor to the French islands. Yet it was difficult to do this without cutting the supply to the British islands as well. The wars between England and France broke out and continued and were settled, and then broke out again; but the slave trade persevered.

Unable to stifle French competition, the British next turned their attention towards safeguarding the monopoly of their trade with the North American colonies. These colonies were now rapidly expanding with the aggressive vigor of their settlers and the increasing wealth of their slave-grown tobacco and other products. But here the British monopolists ran into another diffi-

Abolition

culty. The North American colonies had begun to feel themselves a new nation of their own, a distinctive unit whose interests were not necessarily the same as those of the home country. What these colonies increasingly wanted was free trade. The British monopoly worked against them. They found it irksome — and eventually unbearable. They were producing more lumber and foodstuffs for the hungry and often treeless Caribbean than the British islands needed or could pay for; and yet they were barred by British order from free trade with the French islands.

The British held to their monopoly. Their principal motive was simple. Questions of prestige apart, free trade between the North American colonies and *all* the Caribbean sugar islands would have driven down the price of British-produced sugar. It was here that the West Indian interest, applied in London through a powerful and ruthless lobby, made its second enduring contribution to history: having swollen the oversea slave trade into an all-consuming appetite, the "West Indians" now helped to thrust Britain into war with the American colonies.

The turning point was probably the Molasses Act of 1733. This measure, promoted by the West Indian planter-slaving lobby, clapped a duty on rum treacle imported by the North American colonies from the non-British islands. This meant that the colonists were supposed to pay through the nose for their needs so that a handful of men in England and the Caribbean might continue to prosper. They had not populated a new continent to suffer treatment of this sort, and they responded at once with contraband trade between themselves and the non-British islands. Not only that; they also decided to sell their fish and lumber to the British islands only against cash. Hitherto they had accepted payment in sugar; now they demanded bullion while at the same time buying cheaper sugar from the French islands.

There followed the foolish and eventually futile reprisals of a

THE YEARS OF TRIAL

British Government under the influence of West Indian planters and their friends. The Stamp Act of 1764 applied prohibitively high duties on the import into North America of all non-British sugar, rum, or molasses; and there began a stiff British attempt to insist on rigid payment of such duties. But by now the Americans had had enough. For this and for other reasons, they replied with revolutionary war and won their independence.

Thus the British sugar interest not only lost the greater part of their market in Europe; they lost their precious monopoly in North America as well. By the last quarter of the eighteenth century their influence in London had shrunk to a mere shadow of its former power, and proved too weak in the event to withstand the onslaught of the antislavery campaign. If the consequences of this loss and defeat were not economically disastrous to Britain, it was precisely because the new industrial system was already far advanced. And the new industrial system, as we have seen, had no need of slaves from Africa.

The way was clear for abolition of the British trade in slaves; but the British were not the only ones in the field. If British investors had lost their economic interest in slaving, others had not; and the same circumstances which worked for abolition in Britain worked against it elsewhere. Even when some years later the trade was abolished by the French, it continued to the Spanish colonies and to Brazil, being promoted by many tough and vigorous operators. It would seem that no fewer than one million slaves were put ashore in Cuba in the years between 1791 and 1840. British parliamentary records suggest that as many as fifty thousand slaves were landed in Brazil during the year 1812 alone; and Brazil was evidently taking an even higher number as late as 1839, though the Brazilian total seems then to have fallen to about fourteen thousand for some years after that. Thus the main period of the European slave trade from Africa ran from about 1550

Abolition

until about 1850, or three full centuries. In this time it helped to work a massive change in the leading countries of Western Europe.

On many parts of America the influence of slaving was even more revolutionary. By 1798, says Ramos, one half of the population of Brazil was Negro — some 400,000 free Negroes and 1,350,000 Negro slaves, not counting mulattoes, in the coastal regions alone. Peru, Ecuador, Chile, Central America, all were filled with sons and daughters of the "Black Mother." By 1810, according to the Colombian historian José Manuel Restrepo, Negroes and free "men of color" in New Granada — which included the Isthmus of Panama — numbered 210,000 out of a total population of 1,400,000. In the Captaincy of Venezuela, a total population of 900,000 included 493,000 Negroes and part-Negroes. There were large Negro populations in several states of the United States, and in every island of the Caribbean.

Against this wider background, we can now look more closely into the consequences of the trade for Africa itself. In the wake of the trade and all its ravages, the European visitor to the western coast of Africa could observe little but ruin. His typical comment was like that of a British naval officer on antislaving patrol in the year 1850. These African countries, he wrote, with comfortable self-assurance, "are now in the same state of barbarism as when they were first discovered. . . . Altogether, the vast project of civilising and christianising Africa has ended in a melancholy failure. . . ." But what were the facts?

three

Manner of the Trade

He that is shipped with the Devil must sail with the Devil.

Defoe: Captain Singleton

The trade of slaves is the business of kings, rich men, and prime merchants.

John Barbot in about 1683

1 How Many?

First of all, what were the round numbers involved in this forced emigration to which the African-European trade gave rise, beginning in the fifteenth century and ending in the nineteenth? The short answer is that nobody knows or ever will know, because the necessary records either are lost or were never made. The best one can do is to construct an estimate from confused and incomplete data.

Between 1580 and 1680, for example, the Portuguese are said to have carried to Brazil a total of not fewer than one million slaves. In the following hundred years the British colonies in North America and the Caribbean seem to have received rather more than two million Africans. For the grand total of slaves landed alive in the lands across the Atlantic an eminent student of population statistics, Kuczynski, came to the conclusion that fifteen million might be "rather a conservative figure." Other writers have accepted this figure, though as a minimum; some have thought that the probable total was about fifty million, and others have believed it was much higher than this.

But the sum of all the slaves landed alive was not, of course, the total of those embarked. Many died on the dreaded Middle Passage. The average duration of a thousand French slaving voyages whose records were examined by Gaston-Martin — and the English average will not have been much different — was about five weeks from the Guinea Coast to the Caribbean. Sometimes the voyage was much longer; now and then it failed altogether. There are no complete figures for losses on the way, although they were certainly significant. Out of 146,799 captives that were bought in Africa on 541 slaving voyages from the port of Nantes in the years 1748-1782, only 127,133 were actually sold. The dif-

MANNER OF THE TRADE

ference is 13 per cent, and most of this must have been caused by death during the ocean crossing.

Nor was the total of those embarked anywhere near the complete number of those affected by the trade. "I want to point out," remarked Kuczynski, "that the total number of victims of the African slave trade was probably several times as high as the number of Negroes imported into America, and this for the following reasons: first, Negroes have been imported ... to Asia and Europe; second, many millions of Negroes died in raids and wars."

It is difficult to get much nearer than this. It is even more difficult, one may note in passing, to arrive at any responsible figure for the Asian-Arab trade. All that one can state in this respect is that the eastern slave trade never reached the size and scale of the western trade, although it undoubtedly went on for many more centuries. Some European writers, possibly out of an understandable but quite unhistorical conviction that "Europe should not bear all the blame," have tended to equate the Asian-Arab trade with the European trade, or even to portray the first as much larger than the second.

This argument will not bear examination. There is not a shred of evidence that the Indian Ocean trade ever carried, or could have carried, a tithe of the slaves that were taken across the Atlantic; while the undoubtedly massive Arab slave trade of the nineteenth century was only of brief duration. The clinching fact is that the eastern world, though always in quest of domestic slaves, never knew an economic situation which could have used captive labor on the scale of the Caribbean and American mines and plantations.

So far as the Atlantic slave trade is concerned, it appears reasonable to suggest that in one way or another, before and after embarkation, it cost Africa at least fifty million souls. This estimate may be about one fourth of Black Africa's approximate population today, and is certainly on the low side.

2 The System Installed

PEOPLE WERE CARRIED AWAY FROM AFRICA UNDER ALL MANNER of conditions, but the general run of the Atlantic trade can be said to fall into three stages, of which the third was by far the most important. These were slaving by piracy, by warlike alliance, and by more or less peaceful partnership.

In the first of these stages Africa faced mere raiding by small parties of Europeans that differed from intertribal warfare only in the new fact that the raiders came and went by sea. Thus the Portuguese raider João Fernandes saw some "Moors" coming towards his landing party and resolved to fight. But "all five were women, and these they took with right good will, as something that increased their capital without toil; and then they conducted them with others to their ships."

Raid soon gave way to alliance, for the Europeans could offer goods that African chieftains greatly desired: horses to begin with and then, increasingly, firearms and alcohol. Nearly a century after "Mamadu, the lord of Mali," had sent to the Portuguese captain at Elmina for help against his enemies, the English became involved in wars by one chief against another.

In 1567 Hawkins set forth upon his third slaving voyage to the lands of Guinea and passed, as before, down the coast by what was now a familiar route: from Cape Verde to the Rio Grande (in the modern Portuguese colony of Guinea); thence to the Islands of the Idols (Ihlas dos Idolos, corrupted to Isles de Los, off the modern city of Conakry, capital of independent Guinea); and so onward, raiding for slaves all the way, to the coastland of Sierra Leone. By the time he had come as far as this he had collected 150 slaves and was ready, having suffered some losses, to sail with them to the West Indies and sell them there to Spanish planters. But events took a new turn.

"And being ready to depart from the Sea coast," runs the account of this voyage, "there was a Negro sent as an Ambassador to our Generall, from a King of the Negroes, which was oppressed with other Kings, his bordering neighbours, desiring our Generall to graunt him succour and ayde against those his enemies, which our Generall graunted him thereto." With reason — for the ambassador added a promise "that as many Negroes as by these warres might be obtained, as well of his part as of ours, should be at our pleasure." The local chief, in other words, cared nothing or knew nothing about any difference between the condition of African captives and that of captives who were sold to the Europeans. He considered selling prisoners to an ally who came by sea in the same light as selling them to an ally on land. Anyone who was not of his own people — a "believer" — was fair game. The precedent would mark a fateful step.

Hawkins thereupon took two hundred Englishmen ashore and joined the "king of Sierra Leone" and the "king of Castros" against the hostile kings "Zacina and Zetecama." The object was to storm and ruin a town which was said to have some eight to ten thousand inhabitants; and they marched on it forthwith, a curious army of mercenaries mingled with feudal vassals.

"This towne was built after the use of the countrye, very warlike, and was walled round with mighty trees bound together with great wythes and had in it soldiers that had come thither 150 leagues. The kings within it had in it of principall soldiers Negroes 6,000, beside thereof innumerable sight of other menne,

The System Installed

women and children." Eager for his booty, Hawkins pressed this feudal assault. But the taking of the town proved no easy matter, the besieged having "made many engins, as false ditches covered with light sticks, leaves and such trumpery, to overthrow our men in and with their envenomed arrows and darts so defended the walls, having made loopes in every place to shoot out at for their safety. . . ." In the end the English fired the town. There was great slaughter, and Hawkins eventually weighed for the Spanish Main with 470 captives.

Such rough and ready systems of alliance occurred elsewhere. The Portuguese often made them. Not many years later, to quote one case, they signed a treaty of "mutual aid" with the paramount chief of the inland empire of the Monomotapa in the lands that were to become Southern Rhodesia. They exchanged their fire-armed discipline and skill against a promise of mining and land concessions. This was the familiar process of one feudal power demanding help from another until the more powerful ally could overwhelm or ruin the weaker. In West Africa, fortunately for its inhabitants, the social structure was generally strong enough to resist more than occasional infiltration of this kind.

Warlike alliance gave way in turn to a regular pattern of peaceful trading. With the growth of triangular trade in the seventeenth century, when slaving was the dominant factor in the African-European connection, collection of slaves on the coasts of Guinea and the Congo became increasingly a business with an accepted though often highly complicated scheme of rules and prohibitions. This business was always that of powerful men on either side, operating directly or indirectly through appointed agents, merchants, and captains; but it was increasingly, on the African side, an affair of chiefs and rulers who understood the value of monopoly and how to defend it.

At the point of sale and purchase it was peaceful more often

MANNER OF THE TRADE

than not; but it was also perilous. What Mary Kingsley at the end of the nineteenth century would call "the steady kill, kill, kill of the West African region" was already at work; and death is never long absent from the slaving record. The ships would sail in from Europe and approach the tropical shore, search for their landmarks on charts that showed a promontory, a cluster of palms, or a "tall tree" here and there, send out a boat to make soundings ahead of the blunted prow, usually with the master or his chief officer in charge, and land at last with their arms at the ready.

Speed was vital for the slavers, since the longer they stayed on the coast the more deaths they would suffer from fevers that were irresistible. Often enough, as the years passed, coastal chieftains with slaves for sale learned to operate signaling systems; they would light fires to call in ships, or else leave their coast in darkness so that the slavers should go elsewhere.

"Sence our coming into this river [of Gambia]," runs a typical early comment, that of Captain John Blake of the English Guinea Company in 1651, "it hath pleased the Lord aflikt us with much Sicknes that wee have buried three and twenty men. My Chefe and my Second maite and botswaine are three of them; both my Guneres maites and botswaines mait, three more, Mr Dobes one of your factores, the rest of them being the lustiest men wee had in our Shipe."

Except for those who drove the trade and throve on it — whether investors in Europe, planters in America, or chiefs in Africa — the game was harsh and merciless on all it touched. Whether from London or Liverpool, Nantes or Amsterdam, the man before the mast was in some respects even more of a victim than the man battened below decks; the choice he faced, as often as not, lay between starvation at home or death on the Coast.

Little by little, as slaving settled into a regular system, the coast

The System Installed

was divided by Europeans into regions considered good or bad according to their speedy or slow delivery of slaves. This had its profound effect on the course of much African experience. And something else happened at the same time — something that was even more binding and pervasive in its consequences. Men became mere trade goods. Not only that; with the expansion of the Great Circuit" enterprise in the seventeenth century, men became the *only* trade goods that really mattered. African chiefs found that the sale of their fellow-men was indispensable to any contact or commerce with Europe. Unless they were willing — and not only willing, but active in delivery — the ships went elsewhere. That is how the system was installed.

Trapped in this unforeseen and fatal circumstance, pushed by their desire for European goods (and firearms often became essential to chiefly survival), or blackmailed by the fear that what one or two might refuse their rivals would consent to give, the rulers of coastal Africa surrendered to the slave trade. They struggled against its worst excesses from time to time; but the trade was always too strong for them in the end.

It would be foolish to moralize. As it was in Europe, so it was in Africa; "the trade in slaves," wrote John Barbot of the Guinea Coast at the end of the eighteenth century, "is the business of kings, rich men, and prime merchants." This is the necessary key to understanding the nature of the system, its success and its consequences, throughout coastal and near-coastal Africa.

Within its "tribal-feudal" context, the slave trade became inseparable from the workings of chiefly rule. Wherever the trade found strong chiefs and kings it prospered almost from the first; wherever it failed to find them it caused them to come into being. Whether in the accumulation of wealth by customs duties, gifts, or trading profits; or in the political authority which slaving lent to those who organized it; or in the military superiority which

MANNER OF THE TRADE

derived from the buying of firearms, slaving built up the power of chiefs where it did not exist before, or else transformed that power, where it was already present, from a broadly representative character into an autocratic one.

All this might have gone differently if only the demand had slackened. But the demand incessantly grew; and, along with this, an ever-renewed insistence on speed of delivery. Hitherto, the slavers had often been obliged to cruise along the coast, picking up a dozen captives here and a dozen there, enduring long weeks and months in pestilential misery and paying the price with an appalling death rate in their own ranks. But now the productive regions shortened the period of collection by laying in a store of slaves ahead of delivery. A handful of European castles on the Gold Coast had already become centers of collection; the more powerful chiefs followed suit and the barracoon appeared — the coastal warehouse where slaves could be kept until ships should call.

Here and there the Europeans themselves established floating barracoons, hulks permanently anchored in creek or estuary for the storage of slaves. Often these storage ships were heavily armed so as to be able to defend themselves from slave revolt, attack from the land, or assault from rivals at sea. Off Dahomey in 1739, for example, the French slaver *Affriquain* found "an English ship of forty guns . . . serving here as fortress and trading station for an English company."

Africans had long watched how Europeans fought each other for monopoly of the maritime side of the trade — for exclusive enjoyment, that is, of the African alliances and thus of rapid access to many slaves. For their part the coastal chiefs were not slow in understanding where their own commercial interest lay. They in turn endeavored to win a monopoly of the landward side of the trade, not so much against each other as against any European attempt to penetrate into the near-interior lands whence most of the slaves must come. On the whole they succeeded. The story of much of the coast during this long period is the record of how coastal societies prevented any contact between Europeans and the peoples of the interior and constructed for themselves a powerful middleman position.

They also fought each other as the Europeans did, sought alliance with this or that European nation, stormed their rivals, enslaved them, sold them off — or were themselves seized and sold. In this grim sequence of cause and effect the slave trade foundered gradually into a ruthless manhunt — ruthless, but not therefore chaotic. For the rules of the connection were well established, and they grew in number. In this the manners of Africa were no different from those of Europe.

3 Rules and Customs

"THIS DAY ABOUTT NINE IN THE MORNING," SAYS THE JOURNAL OF the *Arthur* of London for a slave-and-sugar voyage in 1677, "Came on Board the King of New Calabarr with some others of his gen'tes, and after a Long Discourse Came to Agreem'tt for Current for negro man 36 Copper Barrs: for negro woman 30. . . ."

Many have pictured the slave trade at its zenith as a desperate affair of raid and war; much more often than not, at least at the point of sale and purchase, it was nothing of the kind. That morning's scene aboard the *Arthur* of long and earnest haggling between partners who knew one another well, and had long since learned to tolerate each other's peculiarities and methods of bargaining, was much closer to the general run of the trade. Highly

MANNER OF THE TRADE

organized on the European side, it was scarcely less so among Africans.

By this time, custom regulated the trade in almost all its contingencies and not least in price and payment. Here the slave-ship supercargoes and the coastal chiefs needed all their skill if they were to "see their profit"; and it was clearly understood on both sides that a good half of the success of a slaving exchange would lie in this battle of wits. The inexperienced or the ill-informed went quickly to the wall. Chiefs and supercargoes were required to know not only the state of the trade at any given moment (including the likely supply of slaves on one hand and the likely supply of ships on the other) but also the varying values of many different standards of payment.

Coins were seldom or never used on the coast. Mostly the chiefs and supercargoes dealt in rolls of tobacco, pipes of rum, and firearms, or more generally in lengths of iron or copper or in "pots and basins" of brass. The slavers' log books are eloquent of all this.

"On the twenty fifth in the morning," runs the log of the *Albion-Frigate* in 1699, trading at New Calabar, "we went ashore also to compliment the king, and make him overtures of trade, but he gave us to understand he expected one bar of iron for each slave more than Edwards had paid for his; and also objected much against our basons, tankards, yellow beads, and some other merchandise, as of little or no demand there at the time." Such was the customary opening; the great thing was not to lose heart.

"On the twenty sixth, we had a conference with the king and principal natives of the country, about trade, which lasted from three o'clock till night, without any result, they insisting to have thirteen bars of iron for a male, and ten for a female slave. . . ." This was too dear for the Europeans; they took supper with the king and went back to their ship.

Rules and Customs

"The thirtieth, being ashore, had a new conference, which produced nothing. . . ." The king's representative held forth once again on his difficulties. "He was sorry we would not accept of his proposals; that it was not his fault, he having a great esteem and regard for the Whites, who had much enriched him by trade. That [the reason why] he so earnestly insisted on thirteen bars for male, and ten for female slaves, came from the country people holding up the price of slaves at their inland markets . . . but to moderate matters . . . he would be contented with thirteen bars for males, and nine bars and two brass rings for females, etc. . . ." And at last, on the following day, they fell into agreement.

Such haggling was accompanied, especially at prosperous harbors like New Calabar in the Niger delta, by a vast amount of entertaining, bestowal of gifts, argument, teasing on both sides, and alcoholic refreshment. On this particular occasion there was an almost riotous reception on board the *Albion-Frigate*, everyone being filled "with drams of brandy and bowls of punch till night"; and the king was presented with a hat, a firelock, and nine bunches of beads. His various counselors and subchiefs, garnished in the slavers' records with a fine sequence of names and titles, benefited likewise. Thus: "To Captain Forty, the king's general, captain Pepprell, captain Boileau, alderman Bougsby, lord Willby, duke of Monmouth, drunken Henry, and some others, two firelocks, eight hats, nine narrow Guinea stuffs. . . ."

As the trade expanded and was regularly installed, Africans grew more skillful in extracting profit. They evolved a whole system of "tax and tribute." This varied greatly from place to place, but generally the slaving captains and supercargoes were pushed from one small concession to another. The forceful kings of Dahomey became adept at this game. At Great Ardra, Barbot notes, "'tis usual for Europeans to give the king the value of fifty slaves in goods, for his permission to trade, and customs, for each

MANNER OF THE TRADE

ship; and to the king's son the value of two slaves, for the privilege of watering; and of four slaves for wooding."

In the same way the hire of canoes and crews for transporting goods and slaves back and forth through the coastal surf was also subject to accustomed payment in goods-per-slave, and gifts were expected on top of that. "The factor or supercargo, having finished his sale, is to present the king again with two muskets, twenty-five lbs of powder, and the value of nine slaves in other goods," as well as making presents to lesser luminaries.

Often the manner of payment was bafflingly complex. In one characteristic transaction a young woman was bartered against one roll of tobacco, two patches, twenty-four linen handkerchiefs, one gun, one jug, four pint mugs, and three "garsets," or textile measures. "A man and a fine girl" were exchanged, in another typical bargain against:

> One roll tobacco, one string pipe coral
> One gun, three cutlasses, one brass blunderbuss
> Twenty-four linen hankerchiefs, 5 patches, 3 jugs rum
> Twelve Brittanicas, 12 pint mugs
> One laced hat, one linen handkerchief.

In 1676 — to quote another representative case — the *Sarah Bonaventura*, a ship of the British Royal African Company, bought exactly one hundred men, women, and children — all duly branded with the company's mark, D Y (Duke of York) — for various lengths of cotton cloth, "nittones," "Tapsells," and so on, whether made in England or in India, and five muskets, twenty-one iron bars, seventy-two knives, half a barrel of powder, and various odds and ends.

Much of the trade was carried on in cowrie shells, a standard of value long accepted on some parts of the coast as well as in the interior. "The best commodity the Europeans can carry thither," reports Barbot of the Gold Coast at the end of the seventeenth century, "is Boejies, or Cowries, so much valued by the natives: being the current coin there, as well as at Popo [Ivory Coast], Fida [Dahomey], Benin [estuary of the Niger] and other countries farther east [Congo and Angola]; without which, it is scarce possible to traffick there."

Slaves at Ardra on the Slave Coast, Barbot goes on, "are usually purchased, one half with Boejies [cowries] and the other half with European goods; and when they [cowries] are scarce and dear in Europe, as it happens sometimes, we endeavour to satisfy the Ardrasians with one-third or fourth part of them, and the other parts in merchandise; of which, generally, flat iron bars are next to Boejies the most acceptable."

Sometimes the currencies were elaborated into multiple units. Dahomey is a case in point. In 1793 Archibald Dalzell gave the current values there in the following curious list:

40 cowries =	1 tocky =	⅙d.
5 tockys =	1 gallina =	6d.
1 gallina =	1 ackey =	2s. 6d.
4 ackey =	1 cabess =	10s. 0d.
4 cabess =	1 ounce "trade" = (16,000 cowries weighing 42 lbs).	40s. 0d.

All these complicated reckonings had to be learned by the traders on either side. In addition, prices had to be fixed for the right of watering and timbering ships on the coast, as well as for the yams that the slaves would eat on their ocean passage. Over and above this, extensive systems of credit soon came into operation. "If there happens to be no stock of slaves at Fida," notes Barbot, "the factor must trust the Blacks with his goods, to the value of 150 or 200 slaves; which goods they carry up into the inland, to buy slaves at all the markets."

Even after all this bickering and bargaining was done with,

MANNER OF THE TRADE

there remained the quality of captives to be considered; and, for those who were accepted, the branding of them. Here too custom ruled. "As the slaves come down to Fida from the inland country, they are put into a booth or prison, built for that purpose, near the beach, all of them together; and when the Europeans are to receive them, they are brought out into a large plain, where the [ships'] surgeons examine every part of every one of them, to the smallest member, men and women being all stark naked. Such as are allowed good and sound, are set on one side, and the others by themselves; which slaves so rejected are called Mackrons, being above 35 years of age, or defective in their lips, eyes, or teeth, or grown grey; or that have the venereal disease, or any other imperfection." Only the best were good enough; and this is no doubt one reason for the often amazing resistance, physical and moral, of the slaves who reached the Caribbean and the Americas.

"These being so set aside, each of the others, which have passed as good, is marked on the breast with a red-hot iron, imprinting the mark of the French, English or Dutch companies, that so each nation may distinguish their own, and to prevent their being chang'd by the natives for worse, as they are apt enough to do. In this particular, care is taken that the women, as tenderest, be not burnt too hard.

"The branded slaves, after this, are returned to their former booths," where they await shipment, "sometimes ten or fifteen days." When that happens they are stripped naked before being put into the canoes "without distinction of men or women"; but, adds Barbot, "to supply which [deficiency of clothing], in orderly ships each of them as they come aboard is allow'd a piece of canvas to wrap about their waist, which is very acceptable to the poor wretches."

With this systematic degradation, one brutal innovation leading to another, one cruelty opening the way to the next, it was

Rules and Customs

inevitable that indifference to human suffering should grow. It did grow mightily, and on both sides. On the African side there is much evidence, as we shall see, that this process helped towards a breakdown of social structures and a collapse of security and self-respect. On the European side there was increasing thought for raising the rate of profit at the expense of the slave commodity. Often enough this was carried to a point where it utterly defeated its own end, for the commodity was rendered so wretched and reduced as to deprive him, or her, of any market value or even of life itself. On all this, too, the records speak clearly and without shame.

"Concerning Captain Woodfin's Negroes whereof 160 died and no complaint made of their goodness," report the factors of the British Royal African Company at Cape Coast in 1681 "wee are apt to believe that had he taken in only 400 there had few miscarried. . . ."

A year later Captain Japhet Bird is writing to his Bristol owner from Montserrat in the West Indies: "I arriv'd [here] . . . with 239 slaves which Now all sold better than Expectation; so that I am in hopes to make a Tolerable good voyage Notwithstanding I've had the misfortune of beuring [burying] seventy odd slaves, as good as any Now sold. I am somew't Dissatisfied that it should happen to a young beginnar, but thank god it Can't be said that its owing to Neglect for I can assure you that it have been the Constant care and Indeavour of me for the Interest of those Gentlemen that have Imploy'd me." Seventy slaves might die, but the interest of the gentlemen of Bristol came first; and in thinking so the youthful Captain Bird did no more than honestly interpret the spirit of the times.

Those captains who lost a large number during their voyage to the West Indies — and they were a minority of captains — were understandably defensive in their reports. "This with my Humble

MANNER OF THE TRADE

Servis to you and Rest of the Gentlemen Owners," Captain Edward Hollden of the *Grayhound* galley is writing to Bristol in 1723, "and is to certifie you of my Arivall hear haveing seven weeks Passage from Bony [Niger delta] but very Dismall and Mortall for outt of 339 Slaves I brought in hear butt 214 . . . the Like Mortality I think Never was known for Jolly Likely Men Slaves to Eatt their Diett over Night and the Nex Morning Dead 2 and 3 in a Night for severall Days . . . as for Management I think it Could Nott be Better I allways had their Victuals in good order. . . ."

In somewhat later times there were spasmodic efforts and "inventions" to avert such calamitous blows to the profit of investors. Towards the end of the eighteenth century it was a common practice to bring the slaves on deck and exercise them by making them jump in their irons. "This was so necessary for their health," it was explained in evidence before the House of Commons, "that they were whipped if they refused to do it."

Systematic inhumanity more often than sadism marked the trade. Yet the inhumanity knew no limits. Slaves who fell sick were simply pitched overboard. In the nineteenth century there were many cases of slavers who threw their whole living cargoes into the sea when pursued by British antislaving patrols, since capture with slaves aboard meant the impounding of their ships.

Fear on both sides added to the brutality of everyday custom. Slave revolts at sea were put down with grim ferocity. John Atkins has left an account of how the master of the *Robert* of Bristol, one Captain Harding, dealt with an insurrection early in the eighteenth century:

"Why, Captain Harding weighing the Stoutness and Worth [of the ringleaders] did, as in other countries they do by Rogues of Dignity, whip and scarify them only; while three other Abettors,

Rules and Customs

but not Actors, nor of Strength for it, he sentenced to cruel deaths; making them first eat the Heart and Liver of one of them killed. The Woman [who had helped in the revolt] he hoisted up by the Thumbs, whipp'd, and slashed her with Knives, before the other Slaves, till she died."

Bloody clashes were the order of the day not just between Europeans and Africans, but also among Europeans and among Africans. "That day came into the Road," William Smith wrote of his voyage in 1726, "the *Friendship* Brig, of Bristol, one Barry Commander, who likewise din'd aboard the *Queen Elisabeth*, and towards night, having drank pretty freely, insulted the two Captains, who not being able to bear it, return'd him proper marks of their resentment; which so enrag'd him, that he immediately went aboard his own ship, and in a piratical manner fir'd a shot at the *Queen Elisabeth*, which had like to have carried away her forestay. . . ."

African manners along the slaving coast showed the same reckless attitude. There is the example of one Thomas Osiat, who became the grand *caboceroe*, or principal trader, of Cape Coast, in what is now southwestern Ghana. Osiat had been enslaved as a boy and carried to Ireland. There his master had died and "left him in Care with a widow, whose name was Pennington, who kept the Crown or Falcon tavern near the 'Change in Cork.'" Having in the course of time come home again, Osiat "now lives in very great grandeur, and is of the utmost service to the English, both for carrying on this trade in the inland country, and preserving peace with all their neighbouring powers. . . ."

But Osiat's way of "preserving peace" was peculiar to the times. He fought in many of the skirmishes between Cape Coast and neighboring Elmina, then held by the Dutch. In one of these flurries he "took a great many prisoners, among whom were nine of the petty caboceroes of Elmina, whose heads Tom Osiat (tho' a Christian) caus'd to be cut off, and sent them next day in a bag" to his opponents.

With a commerce of this sort, little else could be expected. Once again the habits of the seamen prove the point. "Men on their first voyages," noted Clarkson, "usually dislike the traffic; and, if they were happy enough then to abandon it, they usually escaped the disease with a hardened heart. But if they went a second or a third time, their disposition became gradually to be accustomed to carry away men and women by force, to keep them in chains . . . to behold the dead and dying. . . ." Clarkson, it is true, was an abolitionist eager to prove that slaving meant sadism. Yet by the time he wrote those words he had traipsed around the docks and quays of London and Bristol and Liverpool, sat and listened endlessly in seamen's taverns, interested himself in many cases of injury, and collected the names of twenty thousand seamen engaged in the trade.

His judgment may stand. The trade was always vicious. But it became worse with the passage of time.

4 Attitudes and Opinions

MISUNDERSTANDINGS GREW APACE. FEAR AND IGNORANCE QUICKened on either side into beliefs that were strange, but also strangely alike. There came into being a "community of legend." Nothing shows this better than the currency of thought about man-eating.

Cannibalism certainly existed in Africa. Some African peoples had long practiced the ritual eating of the flesh of their especially honored enemies. Now and then, no doubt, famine drove men

Attitudes and Opinions

to eat each other. None of this was exclusive to humanity in Africa; although at one or two points, and for reasons that were evidently not disconnected with the slave trade, cannibal habits appear to have gained a destructive hold.

Yet most Europeans who thought of Africa were convinced from early times that it was the general custom in that continent for men to eat their fellows from taste and preference. A good illustration of this fantasy may be found in Cavazzi's celebrated description of the three African kingdoms of Congo, Matamba, and Angola. The artist in that fine quarto volume, published at Bologna in 1687, gave free rein to popular belief. He offered a splendidly graphic line engraving of a cannibal scene: several Angolans butchering human limbs and cooking them on a gridiron.

Now the odd thing is that this cannibal myth worked both ways. The drawing in Cavazzi's book occurs on page 32. But a little beyond, on page 164, Cavazzi is describing how the slaves of Angola have a particular horror of being shipped away. Why? Because, he writes, they are convinced that Europeans want them, not for labor, but for turning into oil and charcoal — or simply for eating. Europeans learned with surprise that Africans generally believed them to be great and irredeemable cannibals.

Many of the old descriptions of the coast record this belief, but none better than that of Olaudah Equiano, an Ibo slave who afterwards lived in London as a free man and whose book deserves respect. Captured as a young boy in about 1756, he retained a vivid memory of his fear that the stewpot was his fate. "When I looked round the ship," he recalled of the moment when he was delivered to the European slavers, "I saw a large furnace or copper boiling, and a multitude of black people of every description chained together, every one of their countenances expressing dejection and sorrow." He "no longer doubted of his fate." He turned to his companions, newly enslaved as he was, and "asked them if we were not to be eaten by those white men with horrible looks, red faces, and long hair?"

The belief was encouraged in the Niger delta, as we shall see, by the famous Aro oracle. Yet it has had a long life in several parts of Africa. Even in the early twentieth century a Scottish missionary's wife in Nyasaland could describe it clearly. "It was commonly asserted that our chief . . . had eaten his child by a slave wife. Some of our boys believed us capable of this abominable practice ourselves. When a very stout man, a land surveyor, called by the natives 'Che Cimimba' (Big Stomach) visited our station and stayed in the Doctor's house, the table-boy there fled in terror lest he should be eaten by the fat man. And another time when the Msungu [European in charge] was smoking a piece of wild boar in a barrel, a boy believed firmly that the 'nyama' [meat] was one of his comrades."

By the eighteenth century this slaving mythology was in full bloom on either side. Yet it remains an interesting fact that this period of the largest extension of slaving was also the period of a revised European estimate of African society. Moreover, at about this time the "noble savage" came on stage. This is noticeable as early as 1744, when William Smith, together with his own memoirs of the coast, published the account of Charles Wheeler, an agent of the Royal African Company who had seen ten years' service, evidently at Cape Coast. Wheeler's description of African life is strong on lascivious detail and was possibly written with an indulgent eye to the eighteenth century public; but there is no doubting the idyllic note. He dwells with fond amusement on his concubine with "jetty breasts" but argues strongly for the "sexual liberty" which, he says, Africans accept. They are never, he claims, tempted to rape as European men, through constant frustration, are tempted. "All the time I liv'd there, I never once heard of those detestable and unnatural Crimes of Sodomy and Bestiality, so much practis'd among Christians."

"A Guinean," says Wheeler, "by treading in the paths prescrib'd by his ancestors, paths natural, pleasant, and diverting, is in the plain road to be a good and happy man; but the European has sought so many inventions, and has endeavour'd to put so many restrictions upon nature, that it would be next to a miracle if he were either happy or good." Not entirely a balanced view, perhaps, but certainly a new one in the literature of the coast. "And I doubt not upon an impartial examination of the premises, it would be found that we Christians have as many idle ridiculous notions and customs as the natives of Guinea have, if not more. . . ."

This note was struck repeatedly in Britain and France as the antislavery campaigns grew stronger. Long-accepted beliefs were challenged by the most unlikely observers. In 1796, for example, a pensioned officer of a brigade of Scottish mercenaries in the Dutch colonial service published his memoirs of an expedition against rebel slaves in Surinam (on the northern coast of South America) during 1772-1777. The frontispiece shows the young man, whose name was Stedman, leaning on his gun while a rebel Negro lies dead at his feet. But there is a ravaged expression on Stedman's face, and the rubric underneath has these surprising words:

> "From different Parents, different Climes we came,
> At different Periods:" Fate still rules the same.
> Unhappy Youth, while bleeding on the ground,
> 'Twas *Yours* to fall — but *Mine* to feel the wound.

Some of the most useful memoirs during the eighteenth century were those of ships' doctors and surgeons, men who were trained to look facts in the face. One such writer, Thomas Winterbottom, observed of the coastal Africans of the region of Sierra Leone in 1796, that they "are in general shrewd and artful, sometimes malevolent and perfidious. Their long connection with European slave traders has tutored them in the arts of deceit, so that false weights and measures, damaged goods, and all the various cheats which the ingenuity of the more enlightened European has strained itself to invent, are now detected almost as soon as they are attempted to be put into practice. It is in great measure owing to this cause that traders who visited the coast of Africa in hopes of becoming suddenly rich, disappointed in finding the natives better acquainted with the value of their country's produce than they at first supposed, and too well instructed by dear bought experience to be so grossly imposed upon as formerly, have drawn of them so foul a picture as they could invent. . . ."

This new tone of cool inquiry, cutting through the mist of legend, was partly cause and partly effect of the antislaving agitations of the last quarter of the eighteenth century. It is of great importance in European literature about Africa. Henceforward, Europeans would be increasingly divided into two opposed views: one, the traditional, tending to hold that Africa had never possessed cultures that were worthy of respect or even of serious investigation; the other, the scientific, tending to argue the reverse.

One may reasonably think that the ending of the slave trade must have reinforced this spirit of inquiry. This happened to some extent. But the trade was followed without much interval by colonial conquest and the "scramble for Africa"; and a new spirit of obscurantist reaction soon carried all before it. Otherwise intelligent men were writing about Africa, by the beginning of the twentieth century, with much the same condescension and contempt as their predecessors of earlier times. "People more animal-like than reasonable," Cavazzi had declared of the Angolans in 1687. "Dancing among these barbarians, having no motive in the

Attitudes and Opinions

virtuous talent of displaying the movement of the body, or the agility of the feet, aims only at the vicious satisfaction of a libidinous appetite." Such words read oddly in our day; yet the records of the colonial period are full of remarks no less absurd.

By 1900 the average European opinion about Africa — though there were some memorable exceptions — showed scarcely a trace of the stubborn curiosity which men like Winterbottom had deployed a century earlier. Sir Harry Johnston is a case in point. He knew some parts of Africa fairly well; yet none of his experience stopped him from accepting the doctrines of the day. Indeed, he swallowed them whole. For him, as for others, all signs of civilization in Africa were to be attributed to outside influence. "Undoubtedly," he wrote in 1910, "the influence of the Portuguese . . . wrought some surprising movements all along the coast regions of West Africa and in the southern basin of the Congo, by which organised kingdoms arose which created and stimulated commerce, and which in their general effects on the people were perhaps less drearily horrible than the anarchy of cannibal savages." Yet the truth — as any diligent inquirer could have known even in 1910 — was precisely the reverse. For the kingdoms of the Congo had preceded the Portuguese; and the Portuguese, far from creating them, had in truth destroyed them.

The tide of reaction flowed far and wide; and some of its racialist inundations are mournfully with us to this day. Johnston was a man of liberal reputation in the England of his time, yet he could airily dismiss the consequences of the slave trade for Africa as small or nonexistent. No doubt unconsciously, he repeated the opinions of the Liverpool slavers of the eighteenth century who had claimed that the trade could even bring "an access of happiness" to Africa. "So far as the sum of human misery in Africa was concerned," he wrote, "it is probable that the trade in slaves between that continent and America scarcely added to it. It even to some extent mitigated the suffering of the negro in his own home; for once this trade was set on foot and it was profitable to sell a human being, many a man, woman or child who might otherwise have been killed for mere caprice, or for the love of seeing blood flow, or as a toothsome ingredient of a banquet, was sold to a slave-trader. . . ."

Such language passed for serious comment in high colonial times. Only at the end of the imperial epoch, still many years ahead when Johnston wrote his books, would Europeans and Americans begin to look at Africa systematically, and as a subject in its own right rather than a mere object of pity, amazement, or contempt.

5 Where Did They Come From?

THE MODERN READER WILL NOT THINK IT LIKELY THAT REMOVING fifty million souls from Africa could have brought "an access of happiness." True enough, this enormous total — and possibly it was much larger — is not very great when divided into an "annual average" over the three main centuries of the trade. There are several reasons, however, why it would be misleading to regard it in this light. One reason is that the most intensive years of slaving were concentrated between about 1700 and 1850. Another is that the areas from which slaves were consistently taken in great number were relatively few, and perhaps relatively small.

Even so, barely a single tribal name is missing from the records.

Where Did They Come From?

There is the convincing case of Mexico. African labor in Mexico early took the place of "Indian" labor; no wonder, for the Indian population was cut down by more than half in little over a century. As early as 1570 there were said to be as many as twenty thousand African slaves in Mexico. In 1584 the king of Spain passed to his viceregal council in Mexico an order that "the Indians, a weak people, be left to their own business, and that the labour of the mines, construction, fields and mills be undertaken by mulattoes, negroes and mestizos." And so it was.

Most of the Africans who came to Mexico in those early days were probably of the Mande group of peoples who lived then, as they still do, in the lands behind the far western bulge of the Guinea Coast. These captives were generally known as Mandingos, and this word "Mandingo" has survived in Mexico as the popular name for a devil. But the careful records of the Inquisition in Mexico — records that were kept as part of the process of "safeguarding Christianity" by ensuring baptism — show that the land was fertilized by many African peoples.

Some of these were brought into the country not under their own names but under those their captors knew them by. Thus Nupe captives who were taken and traded by the Yoruba people of western Nigeria were generally called Tapas, and as such they were delivered by the traders to the markets of the New World. In their turn the Yoruba, enslaved by the Fon people of Dahomey to the west of them, were known as Nagos, and entered America under that name. The Susu people from the coast of the modern Republic of Guinea do not appear in the Mexican records; instead they were registered as Xoxo. Bambara captives from the Middle Niger were known to the Inquisition as Bambura; the Tuculor of Senegal as Tucuxui; the numerous Foulah, or Fulani, under various labels and derivations. Among tribal names that suffered no distortion one may note the Kissi and the Senufu, who came

MANNER OF THE TRADE

from the lands of the forest belt behind the coast of present-day Liberia and the Republic of Guinea.

Often enough, the captives were given two names, the first being that of the market where they were purchased on the African shoreline, and the other the name or nickname of their tribe. Thus the records speak of Mina-Popos going to Cuba (Ivory Coast captives bought at the castle of Elmina), and of Mina-Nagos going to Brazil (Yoruba people acquired at the same market). Ibo slaves from eastern Nigeria generally arrived in Mexico as Calabares, captives purchased at the markets of Calabar in the Niger delta.

Most of the slaves were undoubtedly from western Africa. They were taken from about a score of principal markets, and from many smaller ones, on a 3,000-mile coastline between Senegal in the north and Angola in the south. A few were taken from East Africa even in the sixteenth century. The Mexican Inquisition archives mention at least two of the East African city-states: Melin, obviously Malindi, and Mozambique (by which was meant the island capital of that name, and not the later Portuguese colony). Those carried from the Mozambique coast were called Kaffrarians, after the Arabic word *kāfir*, meaning "pagan." Sometimes they were more clearly labeled. Thus "Zoza" slaves in Mexico were probably Xosa from the far southeastern part of South Africa. And other victims came from places still farther afield; the Mexican records tell of slaves from Burma, Malaya, Java, and even China.

Once in the New World, African peoples were often strong and numerous enough to revive and re-create the customs and beliefs of their homeland. Some of the West Indian islands and Brazil show this very clearly; nearly all the slave-populated lands of the Americas show it to some extent. Transported to Brazil in large numbers, Yoruba captives evolved a compound of their own

Where Did They Come From?

beliefs and Christianity. Children of a strong and venerable culture, they printed a deep African accent into the everyday culture of the cities of the coast. Thus the *orishas* of the Yoruba — the national gods — have been reborn in Brazilian Bahia as Christian saints. At Rio de Janeiro the god of war, Ogun, has become St. George, the sainted knight of the Catholics. And in their cult houses (their *macumbas*), the Africans of Rio, says Ramos, sing: "Ogun! Ogun! My father! Oh Jorge, *sarava* (save) Ogun!" Yemanja and Oshun, goddesses of the Yoruba, have in their turn become fused with Our Lady of the Conception, and other female *orishas* have here and there undergone the same transformation. Even African languages have sometimes survived, though in truncated form.

Thus a study of the ex-slave communities of the New World can still throw much light on their African origins. Modern research seems to indicate two conclusions. The first is that few African peoples were spared their tribute of slaves. But this is considerably qualified by a second conclusion: that most of the slaves came from lands that were near the coast.

Some writers have depicted the slave trails reaching right across the continent, plunging their merciless thrust into the most remote corners of the far interior. This certainly happened during the brief and bloody Arab slave trade from Zanzibar in the nineteenth century. Even in earlier times it was now and then the case, captives from the inland countries being handed from one set of traders to the next until they were finally delivered to Europeans at the coast. "They sold us for money," recalls the narrative of a West African ex-slave who wrote his memoirs in 1831, "and I myself was sold six times over, sometimes for money, sometimes for a gun, sometimes for cloth. . . . It was about half a year from the time I was taken before I saw white people."

Another memoir tells how a French slaving captain purchased

at Cabinda, near the mouth of the Congo River, "an African woman who seemed to him pretty familiar with Whites, or at least showed no surprise or fear at sight of them. Struck by this unusual confidence, the slaver asked her the cause of it. She replied that she had already seen White men in another land where the sun rose out of the water instead of hiding itself in the sea, as it does in the Congo. Pointing to the east, she added the words *monizi monambu* — I have seen the edge of the sea. She had been *ganda cacota* — many moons — on the way." This story, adds the writer, appears to confirm what the seventeenth century Dutch geographer, Olfert Dapper, had said about slaves of Mozambique being sold in the Congo.

There is nothing improbable about Africans having repeatedly and even regularly traversed the continent from one ocean to the other. From his experience at the end of the seventeenth century, the trader James Barbot had already observed that peoples in Angola extended their trade as far eastward as the frontiers of the kingdoms of Mombasa, Kilwa, and Sofala, all of which are on the East African coast. Slaves were brought to the Angolan coast, he noted, from "150 or 200 leagues up the country."

"All that vast number of slaves which the Calabar Blacks sell to all European nations," James's uncle, John Barbot, was writing at about the same time of the Niger delta trade, "are not their prisoners of war, the greatest part being bought by those people of their inland neighbours, and they also buy them of other nations yet more remote from them."

Both the European and American records generally agree, though with exceptions, that the coastal peoples seldom supplied slaves from their own ranks. They purchased or otherwise got hold of them, as one would expect, from the peoples in their rear; and these in turn, while delivering some captives from their own region, looked for their main supply to other peoples still farther into the interior. How far did this shunting process go? The answer seems to be that it went much less far than the slaving totals would at first sight suggest. From one century to the next, the bulk of the slaves were evidently drawn from a belt of territory that reached inland from the coast (but seldom included the coast itself) for several hundred miles, but seldom further.

Thus the great slaving kingdom of Dahomey seems never to have taken prisoners, at least in any significant number, from regions more remote than a couple of hundred miles into the interior. Another large source of slaves was the Gold Coast. Here the slaving middlemen were the Fanti people, who purchased captives from the Ashanti to the north of them and sold them to the Europeans at the coastal forts. "Yet all evidence from recognisable survivals such as the many Ashanti-Akan-Fanti place names, names of deities, and day names in the New World," Herskovits reports, "are evidence that the sources of the slaves exported by the Fanti were in greatest proportion within the present boundaries of the Gold Coast colony [modern Ghana]."

Summing up for West Africa, one may say that the strong peoples of the coast and its immediate hinterland raided or purchased northward, but not very far. They drew their regular supplies from the relatively abundant peoples of the forest belt and to a lesser extent from the sparser peoples of the grasslands beyond the forest. Somewhere in these grasslands a "slaving watershed" seems to have existed; to the south of it captives were drained off the coast, while to the north of it they were channeled to the Niger and thence taken either to Senegal or the island of Goree for the transatlantic trade, or sold for transport across the Sahara to the markets of North Africa. But the main impact of the trade was felt on the southern side of this "watershed," and it is there, near the coast and along the coast, that one must look for its principal effects.

MANNER OF THE TRADE

6 Three Regions

GLANCING THROUGH THE RECORDS OF THIS LONG-ENDURING TRADE, there is at first the impression of a hopeless muddle. Sudden quarrels are smoothed into unexpected peace. Bloody insurrections shatter long-established custom. Chaotic and haphazard strokes of fortune are interspersed by days of the most detailed and calculated haggling. On top of all this there is a flood of strange names and tortuous jargon. Yet the confusion is in fact less baffling than it seems. It can be straightened out with patience into a fairly clear sequence of cause and effect.

To begin with, it soon becomes obvious that the African-European relationship had a powerful influence on the growth and manner of trade. Currencies expanded. Methods of calculation grew. There was a new sophistication in methods of dealing, but along with this, a new fraudulence. Africans learned from European tricks; and the tricks became many and various.

In much of this the African-European connection was no different in its general effects from the African-Arab or the African-Indian connection. Indeed, one should think of the main continent of Africa in these centuries as of a vast island surrounded by three oceans: the Atlantic and Indian oceans of water and the Saharan ocean of sand. Within this island there was barter and exchange by standard weight or value. Cities dealt with cities, rulers with rulers, one trading community with another; and often enough their dealing reached from one end of the continent to the other. Along all three "seaboards" there grew up new trading towns and merchants who specialized in oversea or oversand commerce: Walata, Djenné, Timbuktu, Gao, Kano, and others on the southern "shore" of the Sahara; Kilwa, Malindi, and their like on the coast of East Africa; and new settlements and city-states on the Guinea seaboard of the Atlantic.

Yet this trade, internal or external, had its narrow limits. The vast majority of the population still lived on an economy of subsistence, providing largely for their own needs, exchanging their products for other goods offered by their neighbors but seldom going beyond barter. As long as most of the people lived by subsistence, their interest in trade was small. Where cities were founded and grew strong — here and there in the forest belt, along the Middle Niger, across the fertile savannahs of Hausaland and Bornu — there were concentrations of craftsmen, royal courts, an aristocracy given to good living and display, and markets for incoming and domestic traders. Necessities as well as luxuries were bought and sold in this way: Saharan salt against southern gold, Saharan copper against southern kola nuts, as well as a considerable commerce in textiles and a regular interest in slaves. But the trading systems were seldom more than a minor aspect of the economic life of these regions.

Aside from its few staples, trade was thus a highly specialized affair, particularly in its "international" form. Primarily, it served the rulers and prime merchants and their cities. When Leo Africanus reported in the sixteenth century that Timbuktu made "a big demand for books in manuscript, imported from Barbary," and that "more profit is made from the book trade than from any other line of business," he was not necessarily guilty of any exaggeration. But he certainly did not mean that people all over the Western Sudan were buying books. He meant only that Timbuktu itself was an important center of Muslim learning and well able to afford private libraries. Much the same may be said of East Africa's large imports of porcelain from China; those fine pots and vases were destined for the homes and tables of the rich and powerful, and not for the huts of lesser men.

MANNER OF THE TRADE

The lesser men, for their part, had no zeal for accumulation. It was to be one of the great complaints of European settlers in Africa that the "savages" were immune to the offer of monetary reward — that their objection to earning money lay not only in their unfamiliarity with it and with what could be done with it, but also and above all in their unwillingness to work beyond the mere point of providing for themselves and their families. Schooled in a sterner tradition, these settlers saw in such "stubborn idleness" a main proof of damnation. For them, more often than not, there was only one road to heaven — whether the heaven of immortality or the more immediate heaven of respectability — and that was to accumulate.

Both Protestants and Catholics saw matters in this way; but the Puritans said it most clearly. "The standing pool is prone to putrefaction," said Richard Steele in *The Tradesman's Calling*, published in 1684, "and it were better to beat down the body and keep it in subjection by a laborious calling, than through luxury to become a castaway." Such ideas would serve later on as a moral veneer for methods of coercion. Speaking on his Glen Grey Act of 1894 — a measure which imposed an annual money tax on Africans in South Africa so as to force them to leave their villages and go to work for European-paid wages — Cecil Rhodes uttered a comment which may stand as typical. "You will," he told the Legislative Assembly of the Cape Province, "remove [the Africans] from that life of sloth and laziness: you will teach them the dignity of labour and make them contribute to the prosperity of the State: and make them give some return for our wise and good government." Across a crazy paving of such ideas as these the clumsy steamroller of subjection and "trusteeship" has gone testily through the years; and only of late have men begun to question its right of way.

Most Africans found such notions, whenever they came across

Three Regions

them or were forced to take account of them, absurd and inexplicable. The majority of peasants and stock breeders lived in communities where the idea of private property had scarcely appeared, let alone the much more objectionable notion of private enterprise. "All the land occupied by the tribe," writes Schapera of the Bantu-speaking peoples of southern Africa, but his definition will apply more widely, "is vested in the Chief, and administered by him as head of the tribe . . . the land is not his personal possession. . . . The natural resources of the land — earth, water, wood, grass, clay, edible plants, and fruits — are all common property, never reserved for the use of any particular persons. . . . It is only in regard to land for residence and cultivation that private rights are universally recognized. . . ."

Such systems varied in detail. That is understandable. But they were common to much of Africa, the product of trial and error over many centuries. They carried with them and required a general sense of collective responsibility, codes of law that were none the less effective for being unwritten, well-understood sanctions and rewards. There seems little doubt that the economy and ideology of subsistence was raised among a majority of African peoples to a point where it had solved, if far from perfectly, all the root problems of survival at a preindustrial and prescientific level.

Trade was therefore useful but inessential. It grew with the development of Iron Age states and centralized rule. It became the prop and stay of merchants and craftsmen. It supplied the luxury and prestige of courts and rulers. Here and there, too, the growth of trade developed towards the growth of capitalism. Islamic scholars exercised their wit in finding ways to evade religion's ban on usury in much the same way (and with much the same success) as Christian scholars in Europe. But the problem remained within narrow limits.

MANNER OF THE TRADE

Even where trade was promoted by the mighty, there was still no accent on accumulation, in the capitalist meaning of the term. The proof and power of wealth came from display, not from investment. Sometimes there was glittering display. When Sultan Musa passed through Cairo on his way to Mecca in the fourteenth century, he presided over a spending spree of prodigious dimensions and practically wrecked the value of the Cairo currency by paying lavishly in gold that he had brought with him. Earnest bankers in European cities, catching the distant echo of that event and others like it, came mistakenly to think that the whole country beyond the desert must be replete with wealth. But in fact the prodigality of rulers like Mansa Musa, in Suret-Canale's words, pointed "less to the wealth of the mines of Bouré than to the enormous accumulation that the social condition of the country made possible — and to the exercise of the old tribal principle that wealth is an instrument of power because it can buy the loyalty of others, rather than the labor of others."

So long as trade conformed to this pattern, its profits merely enhanced the pride and reputation of local rulers. It added another element to everyday life, but one that was easily absorbed by systems which possessed great inner stability. But once the European connection developed into a massive exchange of slaves for firearms, this old stability was undermined. Trade began to have special and disrupting consequences. These were generally not present with the trans-Saharan or East Africa–Eastern connections. The latter also dealt in slaves and firearms, but marginally; the supply of slaves was never so great as to menace the internal security of the countries concerned, nor was the delivery of firearms large enough to change the balance of military power.

To unravel the course of this European connection, often devious but never dull, I have selected three regions where its impact was decisive, but of widely varying effect.

Three Regions

These are the region of the old states of the Congo, reached by the Portuguese in 1482; the region of the East African coastal city-states and trading empires; and, thirdly, some parts of the Guinea Coast.

All three regions have a large place in the records, but there is another and perhaps stronger reason for choosing them. This is that they present contrasts and parallels which are often strikingly instructive. Through these, I suggest, one can measure with a greater accuracy than in any other way just what the consequences of European enterprise in Africa really were.

Frontiers of Kingdoms, after D'Anville (1749) and Fage (1958)

four

Mani-Congo

> I fetch my life and bearing
> From men of royal siege . . .
>
> *Othello*

> With an assortment of sundry goods amounting to about fourteen hundred pounds sterling, it may be reasonably expected to get about three hundred slaves or more, which brings them to near the rate of five pounds a head.
>
> *James Barbot* in 1700

1 Discovery

SOMETIME IN THE SECOND HALF of the year 1482 an expeditionary fleet of three Portuguese caravels anchored off the Gold Coast castle of Elmina, then less than a year old, and sent in boats through the surf for food and water. They were bound on a long journey. Replenished by their fellow-countrymen in the new-built castle on shore, they at once set sail for the eastward, pressing on to fresh discovery.

For the first few hundred sea-miles after leaving Elmina, they were on a route that was already roughly known. Several Portuguese ships had come this way since Ruy de Siqueira, ten years earlier, had first entered the Bight of Benin. But near this bight their commander changed course for the southward. He and his crews passed Cape Saint Catherine — Cape Lopez in the Gabon of today — and entered seas that no European mariner, and probably no mariner of any continent, had ever sailed before.*

In the annals of European discovery the commander of this expedition, whose name was Diogo Cão, undoubtedly deserves a high place. He was the true forerunner of Bartolomeu Dias and Vasco da Gama, who would soon afterwards sail around the Cape of Good Hope into the Indian Ocean. It was Cão's central task to

* Herodotus had recorded a Phoenician circumnavigation of Africa, but the fact seems more than a little doubtful.

bring back the answer to one great question of consuming interest: How far to the southward did this continental coastline reach before yielding passage to the eastern seas? For it was to complete their turning of the Muslim flank along the Mediterranean coast of Africa that the princes of Portugal mainly promoted the discovering voyages which gave them fame. Once their ships could sail right around and behind the Muslim barrier, they could send expeditions to the lands and peoples of the East. They were convinced that this was possible, since earlier maps had shown a southern termination of the continent; and for some time they believed that this eastward channel must lie not far beyond the Gulf of Guinea. But Diogo Cão proved them wrong.

He failed to sight the southern cape. His farthest point on this first voyage was Cape Lobo, about a hundred and fifty miles beyond modern Lobito. There he erected a stone column — "in the year of the world's creation 1681, and that of Our Saviour's birth 1482" — to the honor of his king and himself. But on the way to Cape Lobo he had already discovered something else — the estuary of a vast river flowing from the interior of Africa. It was this discovery that made his name and fortune. So great was this river, he reported, that its mud-laden waters discolored the ocean for many miles from the shore.

Lisbon sent him back to this river — the Zaire, or Congo. An estuary as wide as this must surely offer an overland route to the first of the great eastern lands on the Portuguese list for discovery, the "empire of Prester John." On his second voyage Cão sailed up the estuary, landed near the Matadi of today, and there met with some of the people of the country. The encounter was peaceful. Failing a common language, neither side could learn much of the other, but the Portuguese understood they were in the territory of a powerful ruler whose capital was distant from the coast. Cão left four Franciscan monks with orders to visit this

Discovery

monarch if they could, and renewed his voyage to the south.

Returning northward some months later, he again sailed up to the head of the estuary but found his monks were missing. He accordingly seized hostages from the people on the shore and carried them back with him to Portugal. The records say that these Congolese discoverers of Europe were well treated on their involuntary journey, and had already learned to speak some Portuguese before being delivered to the king in Lisbon. They were certainly well received by the king, clothed, converted to Christianity, and encouraged to act as future interpreters. In 1487 they were sent back to the Congo with Cão's third expedition. And now Diogo Cão himself, together with a retinue of fellow-countrymen and these Congolese interpreters, was invited to visit the ruler of this land, the Mani-Congo (or Mweni-Congo, lord of Congo), at his capital of Mbanza in the hills behind the coast.

There the Europeans found this African ruler seated on a royal stool of ivory, surrounded by his counselors and men-at-arms; and the meeting was a great success. Each side recovered its lost ones: the king his subjects who had spent nearly two years in Portugal, and Cão his four Franciscan monks. The long history of Portugal in southwest Africa had begun.

It began in friendship and alliance. Within a few years of this visit to Mbanza, the "royal brothers" of Portugal and Congo were writing letters to each other that were couched in terms of complete equality of status. Emissaries went back and forth between them. Relations were established between Mbanza and the Vatican. A son of the Mani-Congo was appointed in Rome itself as bishop of his country.

Not for another two hundred years would the Portuguese succeed in destroying the Mani-Congo's independence. Not until 1883 — four centuries after Diogo Cão had first gazed in wonder at the wide brown flood of the Congo where it surges into the

Atlantic — would this African state be formally annexed by Portugal to the neighboring colony of Angola. The whole early history of this intercourse makes a clear and often startling illustration of the organizational similarity of these two states; and, at the same time, of the inner contrast in their forms of rule and growth that would lead, little by little, to Portuguese dominion. Here, if briefly and fitfully, there was the promise of a genuine partnership between Europe and Africa, as well as a demonstration of why the promise failed.

2 Royal Brothers

NOTHING MORE CLEARLY SHOWS THE CURIOUS PERVERSITY OF THE European-African connection, as it developed through the years, than this history of the Congo. The connection undoubtedly began with something of a golden age of peace and friendship. It just as surely degenerated into violence, hatred, and distrust. So complete was this decay that when the nineteenth century finally brought colonial conquest, the conquerors seemed to have utterly forgotten the experience and accumulated knowledge of earlier Europeans. They proclaimed their "mission to the heart of darkness" as though nothing had previously been known of any of these states or peoples. They and their backers in Europe saw this land as a twilight zone of mystery and mumbo jumbo where the ancient African had somehow managed to survive in primitive squalor and simplicity, a little better than the animals but not much — and not enough, in any case, to justify regarding him as a man who deserved the same respect as other men.

No one expressed this approach and attitude more clearly than

Royal Brothers

Joseph Conrad, although he, of course, did it only to expose the bitterness of the case. His Marlow would remember of a journey in about the year 1900 how the wide reaches of the Congo River opened before his river vessel and closed behind it "as if the forest had stepped leisurely across the water to bar the way for our return. We penetrated deeper and deeper into the heart of darkness. It was very quiet there. At night sometimes the roll of drums behind the curtain of trees would run up the river and remain sustained faintly, as if hovering in the air high above our heads. . . ." No good thing, surely, could ever have come out of such a place.

The impressions of the early Portuguese had been altogether different. They found much that was strange and puzzling, but nothing that seemed to allow an easy contempt or special sense of mystery. They ran into many amazing beliefs and superstitions, but few or none that seemed more disconcerting than others they could find at home. Victorious Congolese armies tended to see signs and ghostly symbols in the sky, yet there was nothing out of the way in that. The Portuguese themselves regularly saw angels, and so of course did other Europeans. More often than not they found it easy to accept the peoples of the Congo as natural equals and allies.

Of this, the most striking evidence is to be found in the correspondence exchanged between King Manuel of Portugal and his remarkable Congolese contemporary, the Mani-Congo Nzinga Mbemba, who was baptized as Dom Affonso. This outstanding African ruler seems to have become a Christian soon after the first large Portuguese missionary expedition reached the Congo in 1490; after defeating his rivals, probably with Portuguese armed assistance, he became Mani-Congo in 1506 or 1507 (the date remains uncertain) and entered at once into a close alliance with his "royal brother" of Portugal. He reigned for some forty years and was long remembered with honor and respect. Even as late as the nine-

MANI-CONGO

teenth century a Portuguese missionary could say that "a native of the Congo knows the name of three kings: that of the present one, that of his predecessor, and that of Affonso."

Some twenty-two of King Affonso's letters, preserved in the royal archives of Portugal, are known for the years 1512 to 1540. Written by various secretaries — the most important of whom, baptized as João Texeira, was evidently Congolese* — they show a good command of the Portuguese language and bear on a wide variety of topics. They also illuminate the relations of equality that marked this early contact.

"Most powerful and excellent king of Manycongo," King Manuel wrote from Lisbon in 1512, "We send to you Simão da Silva, nobleman of our house, a person whom we most trust. . . . We beg you to listen to him and trust him with faith and belief in everything he says from our part. . . ." And King Affonso, who was still Nzinga Mbemba to his subjects, generally began his own letters with the words: "Most high and powerful prince and king my brother. . . ."

What medieval Lisbon thought of this remote land and its people may best be seen from the famous *regimento* of 1512. This "set of instructions" was composed by the Portuguese court for the better ordering of Manuel's relations with the Mani-Congo. It consisted of thirty-four points "in none of which," as James Duffy has lately pointed out, "is there a suggestion of authoritarian constraint on the people of Congo." The *regimento* remains one of the most interesting documents in the tortuous saga of Europe in Africa. It reveals a strikingly keen appreciation of the difficulties of conducting a commercial alliance with a distant people of whom little was known, and foreshadows many of the bitter problems which were soon to beset the enterprise of European discovery.

The "instructions" from Lisbon were in four parts. All of them

* I am following here the opinion argued by Cuvelier.

portray the central misunderstanding that dogged these early efforts in the Congo. Affonso asked for friendly help and was willing to pay for it in whatever goods the Portuguese might care to buy. But the Portuguese, having won over an African ruler to Christianity, thought that the best way they could respond (while duly furthering their own interests) was to transfer Portuguese institutions bodily to the Congo. Simão da Silva, bearer of the *regimento*, was recommended as a resident adviser to Manuel's royal "friend and brother." Not foreseeing the consequences, Affonso eagerly accepted this; later on, when the consequences became clearer, it was too late to reverse the course of events. Yet it is fairly certain that the Portuguese themselves had as yet no thought of outright invasion of the Congo; their *regimento* was intended as a gesture of friendship to a newcomer by one of the leaders of the Christian world. In sending it, Manuel seems to have had in mind that he was dealing with a pagan but strongly organized people — now, fortunately, with a Christian king at their head — who were fully masters of their own land, nonliterate but not therefore savage or especially barbarous, and capable of taking the graft of Portuguese culture without any long period (this idea would develop much later) of "trusteeship" or direct Portuguese government.

In the first two parts of the *regimento* it was provided that the Portuguese should help the king of Congo towards a better organization of his realm, introduce Portuguese notions of law and warfare, build churches, teach Portuguese court etiquette, and, writes Duffy, move in all matters "with tact and discretion, to offend no-one, but to create where possible an African parallel to Portuguese society." It was also suggested that the conflicts and quarrels of Europeans and Africans should be settled amicably, but local Portuguese were to have "extraterritorial rights" and be dealt with in case of need by Portuguese law. Offenders were to be sent home for punishment in Lisbon.

MANI-CONGO

Such was the "civilizing mission." Manuel was also mindful of the material profits. The last two parts of the *regimento* insisted that the Mani-Congo should supply cargoes for the ships of Portugal. "This expedition," noted Manuel, "has cost us much: it would be unreasonable to send it home with empty hands. Although our principal wish is to serve God and the pleasure of the King [of Congo], nonetheless you [Simão da Silva] will make him understand — as though speaking in our own name — what he should do to fill the ships, whether with slaves, or copper, or ivory." Lastly, da Silva was told to collect information of every kind, whether political, military, or commercial.

By the better organization of the Congo kingdom, Manuel intended a tighter and more reliable feudal hierarchy. He knew that Affonso had won his throne in the Congo only against violent opposition from other claimants, and he seems to have been convinced that if Affonso were going to survive the ambition of his turbulent feudatories, he must take an altogether firmer grip on his fiefs. Manuel himself, after all, had the best of reasons for distrusting feudal chieftains, his predecessor having put to death a number of rebellious noblemen. He accordingly abounded in good advice tending towards autocratic rule and thoughtfully added an appendix to the *regimento* that set forth the titles and armorial bearings which the king of Congo should adopt and bestow on his nobles. Here in this curious list there figured "principes, ifamtes, duques, marquezes, comdes, bixcomdes, barões." *
The six greatest feudatories of the Mani-Congo — chiefs of the regions of Mbata, Nsundi, Mbamba, Wembo, Wandu, and Mbala — were to be dukes; lesser notables were to be marquises, counts, and barons; while the children of the king were to be princes and princesses. Manuel also sent a specimen signature "which it seems

* "Princes, royal heirs, dukes, marquises, counts, viscounts, barons."

Royal Brothers

to the King our lord that the King of Manycongo should make and sign from now on."

It is hard to know what the Congolese really made of all this. Affonso accepted it, at least outwardly, in its entirety. On receiving the *regimento* — presented by a "husbandman" called Alvaro Lopes, da Silva having died on the way — the Congo ruler at once sent down 420 slaves for choice by the Portuguese at their anchorage near the mouth of the Congo, and of these the Portuguese selected 320 and duly carried them off. There is also extant a long manifesto or circular letter which Affonso addressed to the "chief lords" of his kingdom; but once again it is difficult to guess how far Affonso could have been sincere.

The king of Portugal "sent us the arms painted in this letter," Affonso told his chiefs and counselors, according to this manifesto, "for us to use them as ensigns on our shields, as the Christian kings or princes of those lands generally carry so to show to whom they belong and whence they come. . . . Those arms which he so sent to us represent the Cross seen in the skies, and also the Apostle St. Tiago with all the other Saints with whom he fought for us . . . together with that part of his own arms which he added to the mentioned ones which the Almighty God our Lord gave through his Angel to the first King of Portugal while he was fighting in a battle against many Moorish Kings, enemies of his holy faith. . . ." This was no doubt a letter written for consumption in Lisbon.

Sincere or not, Affonso increasingly adopted the Christian ideas and arguments of his "royal brother" in pressing frequently for help, and in complaining when help as frequently failed to arrive. There must in any case have seemed no other way of winning access to European knowledge and techniques; and Affonso's letters leave no doubt that he was fully sincere in wanting both of these new things. Whenever he had the chance he sent cargoes of young men to be educated in Portugal, persisting in this even when he had learned by experience that many would be lost to Portuguese enslavement on the way.

He also strove to bypass the Portuguese maritime monopoly and enter into direct relations with the other "important European" of whom the Portuguese had given news, the Pope in Rome. Manuel at first was not averse to this, since the appearance of a Congolese embassy in Rome would necessarily reflect great prestige on the Portuguese discoverers. He suggested that his brother of the Congo should send a mission to Rome, helpfully explaining that twelve noblemen with six servants would be the right number. One of Affonso's sons, baptized as Dom Henrique and then being educated in a Portuguese seminary, should lead this mission and, as ambassador, should formally address the Pope in Latin. King Manuel would request the Pope to make Prince Henry a bishop.

All this, however unlikely it may now appear, came to pass with little delay. Accompanied by gifts of ivory, rare skins, and the fine-woven raffia textiles of the Congo (and, as far as Lisbon, by the 320 captives whom the Portuguese captains had chosen), the mission arrived in Portugal and was sent overland to Italy, crossing the Alps and making its way slowly down to Rome, where it safely arrived in 1513. With it went Prince Henry, who was then eighteen years old.

Five years later, on May 5, 1518, Henry of Congo was elevated to the rank of bishop on the formal proposal of four cardinals, Pope Leo X having two days earlier published a bull to that effect: *Vidimus quae super Henrici.* . . . Three years later Henry returned to his native land. He appears to have died in 1535, having achieved little or nothing. Like the rest of his people — and like his memorable father — Henry was the victim of an impossible contradiction. The "civilizing mission" and the "commerce" of the *regimento* had been supposed to march gently hand in hand, each aiding the other. In fact they were sharply and even violently opposed from the very first; but it was the commerce that won.

Yet "relations of equality" persisted as long as Dom Affonso remained alive. So did the Christian texture of his correspondence. "Most high and most powerful prince and king my brother," he was writing in 1517, "it is due to the need I have of several things for the church that I am importuning you. And this I would not probably do if I had a ship, since having it I would send for them at my own cost. . . ." He had repeatedly asked Manuel to give him a ship or the means of building one; but Manuel, being determined to keep the maritime monopoly strictly in his own hands, had as regularly refused to oblige. "The things needed for the church are the following . . . a silver cross, a monstrance for the Corpus Christi, curtains for the altar, half a dozen surplices . . ." and other items of the kind.

In 1526 Affonso had news by a Portuguese vessel of the death of the queen of Portugal. He at once hastened to send Manuel assurances of "the great sorrow and mourning" he felt because "the Queen Dona Leonor our Sister had passed away from the present life, and only Our Lord knows how sorry and regretful we were for that. . . ."

In the same year he wrote again, with fresh requests for "technical aid," asking this time for medical staffs:

> Your highness has been kind enough to write to us saying that we should ask in our letters for anything we need, and that we shall be provided with everything, and as the peace and health of our kingdom depend on us, and as there are among us old folks and people who have lived for many days, it happens that we have many and different diseases which put us very often in such a weakness that we reach almost the last extreme; and the same happens to our children, relatives and others owing to the lack

in this country of physicians and surgeons who might know how to cure properly such diseases. . . . We have neither dispensaries nor drugs which might help us in this forlornness. . . . We beg of you to be kind and agreeable enough to send two physicians and two apothecaries and one surgeon. . . .

Like other of Affonso's efforts to introduce European techniques, this appeal for doctors seems to have been fruitless. Yet even as late as 1540, when the early partnership had run hopelessly into the sands of commercial greed, and Affonso had seen all his plans and ambitions reduced to nothing, the Congo monarch was still writing to Lisbon — now to John III, who had meanwhile succeeded Manuel — in the same language of Christian persuasion. He argued that the king of Portugal's assumption of the title of "Lord of Guinea" should be a reason for showing special consideration for the needs of the Congo, "since we have helped you to sustain this title with unfailing support." He gently complained of the repeated disappointments that he had suffered at Portuguese hands. He renewed his appeal for help:

It will not seem wrong that . . . as adequate income should be awarded us for our legitimate necessities . . . since we have to spend a lot of money [in furthering the interests of Christianity] and have nobody to help us, unless we turn to Your Highness and ask for assistance for the sake and honour of Our Lord Jesus Christ's passion: We beg of you to lend us five thousand cruzados to provide for the expenses of our brother and ambassador Dom Manuel, who on our behalf goes to see the Holy Father, accepting in exchange one hundred and fifty *cofos* of coins of our Kingdom [three million cowries] with which slaves can be bought [and the King of Portugal thus repaid].*

* The actual words read: "units can be ransomed," *units* being a Portuguese euphemism for "slaves," and *ransomed* being another for "bought."

But to John III and his counselors the request did seem wrong; and it fell, like the others, on deaf ears. By this time the Portuguese court had taken the measure of their own interests in the Congo, and these were not the same, by a long chalk, as the interests of the people of Dom Affonso. To see why this was so, one needs to look at the old Congo as it really was.

3 Congo, Ngola, Matamba

Much can be learned of the old states of the western Congo basin and the neighboring coastal regions, for the Portuguese were curious travelers and, from time to time, acute historians. Many early missionary writings have survived. Lately, too, the modern science of archeology has added useful knowledge to the record, filling out the picture of the way these peoples lived before conquest by the Portuguese, and suggesting how they were related to their neighbors in the north and east.

The last of the "Lords of Congo" died some fifty years ago, unhonored and unsung, an obscure nonentity whose authority had vanished and whose prestige lay hidden in the half-remembered traditions of a captive people. His baptismal name was Dom Martin, and he counted in the world of Africa for nothing but a memory. Yet it was a great memory. Dom Martin came of a long line of rulers. He himself was the fifty-fifth Mani-Congo. His "founding ancestor," whose name was written by the early Portuguese as Nimi a Lukeni, appears to have begun his rule near the end of the fourteenth century and was perhaps contemporary, to make a European comparison, with the early years of Joan of Arc.

Two sons of the sisters of Nimi a Lukeni came after him, suc-

MANI-CONGO

cession being matrilineal then just as it is today among some of the peoples who occupy this country; and then another Mani-Congo whose name is lost, at least to the Portuguese records. Fifth in the line was Nzinga a Nkuwa, who was Mani-Congo when the caravels of Diogo Cão turned eastward into the estuary of the great river in 1482, and whom Cão's missionary fellow-venturers christened as João after their own sovereign lord. Nzinga a Nkuwa was followed by Nzinga Mbemba, who, as Dom Affonso, became King Manuel's "royal brother."

The lands of the Mani-Congo's dominion varied in extent. As in Europe a little earlier, this was a time of constant if limited warfare between powerful rulers whose authority was broadly feudal in character. At their greatest extension, probably not long before the arrival of the Portuguese, the Mani-Congo was the liege lord of territories of fealty and tribute whose boundaries may have measured about three hundred miles from north to south and perhaps two or three hundred from west to east. To the north of the Congo estuary these lands included Loango, roughly coterminous with modern Cabinda, and the states of Congo, Ngola, and Matamba to the south of the river, all these three lying in northern and western Angola as we know it now.

The "home kingdom" of Congo was the extreme northern part of modern Angola. Its frontiers, at their greatest extent, may have reached inland from the Congo estuary for about two hundred and fifty miles. There is no means of knowing the exact size of the population of all these countries; about four or five million today, it was probably not much less five hundred years ago. There seems some likelihood that it was considerably larger, in any case, than the population of Portugal.

Self-confidence and a vigorous sense of independence were the characteristics that repeatedly struck the Portuguese about these rulers and their counselors. They thought themselves, wrote a

Congo, Ngola, Matamba

seventeenth century Italian, "the foremost men in the world," and nothing would persuade them to the contrary. "Never having been outside of Africa, they imagine that their country is not only the largest in the world, but also the happiest, most agreeable and most beautiful." Powerful in war, quick to defend themselves, jealous of their rights, and suspicious of foreign intervention, they were seldom or never defeated in outright battle by the Portuguese. Pushed back by European fire-power, they retreated to their mountain strongholds, nursed their wounds, recouped their losses, and returned time after time to the attack. Many of their leaders became famous in the later folklore of colonial Angola.

Where had the Mani-Congo and his people come from? Their own traditions suggested that they — or at least their ruling families — were relative newcomers to the country when they first encountered the Portuguese. Picking up two hundred years later what Lisbon had learned of these traditions, Oliveira Cadornega has an interesting passage in his *Description of the Kingdom of Congo*, published in 1680. "About the origins of this kingdom . . . this nation has always been considered as foreign . . . [and as being people] who had come from the interior to dominate this kingdom: as it happened, we may say, with the Romans, Sueves, Vandals, Goths and Semi-Goths who occupied our Lusitania, Spain and other kingdoms and domains. . . ."

This comparison was strikingly perceptive. For the African period that was contemporary with the overrunning of Roman Europe by "barbarians" from the east and north was also, as modern research confirms, a time of great movement of peoples. These were the centuries that saw many new waves in the great migration movements of Bantu-speaking and other African peoples who have to a large extent populated the nations of central and southern Africa that are known today. They moved across

MANI-CONGO

lands that were relatively empty of people in directions that were mainly from north to south but were also, as peoples doubled and redoubled on their tracks, in lateral and northerly directions too.

In this way there came into the western Congo, in their turn, the ancestors of the Mani-Congo. Probably they were no more than a small group of closely organized and well-armed intruders, tempered and toughened by their travels and adventures. They would have conquered their lands in Congo in much the same sense as Duke William and his four thousand knights had seized control of Saxon England some three or four hundred years earlier, subjugating the peoples whom they found, settling among them, intermarrying with them, and gradually building a new state and social system. Little by little they spread their influence among their neighbors, contracted "royal marriages," and established the right of tax and tribute. Sometimes these neighbors revolted against such impositions, as fief-holders regularly did in Europe, and the Mani-Congo was obliged to call out his levies and go to war for his rights. It was precisely this endemic rivalry between "king and barons" that made the early Portuguese alliance attractive to Nzinga a Nkuwa and his successor, Dom Affonso, and gave the Portuguese their early chance of military intervention here.

Recent archeological research indicates that these southwestern states (Congo, Ngola, Matamba, and their like) were offshoots of the main stream of Iron Age development in central-southern Africa during the first centuries of the present millennium — a development that culminated, so far as southern Africa was concerned, in the plateau states which built Zimbabwe and other notable stone structures. There is evidence of close similarity between the organization and culture of the Congo states and those of Rhodesia and Mozambique.

Among this evidence there is that of the "royal palaces." The

Congo, Ngola, Matamba

paramount rulers of the Rhodesian states were generally established in large dwellings, often of stone, and sometimes, as at Great Zimbabwe or Khami, of elaborate construction with one large wall encircling another — a labyrinth of mystery built less for safety than for means of celebrating the divinity of an elected king. Commenting on the large stone ruin of Khami, near Bulawayo, Robinson has defined its evident function as being "to provide a suitable residence for the chief and his followers. The site for such a residence had to possess certain qualifications. First, it must be centrally placed in relation to the other important dwellings. Second, it must occupy a prominent and dominating position, and provide outstanding sites for important huts. Third, it must be sufficiently fortified to defy attack by jealous rivals. Fourth, it must be near permanent water. Fifth, it must be so constructed that in spite of its prominence it provided sanctuary for the tribal relics, and privacy of movement for the chief and his advisers."

Obviously, the need for security would vary with time and circumstance. At Great Zimbabwe (in Southern Rhodesia) the "palace" of the divine ruler was guarded by a strong fortress established on the hill above. At Khami (also in Southern Rhodesia, but further westward) there seems to have been little or no fear of attack. Elsewhere, and notably at Mapungubwe in the northern Transvaal, the central dwelling was placed on a steep-sided "table mountain" up to the top of which its dwellers had carried many thousand tons of soil. Later European explorers found that many of the villages of Mashonaland, to the north of Mapungubwe and Zimbabwe, were also placed on the tops of hills. Moshesh, the great nineteenth century leader of the Basuto, followed the same tradition when he built his royal village on the flat summit of a mountain.

MANI-CONGO

What is known of chiefly dwellings in Angola, west of Rhodesia, shows the same pattern of need and intention. Here and there the parallels are remarkably close. "The king of Angola or Dongo," James Barbot noted in 1700, "resides a little above the city Massingan, on a stony mountain seven leagues in compass, in which are many rich pastures, fields and meadows, yielding a plentiful provision for all his retinue; in which there is but one single passage, and this according to their method well fortified; so that he needs fear no enemies. . . ."

That the states of the Congo were an integral part of the Central African Iron Age is confirmed by evidence from other groups of stone ruins and graves which have lately come to light two hundred miles south of Massangano, near Amboim on the Angolan coast, and southward again near the port of Benguela. Some of the larger graves are thought to be those of chiefs, although close archeological investigation, as everywhere in the Portuguese colonies, has still to be undertaken. "The importance of the chief," Clark has written of them, "is shown by the amount of ornament on the stone-work. The same geometric patterns are repeated here as in the Rhodesian ruins. Monoliths are also found on these graves and are said to be symbolic of the power of the chief, a suggestion that throws an interesting reflection on the purpose of the Zimbabwe bird monoliths. . . ."

Thus the states of the Congo must be seen as members of the great community of Africa's Iron Age: loosely articulated constellations of state power and social organization that spread across the central and southern continent through the middle centuries of the present millennium. Beyond them to the eastward, across the heartlands of the Upper Congo, there were the long-established and powerful states and empires of the Lunda and Luba peoples Eastward again, over the frontier mountains of the Congo, there were the feudal states of the Banyoro and their like, while to the southward lay the lands of the Monomotapa,* first thought by the Portuguese to be Prester John himself, and the country of the southern and southwestern Bantu. North and west of the Congo there were others no less famous, Oyo and Benin, Kanem and Songhay and Akwamu. This was a world that was specifically African in its outlook, beliefs, culture, and organization — a congeries of states and empires that had tamed a continent.

4 Law and Order

IT WAS NATURAL THAT THE PORTUGUESE SHOULD INTERPRET THE organization of the states they found as clearly feudal. They were mistaken, of course, in part of this interpretation. This was African, not European, feudalism: a distinction with a great difference. In later years the Portuguese discovered their mistake and were suitably mortified. "The government of Bailundu," exclaimed a nineteenth century report on one of the peoples of inland Angola, "is democratic. These heathen mix with the infamous humiliations of the orientals, the unbridled coarseness of the English people at election time in England. The kings defer to and flatter their counsellors: these are they who elevate a king to the throne and also cast him down."

Yet to the medieval eye the general picture of government in the Congo was remarkably close to that of government in Europe. Lesser chiefs were found to pay tribute to greater chiefs, and greater

---

* Mono is clearly *Mweni* (lord). Various meanings have been ascribed to Motapa. The area was central Southern Rhodesia; the people were Bantu-speaking.

MANI-CONGO

chiefs to owe fealty to the Mani-Congo himself. Marriages of chiefs were often contracted with the aim of sealing loyalties or alliances. The whole land of the Mani-Congo's dominion was divided into "provinces," each with its governor or paramount ruler; in the late seventeenth century there were eighteen such provinces, but the number seems to have been much the same at the time of European arrival about a hundred years earlier. There is plenty to indicate that these feudal arrangements, though orally defined and casual in their integration, were part of a solidly grounded state system. They represented far more than a loose confederation of tribes, as later Europeans, victims of the myth that Africa has no past, would sometimes assert.

This organization was described in some detail by the Portuguese and Italians who lived and worked in Angola during the seventeenth century. Provincial governors — and all men who had "fiefs of the king" — had to go to court once every three years and renew their vows of loyalty to the Mani-Congo. Every time a new Mani-Congo was enthroned he had to redistribute fiefs and powers. "For the conferment of offices and dignities," an Italian Missionary, Cavazzi, explained in 1687, "they have another rite which shows the majesty of the king and the great submission that is given by those whom he honours. Early in the morning they announce the ceremony with a triple discharge of muskets and other military noises: at the third discharge the king comes out and seats himself on his throne. Everyone prostrates himself in an act of adoration rather than of courtesy," and after due ceremonial the chosen subject is invested with "a bonnet, a scimitar, a standard, and a carpet with permission to use it."

Perhaps the ceremonies had grown in pomp with Portuguese example, and the muskets of course were of European provenance; yet the meaning of the investiture could not have greatly changed since pre-European times. The lord of Congo, in common with

Law and Order

other rulers of Africa's Iron Age, was conceived as having divine powers. He was believed to embody in himself the immortal substance of god, for the Congolese, again in company with other African peoples, were monotheist in their religion. Mani-Congo Nzinga a Nkuwa, like his forebears, was customarily forbidden to eat in public, as were other divine rulers; and it became a sore point of religious strife when his successor, Dom Affonso, decided to abandon the rule and eat as a Christian in the sight of his court.

According to Father Carli, who wrote a little earlier than his fellow-Capuchin Cavazzi, the most important fiefs were those of São Salvador (Mbanza Congo, the capital province), "where the king resides"; Bamba, "where the great duke Don Theodosio rules"; Sondi, "where there is another duke"; Pemba, "where a marquis lives"; and Songo, "in which there is a count who has not given fealty to the king of Congo for some years." North of the river, the state of Loango likewise had its divine king who was forbidden to eat in public; and here, too, there prevailed a clear hierarchy of duties, rights, and responsibilities.

Methods of government reflected this feudal organization. Writing in the second half of the eighteenth century, the Abbé Proyart mentions a number of "ministers" of the king of Loango: the *mangovo*, who was in charge of "external relations"; the *mafuka*, who was responsible for trade with the Europeans; the *makaka*, who was "minister of war"; and the *makimba*, who was "minister of rivers and forests." To the south of the river, the Mani-Congo had much the same kind of government at his disposal. Pigafetta, drawing on Portuguese sources for a book that was published in 1591, also describes the Mani-Congo's postal system: "runners who stand ready to go from one place to another with the King's messages and to carry the post."

Military levies were raised in a manner which early European travelers found perfectly familiar. "The sovereigns of these countries," Proyart would note a good deal later, yet validly for the earlier period too, "maintain no regular troops. When a king has determined on war, his Makaka, minister of war and generalissimo of his armies, transmits orders to the princes and governors of provinces, to levy troops; the latter never fail to lead to the rendezvous the quota that is demanded of them." Portuguese reports in the seventeenth century credited the Mani-Congo with power to raise some eighty thousand men.

European opinions varied on the degree of bloodiness of these feudal wars. Father Girolamo de Montesarchio thought that generally there were few men killed, and spoke of a pitched battle between the lord of Sevo and a rebel army numbering many thousands when only forty fatal casualties had occurred. Cavazzi, on the other hand, believed that the wars were very destructive of life. A hundred years later Proyart noted of Congo warfare that it was "very rare that the armies advance . . . to encounter each other with the intention of coming to blows. The great art of making war is to avoid the enemy and to pounce on the villages known to be abandoned, in order to pillage them, reduce them to ashes, and take prisoners there." But there is no doubt that by Proyart's time the old feudal and ceremonial manners of Congo warfare had degenerated into the ravage and rapine of wholesale slaving for export. Bloodshed for the sole purpose of taking captives had by then become an everyday affair.

Solidity of state organization was reflected in other aspects of daily life. It would be said in later times that anarchy and chaos had reigned supreme; the colonial system, it would be argued, had brought the blessings of law and order to peoples incapable of fashioning their own. The truth was otherwise. In evidence of this, a former Apostolic Delegate of Matadi on the Lower Congo, Monsignor Cuvelier, has lately suggested a comparison of the laws

Law and Order

of Congo with those of Portugal. True enough, the laws of Congo were somewhat modified (at least in theory) by the *regimento* of 1512; but these Portuguese innovations were never applied to Loango, north of the river, and a comparison of the legal position in Loango with that of Congo shows that the *regimento* made little or no impact on such matters as the scale of punishment.

Another reason for misunderstanding was that Congo law was never written law; moreover, it reflected the easygoing judgments of a much less rigidly organized society. Affonso certainly found the Portuguese legal codes bafflingly severe. "What," he is said to have jocularly asked a Portuguese adviser on one occasion, "is the penalty in Portugal for anyone who puts his feet on the ground?"

Writing to his brother of Congo in 1511, the king of Portugal had opined that the Congolese might find Portuguese law unduly severe in comparison with their own law; and it is easy to see why. Like other Europeans, the Portuguese punished some forms of theft by death; for other forms, the thief must hand over nine times the value of the property he had stolen. Elsewhere in Europe the developing notion of private property caused theft to be punished with an ever-increasing brutality: in the England of 1740 a child could be hanged for stealing even so little as a rag of cotton.

In the Congo, by contrast, where communal ideas of life were still very much alive and notions of private property vague in the extreme, comparatively little importance was attached to theft. Small thefts were punished by fines or "public shame," or else by reduction to domestic servitude or payment of a slave. Larger thefts were generally punished by enslavement or by a fine equal to the value of a slave. Such slaves were not chattel slaves, of course, but domestic slaves who could usually expect to win their freedom.

MANI-CONGO

On murder, the sanctions were evidently much the same in Portugal and Congo: death except in case of reasonable self-defense. High treason and rape were also punished in the same way in both countries. And it is an interesting comment on the vigor of native Congo law that much of Manuel's *regimento* was in fact preoccupied with the problems of engrafting Portuguese law onto native law, while at the same time providing that Portuguese subjects in the Congo should be judged in Portuguese and not in Congo courts.

Another common belief in later times was that colonial rule had enabled Christianity to destroy the savage and superstitious fear of the supernatural in which, it was held, Africans were hopelessly plunged. Until the coming of Europe, it would be said, the heathen in his blindness had bowed down to wood and stone and suffered appalling mental tribulations in the process. Whatever the truth about African animism — and anthropology has stripped off much of its European-woven clothing of legendary horror — this view of the matter did less than justice to the extravagant nature of contemporary Christianity.

Here, for example, is Father Merolla's description in 1683 of his method of dealing with "hellish delusions" in the Congo. The delusions in question concerned female purification rites and habits. Perfectly harmless and possibly hygienic, as we should think now, they were coupled by Father Merolla, who was an otherwise intelligent Capuchin priest, with the whole body of "foul superstition" in which Africans were believed to flounder and perish.

He began his task of enlightenment with a powerful sermon. He admonished his flock to turn away from heathen practices and concluded, so as to improve the lesson, with a little demonstration of a practical sort. "The better to move the people," he relates, "I had placed on the altar the image of this blessed saint [the Virgin],

Law and Order

covered and with a dagger through her breast from which the blood flowed. This done, I began to discourse against those women that observed the hellish delusions before mentioned [such as . . . not to speak to any man, to wash so many times a day . . .], proving that thereby they not only offended the Saviour but likewise did great injury to his immaculate mother. At the same time I drew aside the curtain and revealed the image. . . ."

One may wonder what a seventeenth century African could have thought of that blood-stained Virgin. Many years later, when a British expedition penetrated to the city of Benin (far from the Congo, yet visited by the same Christian missionary zeal in the sixteenth and seventeenth centuries), a degenerate animist theocracy was found to have practiced crucifixion as a means of propitiating God. It would be interesting to know how far the image of a god demanding such sacrifice was derived from the muddle and misunderstanding of early missionary teaching like that of the good Father Merolla.

Trade in the early Congo states undoubtedly existed, though in the primitive forms associated with a subsistence economy. One cannot be sure how much trade there was, nor with whom; there seems to have been some contact with the Kuba states to the eastward, and probably with the states of the central (Rhodesian) plateau. Early records show in any case that the Mani-Congo was far from being the impoverished beggar his successors would become. His revenues were large. They were paid in kind and also in currency: the goods in kind being domestic slaves, ivory, textiles woven in raffia, and skins; the currency of the realm being the cowrie shell, as it was also that of some of its neighbors. There were officials whose duty was to gather the royal dues: the *mfutila*, charged with collecting tribute, the *mani-mpanza*, and the *mani-samba*.

In the matter of cash the Mani-Congo was unusually fortunate.

MANI-CONGO

He appears to have possessed a "mint" of his own. "The island of Loanda," noted Pigafetta, "is the mine from which the king of Congo draws what I should call his metallic riches — more valued than gold or silver by him and by neighbouring peoples. Women are used to go into the sea and fill their baskets with sand from which they extract small shells: these are washed, weighed, and carried to the treasury of the king."

In Loango, north of the river, the currency seems also to have consisted in local textiles (of palm fiber, not of cotton); but cowries were used extensively by all the peoples of the estuary. These *nzimbu* were put through a sieve at the royal treasury. The smallest were rejected, but large ones might still be worth ten times as much as small ones that were considered big enough for use. To avoid the labor of repeated counting there were fixed measures in the form of containers which could hold 40, 100, 250, 400, or 500 shells. The measure that consisted of containers amounting to 1000 shells was called a *funda*; that amounting to 10,000 a *lufuku*; while a *cofo* was a measure holding 20,000.

From early times the Portuguese established a regular rate of exchange between cowries and their own currency. Thus Father Garcia Simões, writing in 1575, reported that ten cowries at Loanda were worth one Portuguese real. These exchange conventions were remarkably durable. In 1619 it was said at São Salvador, the Congo capital, that 25 *cofos* (half a million shells) were worth 187½ cruzados. Since the cruzado at that time was reckoned at about four shillings of English money,* a *cofo* would have fetched about thirty shillings, no mean sum in the early seventeenth century. Two years later, no doubt defending his currency, the Mani-Congo was claiming that the *cofo* was in fact worth 25 cruzados, or five pounds sterling.

---

* Boxer gives this exchange value for 1635; according to Dames, the cruzado of 1510 had been worth nearly ten shillings.

Law and Order

Here lay one of many reasons for dissension between the Mani-Congo and his Portuguese visitors. Oversea traders were quick to see their advantage in devaluating the Congo currency. They began to bring in cowries from abroad. The effect was such that the Mani-Congo tried to prohibit the practice since, in Felner's words, "the money of the country had fallen so much in value that the king was losing two thirds of his revenue." The prohibition seems to have had some effect. By 1622, according to the Mani-Congo Pedro Affonso, a *cofo* could be exchanged for only five cruzados; and a report of 1649 returns the same value. In this latter year Cadornega gave four cruzados for one *cofo*, and the rate appears to have stayed at about this level, falling only slightly, for many years thereafter. Exchange in cowries continued late into the nineteenth century. The Congolese had not defended their currency in vain.

What this stable and comparatively prosperous society clearly needed was neither the autocracy of Portugal, religious paternalism, nor military intervention, but trade and knowledge that could have stimulated internal changes in a social structure which owed almost nothing to the outside world. The Portuguese were in any case poorly placed to offer such help, for they themselves labored under forms of government and commerce that were beginning to be outmoded and grossly inefficient even for the sixteenth century. All they were able to achieve, in the event, was a doubtful sovereignty for themselves and ruin for their former partners in alliance.

MANI-CONGO

5 From Alliance to Invasion

FOR THE MANI-CONGO AND THOSE WHOM HE RULED AND CLAIMED to rule, the crisis came with cruel speed. It was down on them even before the ink could dry on Manuel's *regimento* of 1512. Formally, the early partnership of Diogo Cão's time might continue; in any real sense of the word, it was dying fast. As the early years of Affonso's rule brought experience of what the Portuguese really intended, it became clear that his allies were pursuing dangerously different aims from himself. What he wanted for the Congo was aid in the form of priests, schoolteachers, carpenters, boatbuilders, and the like — the skills and education that could really give him and his people an opening to the new world of Europe. But what these newcomers wanted for themselves, increasingly and soon exclusively, was slaves. They saw no profit in sending "technical aid." Little or none was ever sent.

How much could Affonso have understood of Portuguese motives and intentions? It is impossible to know, although his letters suggest that he had grasped a great deal of the essential truth. Certainly he persevered. Eager to learn, bold to innovate, tolerant of what he failed to understand, Affonso was also under political compulsions that he could never afford to ignore. His vassals were often on the verge of revolt; it would only need Portuguese encouragement to push them to the deed itself. So the Portuguese had to be mollified and kept friendly. Affonso could not afford to throw them off.

Yet he allowed himself a tone of increasing reproach as the years went by, and he continued playing the Christian card to the top of his bent. He was bitter, but he was also dignified. "It is unworthy to remind you," he wrote to John III towards the end of his life, "that you should not forget us, since the reasons why

From Alliance to Invasion

you ought to remember us are perfectly obvious; but I shall take the trouble of bringing some of these to memory in case you have forgotten them."

The immediate cause of Affonso's troubles lay somewhat to the northward of his liege of Loango and two hundred miles out to sea: the island of São Tomé. First settled by the Portuguese in 1490, this island had become a valued staging post for vessels on the journey to and from the East. That would not have mattered to Affonso. But São Tomé was also something else: a settlement of rogues and vagabonds, many of them deported from Portugal, who were governed by a Portuguese vassal empowered to make his fortune if he could. This the vassal of São Tomé could achieve in two ways: first, by exercising a monopoly on trade with the adjacent African coast — that of the Congo states — and secondly, by importing African slaves for plantation labor on the island itself. Both activities were in full swing by the time of Manuel's *regimento*. They bore heavily and in the end decisively on the relations between Portugal and Congo.

Like Nzinga a Nkuwa before him, Affonso found himself faced in practice, not with the "partnership" of the king of Portugal, but with that of the vassal of São Tomé and his thieving traders, concerned now with procuring slaves for their own sugar plantations which were then coming into production, as well as with preventing any other Europeans from gaining access to the Congo coast. The interest of these settlers on São Tomé was to interpose themselves between the Congo states and the outside world, and this they did with utter lack of scruple, great attention to detail, and an unrelenting eye for immediate profit.

Affonso tried to circumvent this fatal obstacle to intercourse with Europe. He attempted this on many occasions and in several different ways; but he never secured any lasting success. First of all, he appealed to Lisbon against the great cupidity and

MANI-CONGO

greed, which he freely mentioned, of Lisbon's vassal of São Tomé, one Fernam de Mello; such complaints echo repeatedly and vainly down the years. Next he tried to persuade Manuel to let him have a ship of his own so that he could communicate directly with Lisbon. "Most powerful and most high prince and king my brother," pleads one of his letters of 1517, "I have already written to you a few times about how much I need a ship, and telling you how grateful I would be if you would let me buy one. . . ." But the robber island had stronger friends at court, and no ship was ever allowed to fall into Affonso's hands, much less a crew to man it.

Failing in that, Affonso asked that São Tomé should be simply handed over to him as a fief, a proposal which only served to inform Lisbon how little he understood of realities in the outside world. By this time it had become a confirmed practice that all slaves from the Congo states — and already the number was considerable — must pass through São Tomé; and the vassal of São Tomé had secured the right to seize a quarter of such slaves for himself, and then a twentieth part of the remaining three quarters. Often he took more, so that the Mani-Congo would as often find that half his "slaving currency" had disappeared in transit to Lisbon. But the notion that Lisbon would ever willingly forgo its claim to São Tomé must have raised many a courtier's laugh at the time.

As the years went by and slaving grew in volume, the situation in the Congo states began gradually to shift towards a chaos not known before. In 1526 Affonso tried a heroic measure. He attempted to control, reduce, and even stop the slave trade. It had begun some thirty years earlier — easily, almost imperceptibly, at that time the mere customary act of one monarch turning over to another, his ally, a quantity of captives. The custom was almost universal in Iron Age Africa. It was not unknown in medieval

From Alliance to Invasion

Europe. African rulers could have had no more anxiety about the giving of slaves than their European partners about the receiving of them; and this, of course, was still at a time when European merchants and sea captains were selling European slaves to the markets of North Africa. Yet oversea slave purchase in the Congo had now gone far beyond any question of royal custom. It had become, even in these early years, a social plague and a daily source of fear and dispute. Affonso tried to cut it down again. His motives were both political and social.

These varying motives were clearly expressed in a strong letter to John III. In the first place, Affonso deplored "the excessive freedom given by your factors and officials to the men and merchants who are allowed to come to this Kingdom to set up shops with goods and many things which have been prohibited by us and which they spread throughout our Kingdoms and Domains in such an abundance that many of our vassals, whom we had in obedience, do not comply because they have the things in greater abundance than we ourselves. . . ." The incoming traders, in short, had undermined the Mani-Congo's trading monopoly, on which rested much of his power and prestige, and thereby weakened his control of the country.

But there was more, and worse. "We cannot reckon how great the damage is, since the above-mentioned merchants daily seize our subjects, sons of the land and sons of our noblemen and vassals and our relatives. . . . Thieves and men of evil conscience take them because they wish to possess the things and wares of this Kingdom. . . . They grab them and cause them to be sold: and so great, Sir, is their corruption and licentiousness that our country is being utterly depopulated." The king of Portugal should not countenance such practices. "And to avoid [them], we need from [your] Kingdoms no other than priests and people to teach in schools, and no other goods but wine and flour for the holy sacrament: that is why we beg of Your Highness to help and assist us in this matter, commanding the factors that they should send here neither merchants nor wares, because it is *our will that in these kingdoms* [of Congo] *there should not be any trade in slaves nor market for slaves.*"*

Probably Affonso wanted only to reduce slaving to its former small proportions; but in any case the hope was vain. Once begun, the trade could be neither stopped nor contained. It was worth too much to the coastal chiefs under Affonso's often purely nominal control. It was far too valuable to the men from São Tomé. Every Christian intention of the Portuguese was forfeited to that inexhaustible commercial appetite, and, on the African side, every reasonable hope of direct and fruitful contact with the world of the far north.

Yet Affonso, for his part, clung to his hopes of aid. Often his letters give dramatic evidence of the plight he was in. In a long one of 1539 he is found explaining to John III, still his "royal brother," that the ship which carries the letter also brings to Portugal five of his nephews and one of his grandsons, two of whom are to be taught to read and write, two to be forwarded to Rome, and two to be prepared in Lisbon for minor holy orders. Then comes a passage that abruptly sweeps away the centuries and brings one face to face with this extraordinary man:

> We beg of Your Highness to give them shelter and boarding and to treat them in accordance with their rank, as relatives of ours with the same blood . . . and if we are reminding you of this and begging of your attention it is because, during the life of the King your father, whom pray God to have in His glory, we sent from this Kingdom to yours, according to his orders with a certain Antonio Veira . . . more than twenty youngsters, our grandsons, nephews and relations who were the most gifted to

* Emphasis in the original.

From Alliance to Invasion

learn the service of God. . . . The above-mentioned Antonio Veira left some of these youngsters in the land of Panzamlumbo, our enemy, and it gave us great trouble later to recover them; and only ten of these youngsters were taken to your Kingdom: But about them we do not know so far whether they are alive or dead, nor what happened to them, so that we have nothing to say to their fathers and mothers. . . .

A sad "partnership" indeed; for these twenty young Congolese students had gone to Europe in 1516, twenty-three years before that letter was written, and ten of them, as the records show, had been seized by the vassal of São Tomé. Yet so little did the court in Lisbon care for religious vows and promises, grandiose and sweeping though they were, that not a single official word had reached the Congo of the fate of these travelers. The case was typical enough.

One reason for this callousness — and Affonso can hardly have grasped its full importance — lay in Portuguese discoveries elsewhere. Throughout Affonso's reign, Portugal was sending almost yearly fleets to the Indian Ocean and others across the Atlantic to Brazil. The Congo had to take third place; and the position was a poor one that was rendered all the worse by the Congo's evident deficiency in precious metals. There was consequently an ever-recurring shortage of transport to and from the Congo. One can see this from the complaints that were voiced by hard-pressed agents on the spot. Slaves might be available in apparently inexhaustible supply, but the ships that were needed to take these slaves away remained few and far between. "During these five years that I have been here," a Portuguese royal agent was writing from the Congo in 1526, "the [available] cargo has never been less than four or five thousand units [slaves], besides many others who die for lack of ships." In later years the same complaint of a lack of shipping would be heard time and again.

MANI-CONGO

Yet after their fashion, and in spite of other interests, the Portuguese also persevered. They were disappointed in their hopes of penetrating the interior by way of the great river, for the states of the Congo resolutely barred the way. They were also duped in their belief that gold and silver could be found in these lands. There remained the slave trade, however, and the need for slaves became hungrier year by year. Affonso's tentative protests had availed for nothing. All his chiefly vassals of the coastal territories, whether great or small, were in the trade by now, and not one of them seems to have cared a whit for the social consequences of slaving or to have tried to follow Affonso's example. The slave trade grew by leaps and bounds until it had engulfed the whole connection with Europe. To European observers it came to seem that the sheer abundance of this African humanity could never be reduced. "And the fabulous amount of people inhabiting these kingdoms," Cadornega was writing in 1680, "can be estimated if we say that the conquest of these kingdoms began about one hundred years ago, and since then there have been despatched from this port in most years [*um anno por outro*] about eight to ten thousand units of slaves, which sum up almost to a million of souls."

One million slaves from Angola in the first century of European contact, together with a further half a million, as other reports suggest, from the neighboring land of Congo — such was the gloomy balance sheet. Already the fabric of Congolese society had begun to crack beneath the strain. Now came a new factor. Impatient for more direct control of this wide seaboard and the lands behind it, the Portuguese turned to thoughts of military invasion.

They began by strengthening their links with the ruler of Dondo to the south of the Mani-Congo's domains. This ruler's title was the Ngola, a word from which the territorial name Angola soon derived. Advised by priests and traders from São Tomé, the Ngola

From Alliance to Invasion

threw off his allegiance to the Mani-Congo in 1556. The Mani-Congo sent an army to punish and subdue him, but the warriors of the Ngola were victorious. Portuguese settlers, driven by their trading interest, actually fought on both sides in that curious battle. Having won a foothold on the mainland by dint of this military intervention, the Portuguese proceeded to enlarge it. Within a few years the king in Lisbon had appointed Paulo Dias as "Governor and Captain General" of this part of the coast, granting him hereditary rights over thirty-five leagues of seaboard and as much of the interior as he could seize and hold. In the event, Dias succeeded in nothing except the founding of the city of Luanda.

Yet from now onward the pattern would repeat itself. Little by little, the Portuguese undermined the feudal order of the Congo states and inserted their own vacillating but destructive power. The story of their intervention and penetration is too long and complicated for rehearsal here. It was slow, erratic, and seldom successful except in ruining the social fabric they had found. Many of its wars and adventures, and many of the personalities associated with them on either side, have remained warm in African memory; none more so, perhaps, than that famous Queen Zhinga of Matamba who held the invaders at bay for year after year. Fighting from her rock-bound strongholds in Matamba, Zhinga held out even when the Portuguese had defeated, at least for the time being, her allied armies of the Mani-Congo and the Ngola.

Pretext for the first invasion of Congo in 1665 was the king's refusal to allow free prospecting for mines of gold and copper, although his predecessor had in fact ceded this right to the Portuguese. The Mani-Congo's call to arms has survived in the Portuguese archives. It reads valiantly now:

MANI-CONGO

> Listen to the mandate given by the King sitting on the throne at Supreme Council of war: and it is that any man of any rank, noble of base, poor or rich, provided he is capable of handling weapons, from all villages, towns and places belonging to my Kingdoms, Provinces and Domains, should go, during the first ten days following the issue of this Royal proclamation and public notice, to enlist with their Captains, Governors, Dukes, Counts, Marquises, etc., and with other justices and officials who preside over them . . . to defend our lands, wares, children, women and our own lives and freedoms, which the Portuguese nation wants to conquer and dominate. . . .

The language, no doubt, was that of Portuguese feudalism, but its application to the Congo was clear enough. An army was raised to fight the Portuguese. It was smashed in battle and the Mani-Congo killed. His successors would never recover from this disaster.

The next two hundred years were a repetition of much the same sequence of intervention and destruction. Although they retained the formal sovereignty of their lands, African rulers found themselves linked ever more firmly to the fortunes of Portugal and Brazil. Here and there the Portuguese built coastal forts — at Luanda in 1576 and Benguela in 1617 — and held them through the slow centuries but for a brief interlude of Dutch supremacy. Yet their direct control of the country, maniloquent proclamations notwithstanding (and there was never any lack of those), seldom extended more than a few miles from the coast.

Why, then, did these African states prove incapable of recovery and progress? How was it that chiefs who were forceful and intelligent and well aware of the nature of their adversaries (and Queen Zhinga was only one of a number of such rulers of this period) failed repeatedly to learn the lesson of their losses and defeats? Where was the root of the evil?

6 Root of the Evil

THE ANSWER TO THESE QUESTIONS LAY PRECISELY IN THE CHARACTER of the trade: a demand for slaves on one side, and, on the other, a monopolist interest among African chiefs in obtaining European consumer goods, especially firearms.

There were, true enough, occasional scruples. In the year 1700, for example, Protestant slaving captains were finding it difficult to buy "units" because African dealers in the Congo harbors "were possessed with an opinion that we were not Christians, and that we used to carry the slaves to the Turks, and other infidels and hereticks, where they were never baptis'd." There was also, at least in theory, a right of appeal against sale abroad. "Every slave in the kingdom," a French observer in Loango was noting in 1776, "is under the protection of the Mfuka [one of the king's chief brokers] and may appeal against his master, should he be inclined to sell him to the Europeans, unless he has given him that right through his own misconduct."

But generally it was true that the slave trade had carried all before it. As elsewhere in the world, those who dealt in slaves could make their fortunes; what was more, they could not make their fortunes in any other way. If "everyone in Liverpool" was investing in the trade, so was "everyone in the Congo." There grew up along the coast a tightly organized and self-defending system of monopoly. It was interested in importing European firearms, strong drink, textiles, and metal goods, and in buying from the peoples of the interior as many captives as were required in payment.

The monopoly was closely guarded. "Those who have made captives," says the same French report of 1776, "sell them to the merchants of the country, or bring them to the coasts, but they are not allowed themselves to sell them to the Europeans: they are

MANI-CONGO

obliged to address themselves to brokers nominated by the [king's] ministers of commerce, who treat with the captains of the ships. . . . The function of these brokers is not limited to facilitating the slave trade: they are also charged with superintending the execution of regulations established by the king or the Mfuka, the most important of which is, that there shall not be sold any slaves to the Europeans except those which have been taken in war, or purchased from abroad."

This pattern of trade and contact left the coastal peoples inextricably enmeshed in a system of spoliation which could not possibly make way to new techniques from Europe. Moreover, it had an additional disadvantage from the standpoint of African development. It isolated the peoples of the interior from any contact with Europe except through the sale of captives. The chiefs of the coastal peoples throve and defended their power by purchasing European firearms; those in their rear, deprived of any direct link with Europeans, were reduced to impotence or involvement in the trade themselves. Increasingly, they chose or were driven to involvement.

From their scattered settlements along the coast, the Portuguese followed the same system and became part of the same pattern. They too dispatched small trading expeditions into the interior. These consisted of servants and slaves — mulatto or African *pombeiros*, as they were called — who might be gone for weeks or months or even years. "These slaves," James Barbot observed in 1700, "have other slaves under them, sometimes a hundred, or a hundred and fifty, who carry the commodities on their heads up into the country. . . . Sometimes these *pombeiros* stay out a whole year, and then bring back with them four, five, or six hundred slaves. Some of the faithfullest remain often there, sending what slaves they buy to their masters, who return them other commodities to trade with a-new."

Root of the Evil

Through many years this was the only mode of Portuguese penetration into the lands behind the coast except for rare military expeditions that failed more often than they were successful. It was these *pombeiros* who opened the long trails across Africa that European explorers would follow afterwards. Now and then these bondsmen, few of whose names have survived, must have set up new records of travel in linking one part of the southern continent to another. At least one outstanding example is known. In 1806 two *pombeiros* called Pedro João Baptista and Amaro José made the first attested crossing of Central Africa. They walked from inland Angola to the Portuguese settlement of Tete on the Lower Zambezi, and thus anticipated Livingstone by half a century. It was a great feat, but it was not in fact particularly difficult. Baptista left a journal which shows (and Livingstone would afterwards confirm it) that the trails were relatively safe and easy once the good will of two or three powerful inland rulers, notably the Muata Yamvo and the Cazembe, was obtained.

These great chiefs of the interior had understandably little interest in trade and contact with the outside world. They had heard of Portuguese penetration to the east and west of them, and they rightly feared it. Besides, they were the rulers of African societies which had attained a valuable balance of social stability after the great migration period of earlier centuries. They had known indirect trade with the Indian Ocean, but it was of little use to them except for occasional luxuries and perhaps a fillip to their prestige. Otherwise their countries were self-supporting, and the exchange of a few domestic slaves would always make good any temporary shortage.

"The territory of Cazembe [around the headwaters of the Congo]," Baptista noted after long residence there a hundred and fifty years ago, "is supplied with provisions all the year round and every year; manioc flour, millet, maize, large haricot beans, small beans, round beans . . . fruits, bananas, sugar-canes, yams, gourds, ground nuts, and much fish from the rivers Luapula and Monva, which are near. [The Cazembe] owns three salt districts. . . . He possesses victuals, oxen . . . [obtained in tribute from lesser chiefs] or in exchange for slaves. . . ." Such was the calm and well-provided "heart of darkness" before the temptations and disasters of export slaving made their fatal appearance here as well.

If these far countries remained long inviolate, pursuing their quiet journey across the years, the coastal countries were nonetheless reduced to misery and despair. It was true, of course, that the impact of the slave trade varied greatly in its effect. Most of the common people were threatened by foreign enslavement or entangled in the brutalities of slaving. But the chiefs and their henchmen generally made as good a thing out of the slave trade as their European partners — better, indeed, for they had little risk in the enterprise, while slaving captains wagered their own lives on every voyage.

In this failure of the African chiefly system to resist the temptations of the trade and to see beyond them to their disastrous consequences for the future, one may grasp just where the decisive weakness of Africa in face of Europe really lay. It was not that the chiefs were entirely without scruple even in the high days of the slaving system. They surrendered to it, but not always without a sense of shame and embarrassment. In the year 1700 a French slaver was buying captives in the Congo estuary. He reported that "as it is the usual custom among Europeans that buy slaves in Africa, to examine each limb, to know whether sound or not; the king of Zaire thus observing . . . burst out a-laughing, as did likewise the great men that were about him. He ask'd the interpreter what was the occasion of their laughter? And was answer'd: It proceeded from his so nicely viewing the poor slaves; but that the king and his attendants were so much asham'd of it, that [the king] requir'd him, for decency's sake, to do it in a private place: which shows these Blacks are very modest."

Yet the enrichment of the ruling groups could not, in the circumstances, lead to any compensating gain for their peoples as a whole. One can see this from the nature of the goods that were bought in exchange for captives. Almost invariably, these were luxuries or the means of war. Nothing really changed or developed in this commerce except the "terms of trade": captives became more or less valuable, as items of exchange, according to the fluctuations of transatlantic demand. Generally, their value grew as the years went by. In 1776 the Abbé Proyart was noting that the "slave Makriota" — no doubt a *ladino*, a man trained in household work and therefore relatively expensive — had cost him "thirty pieces." These "pieces" were variously reckoned: about half were in textiles such as *indienne, guinea,* and *chaffelat*; about a quarter were accounted for by "two guns, two barrels of gunpowder, two bags of leaden musket balls, two swords, and two dozen common sheath knives"; while the rest consisted of "five pots of Dutch ware, four barrels of brandy, and ten strings of glass beads." Perhaps the priest had little difficulty in justifying the purchase of a servant for guns and gunpowder and strong drink, for it was characteristic of the times. But it is obvious that the African purchaser had bought nothing that could help to lift his country to a higher level of economic or social life.

On the contrary, even those who worked the slaving system in the Congo were impoverished. And this was so not only because countless thousands of healthy men and women were sent abroad, nor because the goods bought in exchange were largely for warfare or "conspicuous consumption." More than that, slaving wrecked the native administration of these lands. Even as late as 1592, a century after the Portuguese had first made contact with the states of the Congo estuary, the kings still enjoyed considerable means of government. A report of that year puts the royal revenue in cowrie shells at a value of 60,000,000 reis, but adds that it could go as high as 160,000,000 reis, or 400,000 cruzados. With the cruzado worth not less than four shillings sterling, this would give a minimum revenue for the Mani-Congo of about £28,000. From this, the local missionaries derived a more than satisfactory living; at about the same time, for example, the curé of the main church of Luanda had a salary from the Mani-Congo of 200 cruzados, or £40 sterling, a lavish stipend for the time and place.

This wealth failed to endure. When fresh missionary enterprises were urged in Portugal at the beginning of the nineteenth century, three hundred years later, it was officially objected that "the king of Congo is very poor and naked like the rest. A king of this sort can afford nothing for missionaries nor help them in any way." By the end of the seventeenth century, if not before, a substantial part of priestly revenues in the Congo was in fact paid directly by the slave trade. Thus it had become obligatory on the slavers to pay a "baptismal tax" of 300 reis for every captive they embarked for Brazil; this was handed to the parish clergy as part of their settled income. Later on, the Bishop of Luanda was also allocated a "baptismal tax" of 150 reis for every slave.

One can follow this impoverishment down the years. Its sorry effects struck at local Europeans with much the same force. They were fatally involved in slaving and produced little commercial wealth of any other kind. Fathers Angelo and Carli, two Italian Capuchins, were impressed by the city of Luanda in 1666 as being "large and beautiful enough." Yet even then, relatively early in the trade, they found that for three thousand Europeans there was "a prodigious multitude of Blacks" who "serve as slaves to the whites, some of whom have fifty, some a hundred, two or three hundred, and even to three thousand."

The inevitable happened. Idle and pampered, the settlers of

Root of the Evil

Luanda decayed with the passing of the years until they were left with little beyond their memories of erstwhile fame and fortune. "By the beginning of the nineteenth century," writes Duffy, "the surface splendour of Luanda had begun to tarnish; the fine buildings were falling into disrepair; its streets were unattended; transportation into the interior was in a state of neglect. . . . The population of Luanda and Benguela was made up predominantly of social castaways."

Relations between Africans and Europeans suffered the same decay. The old habits of equality and mutual respect had long since vanished. From allies, the Africans had sunk in European eyes to contemptible providers of slaves. What Africans thought of Europeans may be inferred from a forthright judgment of that enterprising Portuguese settler who sent his two *pombeiros*, Baptista and Amaro, across the continent to Mozambique. Writing of "native opinion" in 1804, this man said that the blacks imagine that the whites "never do anything except for their own profit, and to their [the blacks'] prejudice; that the whites have no sincerity; and only turn their actions to their own advantage against the blacks."

By now, the ordered power which Diogo Cão had found in the states of the Congo had also vanished and for that, as well, the root of the evil was easy to find. "Another great reason for the strife and jealousy existing among the black nations," wrote this same farsighted settler, "is that the whites endeavour to profit by their situation of superiority and power" — a power, one should add, that was largely secured by firearms — "to subject to them other nations inferior in force and position. They are jealous lest the blacks should enjoy the same privileges, and thus be able to remove the yoke in which they are bound. They supply them [the blacks] with some few things they think necessary, adding whatever they think proper to their cost; but preventing the others [the blacks] from obtaining the same articles from whence they [the white traders] obtain them. . . ." One may read in these few words the whole tragedy of that "Christian enterprise" on which the kings of Portugal had once embarked.

Through these years of deepening bitterness and contempt there was laid, little by little, the foundation for future legends of "savage Africa." In the eighteenth century there had still been room for tolerance and sympathy. "The negresses, like the negroes," a French priest could write then, "have their arms and bosoms uncovered, especially when at work; but the custom is general. Nobody thinks of it. Nobody is scandalised at it. And it is wrong for authors to have concluded thence that these [people] brave all the laws of modesty. This nudity of a negress, who from morning to night is occupied in cultivating the field under a burning sun, is less insidious and shocking to public decency, in their country, than the half-nakedness of court ladies in our own." But the judgments of the nineteenth century, the period of outright invasion and occupation, would abound in convictions of a European superiority which was moral as well as material.

Behind all this there lay the driving pressures of the slave trade. No one can be certain how many captives were taken from these lands. The final score was undoubtedly enormous. Up to 1680 and the end of the legal trade in 1836 there were added about another two million from the ports of Luanda and Benguela alone; and more were shipped illegally in the years that followed. Another million must be reckoned for the smuggling trade. This puts the total number of captives taken from the old states of the Congo and Angola at about five million, and the estimate is certainly conservative. Thus the centuries of slaving saw the export to America of populations that were larger, and probably much larger, than all the peoples of Angola today.

Every hope of progress, or even of regaining the old independ-

Root of the Evil

ence, went by the board. "How great was the moral damage of this hunt and traffic for 'black ivory,' " a German scholar would write in 1928, and his verdict may stand for the social and economic damage as well, "it is difficult to say. But gradually the last social links were broken, and the whole structure utterly destroyed."

That this was no exaggeration is shown by the abundant records of the trade. They are full of shadows. In 1804 the Mani-Congo Garcia V, a mere puppet of the Portuguese by now, sent a son and a nephew to make their Latin studies at Luanda so that they could train for the priesthood. Every year until 1815 these two young men, the "princes" Pedro and Affonso, received three slaves from their father with whom to pay for their upkeep. But in 1812, finding himself short of cash, Prince Pedro encountered no difficulty in also selling the royal official whom his father had sent to Luanda with the year's quota of slaves. This was too much even for the Mani-Congo's pitiful dignity. He violently protested and the Governor of Angola accordingly wrote to Brazil, asking his colleagues there to find this Congolese nobleman, if they could, and send him home again.

Nevertheless it was long before the Portuguese could assert control over the lands of the interior or even feel themselves secure along the coast. Their story here, as in Mozambique on the other side of Africa, was one of frantic bursts of bold endeavor followed by long periods of complete stagnation. All through these five centuries there were brave and public-spirited individuals who tried to revive the "civilizing mission," or else curtail the cruelty to which it had decayed. But they always failed. They were defeated by those other Portuguese, more numerous, whose whole glory consisted in cracking the whip of a futile ambition over the heads of people who were no longer able to defend themselves. Chained to their dreams of medieval grandeur, these invaders seem

MANI-CONGO

never to have understood the enormity of their failure or the absurdity of their claims.

True enough, the lands behind the coast were subdued to their command; but the victory was long delayed, and came in the end only by default. The spirit of African independence and self-respect was broken, not by Portuguese military prowess, but by the long ensnarement of the slaving years. Portuguese settlers might flow into these lands, but their numbers were few and they were seldom capable of anything beyond the most primitive enterprise. More often than not, these settlers were luckless victims of ignorance and poverty no less than the Africans among whom they had come to live. Sometimes they were political exiles, bitterly regretting their sojourn in the land. Not seldom they were criminals of the common law, *degredados*, as they were called, whose achievement was to spread in Africa the sadness and despair, and therefore the cruelty, they had brought with them from Europe.

Prisoners of a poor and antiquated European autocracy, the Africans of these lands were condemned to lose their own civilization — limited though it was — without the chance of gaining a better. Even by the 1950's fewer than one in every hundred Africans of Angola had achieved the rank of *assimilado* and thus gained admission to the "rights of civilization."

The record is gray and depressing. Yet in the 1950's, with Africa emerging from the colonial hurricane, new voices were heard in Angola. A nationalist movement was born. These fettered peoples began to shake themselves free. The wheel of history was swinging full circle, and the old vigor of independence now at last found echo in a new resurgence.

five

East Coast Fortunes

The people were formerly said to be numerous, civilised and wealthy; the city extensive and fortified, its habitations elegant and public buildings numerous . . . but whither have they gone?

James Prior: Kilwa in 1812

A new province in the study of history has been opened, and there is a life's work and more to occupy the lives of many men.

G. S. P. Freeman-Grenville in 1960

1 A Riddle at Kilwa

BEGINNING WITH SUCH FAIR promise, European contact with the old states of the Congo had narrowed to the fatal deadlock of the slave trade. But what might not have happened in the Congo if mariners and traders from Europe had followed or been able to follow a different course? What expansion and evolution might these states not have known if their channels to the outside world had linked them with the many-sided growth of civilization, instead of leading into sterile isolation behind the barriers of slaving monopoly?

These questions are not entirely vain. Some valuable parts of an answer can be inferred, at any rate in broad outline, from the rich experience of the East African seaboard during a somewhat earlier period.

Along these African margins of the Indian Ocean (the coasts of Mozambique, Tanganyika, Kenya, and Somaliland, a seaboard rather longer than the distance from Newfoundland to the tip of Florida), the consequences of direct African involvement with the outside world can be measured against a much wider range of fortune than was ever offered to the lands of the Congo. Here there was intimate contact with the mature civilizations of the East, and especially with India. The results astonished the Portuguese when they first sailed up this coast.

EAST COAST FORTUNES

Expecting a wilderness or at best a repetition of Portuguese experience on the Guinea Coast and the Congo, Vasco da Gama and his crews came on strong stone towns and harbors filled with shipping. They met with men who had traveled the eastern seas and knew more of navigation than they themselves. They found city-states and governments that were as wealthy and sophisticated as anything they had seen in Europe.

"When we had been two or three days in this place," recorded the log of da Gama's flagship, the *São Gabriel* (75 feet over-all and 26 feet in the beam), "two gentlemen of the country came to see us. They were very haughty and valued nothing that we gave them. A young man of their company — so we understood from their signs — had come from a distant land and had already seen big ships like ours." The truth was that this eastern traveler must have seen far bigger ships. He would have voyaged in the many-masted ships of India and Ceylon. He might even have known the great ocean junks of China, whose sails were like "great clouds in the sky."

Much of this East Coast civilization was destroyed. Except on the northern reaches of the coast, little or nothing of its material prosperity survived. The city of the "haughty gentlemen" recorded in the *São Gabriel*'s log was probably Quelimane in modern Mozambique. Almost four centuries later a British visitor to Quelimane would find it desolate and in despair and would name it "the most frightful place on earth."

Ruins of a better past could be found, but they could not be explained. In 1823, charting this unknown seaboard for the British Admiralty, a ten-gun brig called the *Barracouta* came to anchor in the great harbor of Kilwa. The *Barracouta*'s officers thought it one of the finest harbors in the world, and Lieutenant Boteler had himself rowed ashore. As he came landward in his longboat, Boteler saw the crumbled ruins of an old fortress on

A Riddle at Kilwa

Kilwa Island, but the rest of the island was screened from view by a thick girdle of mangroves standing in shabby beds of mud. He got to firm ground and pushed his way through the trees. The light of that clear December morning, early in the nineteenth century, showed him nothing that remained of the comfort and sophistication of old Kilwa but a heap of stones. He found a "miserable village, scarcely visited or known," where "the wretched Arab hovels of the present day are blended among the ruins of the once respectable and opulent city of former years." And it was the same wherever they went on this coast. "Even in the most obscure harbours, we could trace the remains of former wealth and civilisation, contrasted strongly with present poverty and barbarism."

Another British naval visitor had formed the same impression a few years earlier. James Prior, surgeon of the *Nisus* frigate under Captain Beaver's command, also found Kilwa a superb harbor, "deep enough for the largest ships, and capable of containing nearly the whole navy of England." Landing there in the year 1812, he noted the "scattered vestiges of human haunts and habitations, cemeteries and ruins," which all proclaimed "this district to have once been open and populous." But the wretchedness and squalor were so complete that earlier reports of civilization seemed hard to believe. Tracing Kilwa's city wall, Prior found himself agreeing with Captain Beaver, who "justly remarked as we walked along, turning the grass to one side in following the line of the foundation, that the older writers gave such flattering accounts of this city in the days of Da Gama, as, from present appearances, to be scarcely worthy of credit."

Yet Prior found the quantity of ruins, here and on the nearby mainland, puzzlingly large. Rambling over the southern arm of Kilwa harbor, he met with stone structures which included a cemetery forty feet square enclosed by a stone wall, and a "place of worship" whose tumbled walls were still "about sixteen feet high, built of stone, cemented by mortar," having "an arched door in the front and two in the rear." A few hundred yards away he stumbled on the remains of a large stone building of many rooms, surrounded by the ragged fragments of what had once been a strong wall.

"The ruins," he wrote, "are the evidences of a former people. But whither have they gone?"

2 Cities of the Seaboard

THE SURGEON OF THE *Nisus* FRIGATE NEED NOT HAVE QUESTIONED the reports of older writers. This country had indeed witnessed a notable achievement. Reassessment during the 1950's has left no room for doubt of it. Many strands of influence and culture had gone into making an East African civilization of long endurance.

Coins from this region offer one surviving field of evidence. So far — and systematic searches have yet to be made — these include five coins of Hellenistic origin (third to first century B.C.), three Parthian coins (first to second century A.D.), two Sassanian coins (third century A.D.), nine Roman coins, and forty-eight from Byzantium, others from Arab and Turkish states, hundreds from China, a few from Ceylon, Annam, and southern India, and thousands from local African mints.

This richness and variety of trading contact with the East is confirmed by the earliest first-hand report, which dates from about A.D. 60. This periplus, or "shipping gazette," probably the work of an Egyptian Greek, offers a brief but factual traders' and

Cities of the Seaboard

mariners' guide to East African harbors and their commerce as far south as a port called Rhapta, which appears to have been near Pangani in Tanganyika. Thus East Africa's coastline, some fifteen hundred years before the coming of the Europeans, was already involved in regular and peaceful trade with the cities of the Red Sea, southern Arabia, the Persian Gulf, India, Ceylon, and countries beyond. By the tenth century if not earlier, Arab writers were well aware of trading ports as far south as Sofala in modern Mozambique.

Archeology has brought wider understanding of a civilization which became famous and important among the cultures of the western Indian Ocean, which flourished over many centuries, and which drew the seaboard of East Africa well within the orbit of the evolving East. Up to 1959 the number of pre-European sites identified along this coast was 127, with 65 of these being in Tanganyika, 20 in Kenya, 28 on Pemba Island, 14 on Zanzibar, and 14 in ex-Italian Somalia. There is little doubt that more will yet be found. All of these cities and ports and settlements, according to Dr. Freeman-Grenville, who has done so much for the medieval history of this challenging region, were linked by common characteristics. "While there are local variations and recognisable regional idiosyncracies, all likewise shared a common architecture which is distinct from the rest of the world."

The little that remains of this architecture may best be seen on one or two islands not far from the coast, notably on the islet of Songo Mnara near Kilwa Island and on Juani Island in the Mafia group off the Tanganyika mainland. Here amid tumbled trees and choking undergrowth, the stone palaces and mosques and merchants' houses of these western terminal ports of the Indian Ocean — product of a trade that stretched in many ramifications to the seas of China and Indonesia — still offer their

EAST COAST FORTUNES

forlorn and ruined witness to a considerable achievement in civilization.

These various kinds of evidence illuminate the interwoven nature of an African culture that owed some of its origins to constructive stimulus from non-African sources. Already, in times of Greco-Egyptian navigation two thousand years ago, the trade in these waters was known to be conducted by mariners from southern Arabia who came down the coast for ivory, rhinoceros horn, tortoise shell, and palm oil — but apparently not for slaves — and who bought these goods in exchange for iron tools and weapons, glass beads, and "a little wine."

Later Arab writers confirmed this nature of the trade, although by A.D. 800 or 900 there seems to have been a steady though never dominant African export of slaves as well. By this time the Indian and Chinese demand for ivory had become of major importance, the African variety being much superior to any other; and it would seem that ivory remained the main export staple for many years. By the eleventh and twelfth centuries the ports of southern China were collecting odd scraps of information about Africa, while Chinese "cash" and porcelain were arriving in the seaboard cities of Somalia, Kenya, and Tanganyika. Several Chinese fleets reached the Kenya coast in the early part of the fifteenth century. Books on "how to treat barbarians" were being published in China, and these "barbarians" undoubtedly included the coastal peoples of East Africa.

"Treat the barbarian kings like harmless seagulls," advised Chang Hsieh in his *Tung Hsi Yang Khao*, published in 1618 at a time when the great period of Chinese ocean-sailing was at an end, but doubtless drawing on past experience. (The reference was to the well-known story of a sailor who had promised his father to catch a seagull and had failed, because the seagulls, knowing of his promise, would never alight on the water.) "Then

Cities of the Seaboard

the trough-princes and the crest-sirens will let you pass everywhere riding on the wings [of the wind]. . . . Coming into contact with barbarian peoples you have nothing more to fear than touching the left horn of a snail. The only things one should be really anxious about are the means of mastery of the waves of the sea — and, worst of all dangers, the minds of those avid for profit and greedy for gain." It was wisdom to which the Portuguese in East Africa could have listened with advantage to themselves, and with still greater gain to those on whom they spent their ravaging fury.

All these influences went to the building of city-states and coastal empires along this coast during the first fifteen hundred years of the Christian era. In Europe of the colonial period it was generally assumed that this achievement had been Arab. The Portuguese of the sixteenth century had given no credit to African initiative and, identifying religion with race, had invariably referred to the peoples of these city-states of Kilwa, Mombasa, Malindi, Brava, and the rest as Moors. Foreign languages were not in their range of study, and there is no known reference to the Swahili language in any of the old Portuguese reports. Writers of the nineteenth century were further confused by the fact of renewed Arab colonization from southern Arabia, and also, one may think, by the prevailing colonialist view that "Africans have no history of their own." Hence it became standard belief in the outside world that the ruins of East Africa were those of Arab colonies to which native peoples had brought little or no significant contribution.

This belief is now in the course of serious revision. It is seen, more and more clearly, that the city-states of the East African seaboard became predominantly African in culture at a relatively early date, though carrying the strong imprint of Arab influence and Islamic religion. One powerful reason for this view rests in the richness and antiquity of Swahili literature and tradition. No one knows how old Swahili may be. But it is certainly not a young language, nor a poor or small one. Its first recorded words appear in Arab reports of the tenth century A.D., and its subsequent literature shows that it early became a flexible and poetic vehicle with a wide vocabulary. Today its spreading influence in eastern Africa, as well as its wealth of slang (resembling, in this, the malleability of English), are modern evidence of old and sound foundations. It abounds in fruity idioms and everyday adaptations. Largely Bantu in construction and vocabulary, it has a rich ingredient of Arabic (and now a notable borrowing from English); and in this, of course, it reflects the essentially syncretic civilization which evolved it and which it helped to evolve.

It would be absurd to deny the formative influence of the Arabs on this old Swahili culture of the coast. Their settlers were here more than two thousand years ago. Their little colonies were the points of contact with the non-African world. Their religion, architecture, and script were only three elements of Islamic culture that helped to bring these peoples of the coast into the circuit of urban civilization.

The essential point is that here — in contrast with the failure of the Portuguese in the Congo — there occurred a genuine and fruitful marriage of cultures. After the thirteenth century, with at least the nominal conversion of much of the coast to Islam, there was also a wide bridge of religion. Ruling men in these cities increasingly felt themselves to be of "Arab descent" and "Arabic culture"; but they felt this as men of Africa, not of Arabia, and in rather the same way as early medieval Europeans might consider themselves to be of "Roman descent" and "Latin culture," but none the less English or French for that. Later on, their rulers would manufacture long genealogies to prove they were sons of

Cities of the Seaboard

the princes of Arabia and Persia; and in this, too, they would resemble European families who "acquired" aristocratic ancestors as the years and gathering wealth allowed.

One can infer this marriage of cultures from many aspects of an often glittering urbanity in Kilwa and some of her sister cities. Mints at Kilwa, Zanzibar, and Mogadiscio made coins of their own; but the inscriptions were always in Arabic just as those of European coins were infallibly in Latin. These mints served the maritime trade, for coins were probably of no use or value in the commerce with the interior by which the coastal cities acquired their ivory and other goods; and all of them are invariably associated with local rulers who had Arabic names (though sometimes Swahili names as well). The first of them seems to have been founded at Kilwa in the twelfth century, though the earliest coins so far recovered are those of Sultan al-Hasan ibn Talut, who reigned in Kilwa between 1277 and 1294. The sheer abundance of these coins suggests considerable prosperity. Thus more than 2,000 coins have turned up from the issues of Sultan Ali ibn al-Hasan (1478-1479); nearly 3,000 of Sultan al-Hasan ibn Sulaiman (1479-1485); and over 2,800 from the Zanzibar issues of one of its fifteenth century rulers, Sultan al-Husain ibn Ahmad. But these rulers were no more Arab (and also no less) than King Henry V of England was a Frenchman.

Kilwa itself is said by tradition to have been founded as an Arab trading center in A.D. 957. Yet the local chieftain who was displaced by Kilwa's traditional founder was called Muriri wa Bari, a name that is manifestly not Arabic and quite possibly Swahili. These pre-Arab rulers of Kilwa must have had close contact with Arab traders and Arab ideas, for Muriri wa Bari possessed a mosque. All that happened here, no doubt, was that incoming Arab settlers took over a going concern in government and commerce; and subsequent rulers of this new Arab line merely

EAST COAST FORTUNES

traced the "foundation" of Kilwa to the time of their forefathers' advent. They intermarried with the people whom they found; their culture rapidly became both Arabic and Swahili but increasingly, as the years went by, Swahili in language and African in context.

Sometime in the twelfth century these energetic traders and warriors of Kilwa seized control of the valuable trade in gold that had long existed between the lands to the south of them and foreign purchasers to the north. Kilwa then became the most important "city-empire" on the coast. Pemba had earlier held this honor, but now Kilwa's power ran south through trading settlements on the Kerimba archipelago to the gold port of Sofala in Mozambique, and north towards Zanzibar. The Portuguese would find Kilwa sovereign along the southern reaches of the coast, a town with "many fair houses of stone and mortar, and many windows after our fashion, very well arranged in streets."

It is a fair inference that through these years of commercial prosperity and expansion the historians and poets of Kilwa and other cities turned to writing in Swahili. But this is not yet proved. Scholars have lately begun collecting works in Swahili, and a fair quantity has come to light. Many more are believed to exist, locked away in cupboards and family chests, forgotten or else guarded from the profanity of the public eye. A still greater number may be presumed lost forever.

Some of this Swahili writing is said to be of high poetic quality. Other documents add to knowledge of the traditions of the coast, sometimes helpfully, sometimes misleadingly. None of those so far found is ancient or medieval, the oldest known document written in Swahili being a version of the *Kilwa Chronicle*. This is an important repository of local tradition originally set down in Arabic and known in that form to the sixteenth century Portuguese. But the early Arabic text is long since lost, and the Swahili version is comparatively new. As things stand today, writes Freeman-Grenville, "no formal Swahili composition, verse or prose," dates from earlier than the eighteenth century. At the same time there is no doubt that Swahili poets were composing lyrical and epic poetry in the vernacular at a date considerably more remote; and it has yet to be shown that they were not writing in the vernacular as well.

This brief outline of a vigorous though purely coastal civilization would be incomplete without some reference to the peoples who knew it from the landward side. Here the problem of describing the past becomes infinitely greater. Much archeological research must be undertaken before the pattern of Iron Age states in the east and east-south African hinterland can be defined even with an approximate accuracy. Yet a number of basic points are established.

Origins of Iron Age culture here go back nearly two thousand years. For not long after western peoples in Africa knew their first tentative experiments in state-making and empire-building, and ancient Ghana took its distant rise, the lands of eastern Africa also began to be settled by peoples who understood the smelting and forging of iron and the use of iron tools for agriculture. They have left the evidence of their being in scattered tumuli, smelting tuyères and hut foundations of stone. These Iron Age folk of eastern Africa underwent the same kind of vicissitudes as those in the west: their lands were repeatedly entered by other African peoples, sometimes at a lower level of culture and sometimes at a higher, and coming from several directions but mainly from the north and perhaps from the west.

Towards the end of the first millennium of our era there seem to have existed a number, conceivably quite a large number, of Iron Age peoples who were organized in more or less coherent groups or units. One can reasonably infer a form of "tribal" government with the elements of statehood — a protonational sense of difference from neighbors, more or less clearly defined boundaries, perhaps a "divine kingship." Popular traditions might be expected to throw light on these early Iron Age "states" of the hinterland, but subsequent invasions and dislocations have erased the old traditions of much of Kenya and Tanganyika. Fortunately, this is not the case in Uganda and its immediately neighboring regions. Here, to history's gain, traditions have survived; and the picture they offer of the past is rich and valuable. One general conclusion that may be drawn from these "Ugandan" traditions is that Iron Age society went through important changes about five hundred years ago. Thus the Babito dynasty of the kingdom of Bunyoro counts nineteen generations to its half-legendary founder, while the Ganda dynasty of Buganda has twenty-two. Sometime around A.D. 1450 to 1500, it would seem, society took an important step towards "modern" organization.

How and why did this happen? Once again the jostling of peoples had brought social change. The instruments of change in this case are known to tradition as the Bachwezi. Little can be said of them, except that they are remembered as people of new and vital strength and skill. "They made strange things that had not been made since man first came to this land," Gray recorded of Bunyoro tradition forty years ago. "They wandered without let or hindrance to places where no man had ever been before. . . . Hunting was their calling, and they were mighty men therein. They were also traders and wandered about in a miraculous manner." When the European explorer Stanley reached the kingdom of Ankole in 1887, he and his party were at first mistaken for Bachwezi marvelously returned to earth for a second time. "We greet you gladly. We see today what our fathers never saw, the real Bachwezi. . . ."

These superb newcomers, the Bachwezi, gathered the peoples of

Cities of the Seaboard

western Uganda into a powerful though short-lived empire. Today they are still thought of in western Uganda, writes Oliver, "as the originators of a pattern of social organisation and a religion which were sedulously, if uncomprehendingly, imitated by the successor dynasties, whose subjects looked back on the Bachwezi much as medieval Europe looked back on the Roman Empire, as the golden age of civilised and pre-barbarian government."

Here again one sees the tribal-feudal structure taking shape. The Bachwezi vanished, perhaps around A.D. 1500, as mysteriously as they had come. But, continues Oliver, they "left their regalia, their drums, their copper spears, their beaded crowns surmounted by tall copper cones and underhung with masks made from the skin of the colobus monkey, distributed about the country in the keeping of the district chiefs. . . . They left their reed palaces, which were faithfully copied upon the sites of subsequent capitals. They left their slave artisans and even, it is said, their palace women, from whom their Babito successors learned the pastoral duties of royalty. They left, in all probability, a working system of administrative officialdom accustomed to ruling small districts as the local representatives of a centralised monarchy; and a regimental organisation . . . under which young men were conscripted into the military service of the king and were maintained by the peasants occupying areas of land designated for the support of the army."

Much the same process of social change within early Iron Age society occurred in other east and south-central regions, as also, of course, in western Africa. Comparable evidence is particularly strong for the plateau lands of Southern Rhodesia. Here there is little or no tradition surviving from the medieval past; in place of that, however, there are abundant stone ruins, objects in gold and other metals, pottery from the East Coast, porcelain from China, beads from India. Where the Bachwezi and their immediate successors left great earthworks, the Iron Age innovators of Rhodesia built stone palaces and temples and strong places on high rocks, the most famous of these being the great complex of structures at Zimbabwe in Southern Rhodesia.

Some of these Iron Age states of the interior had regular and influential contact with the coast from at least the tenth century. Others — but the evidence is notoriously incomplete and may yet be overturned — apparently did not. What can be affirmed with confidence is that the coastal cities had begun to draw these states, or a number of them, into the orbit of Indian Ocean culture and civilization. And the reason for this was that the coastal cities needed ivory and gold and could obtain them only from the interior.

A steady coastal demand for gold and ivory continued through five centuries or more. It unquestionably caused the states of the southern plateau to open their thousands of gold workings. Among themselves, these inland peoples had little use for gold (although they developed a nice taste in gold ornaments), and Arab commentators were constantly surprised how easily they parted with this precious metal. But they desired trade with the coast. Gold was the way to it. And the opening of a large number of gold workings (of which tens of thousands were found when European prospectors came this way in later times) must have done much to stimulate the emergence of social divisions, the birth of an embryonic laboring class, and the development of states that were capable of internal coherence and centralized government.

To the north the influence of the coast may have had much the same effect, though here there was no gold to be tapped and therefore less incentive to penetrate the interior with trading missions. A few archeological soundings in western Uganda have failed to reveal any contact with the coast, but the available evidence is too slender for the drawing of any final conclusions. In

Kenya and Tanganyika the situation is much the same. Almost no systematic research has yet been undertaken into the large question of contact between the coast and the interior. A great site like Engaruka, once a stone-built town of several thousand dwellings that flourished far up-country on the Tanganyika-Kenya border, perhaps three hundred years ago, remains to this day no more than an isolated mystery. Already it is clear, however, that the cities of the coast had extensive and, to them, entirely necessary trade with the states of the interior; that this trade was of greatest importance wherever ivory and gold could be found; and that its general consequence was to provide an indirect link between important regions of the African interior, which had their own inner unity of culture, and the civilizations of the East. Here the effect of outside contact was not isolation, but communication.

3 The Vital Contrast

IN THEIR IMPACT ON AFRICA, THERE WAS THUS A TREMENDOUS difference between the Atlantic Ocean trade and that of the Indian Ocean in medieval times: contraction of wealth in the first and expansion in the second. One clear pointer to the reason for this difference will be found in the different nature of the two commercial systems.

The Indian Ocean trade was never slave-ridden in ancient or medieval times. This is not, admittedly, the standard opinion of European textbooks. There, as Freeman-Greenville has lately pointed out in contesting it, "the main theme is that the slave trade was the principal occupation of the coast until the British asserted their hegemony" at the end of the nineteenth century. But the evidence will not support this view.

True, there was oversea slaving on these coasts from the earliest times. Old Egypt took slaves from the land of Punt; and Punt was probably the Horn of Africa, Somalia of today. Arabia did the same. Negro slaves were known in Parthia and Persia. So many had reached the northern Arab lands by the ninth century that furious slave revolts are traditionally said to have cost the lives of as many as half a million slaves. Many East African captives were taken to India. Others were carried as far as China.

A Chinese document of A.D. 1178, evidently referring to Madagascar, says that "there is an island in the sea on which there are many savages. Their bodies are black and they have frizzled hair. They are enticed by food and then captured" and sold "as slaves to the Arab countries, where they fetch a very high price. They are employed as gatekeepers, and it is said that they have no longing for their kinsfolk." Thus may one see how the legend of "African inferiority" was no monopoly of the West. In the East the slaves from Africa (for they came from the mainland as well as Madagascar) were said "to have no longing for home"; in the West they would be found "docile and therefore fit to be enslaved."

Slaves for the civilizations of the East came of course from all the borders of the Indian Ocean and not merely from East Africa. They were regularly imported into China, for example, over a long period. The same Chinese report of 1178 says that both male and female slaves were bought, "and the ships carry human beings as cargo." A Chinese inspector of maritime customs, writing fifty years later, notes that a slave boy was priced at three taels of gold or their equivalent in aromatic wood. He says that slaves were used during voyages for stopping leaks in the hull, even though they had to go outboard and under the waves as well.

The Vital Contrast

Many of these luckless victims must have come from Africa.

But there is nothing to show that slaving ever overwhelmed this eastern trade or became more than a secondary item of commerce. The available evidence, slight though it is, goes all the other way. "Slaves of the better sort" could be purchased, according to the *Periplus of the Erythraean Sea* in the first century A.D., at Opone; but Opone was Ras Hafun, almost the far northern extremity of the Horn of Africa. For the ports of East Africa to the south of Ras Hafun there is no mention of slaving in the *Periplus*. Nor is there much mention of it by the medieval Arab writers, and in no single case do these writers place any emphasis on East African slaving. On the contrary, they speak of the importance of East Africa as a provider of ivory and gold and other raw materials.

Sofala, for El Mas'udi, who wrote in the tenth century, was the land of gold. He mentions ivory as a principal export from "the land of the Zanj," the Negroes of East Africa. This ivory was taken to India and China by way of Oman in southern Arabia, and "were this not the case, there would be an abundance of ivory in the Muslim countries." For Edrisi, two centuries later, iron was the most valued export of the East African coast. The iron of Sofala, he thought, was much superior to that of India, both in quantity and quality; and the Indians were accustomed to make from it the "best swords in the world." There is nowhere here any reference to an East African export trade in slaves. This does not mean, of course, that no slaves were sent abroad. But it certainly suggests that this part of commerce was an insignificant side line.

Evidence from the Swahili cities of the coast points the same way. The key trades of Kilwa in medieval times were undoubtedly the export of gold and ivory obtained from the states of the interior. Pate Island is said to have dealt in silver as well as ivory

EAST COAST FORTUNES

Others are known to have exported, or collected for the export trade of their more important sister-settlements, a varied range of natural products: copal, ambergris, tortoise shell, copra, coconut oil, and mangroves. All this was the body of Swahili trade and the core of its prosperity.

One can reach the same conclusion from the other end. Where in the East were the vast plantations and many mines that required great armies of slave labor? They simply did not exist, just as they did not exist in the West until the crossing of the Atlantic. Where, again, can one find massive African minorities in the East that are comparable to the African minorities of America? They, too, do not exist. The notion that the old trades of the Indian Ocean dealt in slaves on the same scale as the later Atlantic trade is a pure illusion, the product of an uneasy European conscience and the fact of large-scale Arab slaving in the nineteenth century. What really occurred here was slaving on the same persistent but small scale as between many of the states of the medieval world — a miserable but secondary trade, rarely important in the general balance of wealth and enterprise.

The contrast with the Atlantic seaboard is very sharp. A thousand years of Indian Ocean contact, with slaving never of importance, could raise the peoples of the eastern seaboard to full membership in the family of eastern civilization, and send its fructifying influence far into the hinterland. But less than half a thousand years of Atlantic Ocean contact, with slaving of the highest importance, would reduce the peoples of the western seaboard to a condition of inferiority that even now weighs heavy on the conscience of the world.

These cities of the eastern coast vanished or dwindled through no fault of their own. They were ravaged by the Portuguese. Loot was the key to the discoverers' ambition. Reflecting on da Gama's voyage of discovery, the king of Portugal wrote to the ambassador

The Vital Contrast

of Venice, then the most powerful city of the Mediterranean, that it would now profit Venetian galleys to come to Lisbon for their cargoes of goods from the East, instead of going to Alexandria. To his cousins of Castile, however, he was a little more forthcoming. Giving them news of da Gama's exploits, he explained that "we hope, with the help of God, that the great trade which now enriches the Moors of those parts" — that is, the Swahili Muslims and their oversea partners — "through whose hands it passes without the intervention of other persons or peoples, shall, in consequence of our dispositions, be diverted to the natives and ships of our own kingdom."

He took his dispositions without delay. Fleet after fleet was dispatched to the East, one almost every year for many years to come. Their orders were to seize the Indian Ocean trade, reduce the coastal cities to vassal status, exact tribute from them in gold, and establish Portuguese hegemony. They met with resistance. But the coastal cities, although they too believed that God was on their side, lacked cannon. And the cannon of the Portuguese, together with a ruthlessness and piratical determination never before witnessed in these seas, easily carried the day. Enmity and the threat of violence appeared with the earliest landfalls of da Gama. After 1501, by which time the Portuguese had taken the measure of their intended victims, there followed ten years of bloody invasion and assault. Kilwa, Mombasa, Zanzibar, Brava, and other cities were battered or bullied into submission.

Here and there, as in the Congo, the Portuguese were helped by calls for help from one African ruler against another. This led to the downfall, for example, of the lord of the Kerimba Islands, a long archipelago lying off the coast of northern Mozambique. In 1522 the Portuguese on Mozambique Island, then their principal base on the East Coast, were approached by envoys from Zanzibar and Pemba, far to the north. These envoys explained that their

EAST COAST FORTUNES

rulers had formerly paid tribute to the lords of the Kerimba Islands, but now that Pemba and Zanzibar had to pay tribute to the Portuguese they had stopped paying it to the Kerimbas. This had involved them in war with the Kerimbas, and they now asked for Portuguese protection. Another Portuguese version, written somewhat earlier and possibly nearer the truth, offers a different explanation but confirms the picture of a closely woven system of political and economic power up and down this long coast. According to this second version, the Kerimba Islands had once been subject to Zanzibar and Pemba but had lately transferred their allegiance to Mombasa.

Whatever the truth of the matter, settlers and soldiers on the island of Mozambique saw a golden opportunity in this appeal for aid and alliance. Eighty of them embarked without delay in two *zambucos* — large lateen-rigged coastal vessels — together with "a skiff and a ship's boat." After sailing and rowing for five days, they landed on the principal island of the Kerimbas, overcame its ruler and his troops (he turned out to be a nephew of the lord of Mombasa), and took a vast spoil reckoned at 200,000 cruzados. Whether exaggerated in the records or not, this booty is fairly conclusive proof of wealthy settlements on the Kerimbas during medieval times. We may learn more of these settlements when archeology at last finds time and money to make even a preliminary survey there.*

Within fifty or sixty years of frenzied onslaught on the accumulated wealth of centuries, the Portuguese effort had almost spent itself. Spread-eagled across the world, imperial Portugal lay dying, not from lack of courage or ambition, but from a shortage

---

* Research on the Kerimbas would surely throw new light on the broad-ranging scope of the Indian Ocean trade. A British naval survey of 1823 — carried out to sailing-ship requirements — found that the Kerimbas had excellent harbors affording "perfect security in the heaviest gales." These sheltered harbors must have been greatly used in previous times.

of men and from an even graver incapacity to move with the times and learn new ways. The Dutch overhauled them. The French and English elbowed them aside. Here and there along the coast they continued to enjoy supreme power; here and there they pushed bravely into the lands behind the coast. But the world soon passed them by. And the cities of the coast, still enduring though often sorely harassed, inescapably shared this decline.

4 In the Wake of the Storm

WITH THE RAVAGING OF THE INDIAN OCEAN TRADE, EAST AFRICA falls from recorded history for almost two centuries. Much can be reconstructed, but the European materials for the coast remain painfully thin — little more, indeed, than petty correspondence from sleepy Portuguese settlements, chance travelers' tales, and the bald facts of Turkish penetration from the Red Sea.

Weakened by their loss of trade, by Portuguese storming and sacking and the payment of heavy tribute, these cities greatly suffered. Yet the story is not all sadness. North of Mombasa, at least, the cities seem to have recovered a good deal of their earlier life and vigor. More than that, they developed their Swahili language into a written culture of considerable distinction. Here along the northern segment of the coast, Portuguese impact had been sharp but exceedingly short-lived. Once this impact was absorbed, some of the old settlements and city-states became focal centers for a new Swahili consciousness. Out of this consciousness there came the written language that has since become a flexible and efficient vehicle of speech for tens of millions of people in Africa.

It would be wide of the mark to see in this revival an early movement of cultural nationalism. The peoples of the coast felt themselves as part of the wide Islamic world, and the ideas of national resurgence can be ill applied to this time and place. Yet the effect was not so very different. Poets and historians began remembering the past in a new way, dramatically, nostalgically, prefiguring the present and a better future. And although recovery of their writings from private individuals and families is still at an early stage, enough is known of their outstanding quality to have moved one careful English critic of Swahili, in a recent letter to the present writer, to declare that "some of this poetry was the equal, if not to Dante, in certainty to Milton."

The claim that seventeenth century Swahili poets in Mombasa and Malindi and neighboring cities were writing like Milton may seem tall in English ears. Yet there is nothing inherently difficult about it. These writers undoubtedly worked within a rich and various tradition. They and their fellow-citizens had lived and were still living through a heroic age, a time of cultural awakening by assault from outside, a period of repeated danger from the sea and of sudden alarms and disasters and escapes. To many of them it must have seemed that they had wonderfully outfaced these perils and misfortunes. It was the kind of soil from which great poetry can spring.

Not all the Swahili cities were in this condition. Those in the south were overwhelmed, for it was to the south that the Portuguese had their main strength. Kilwa suffered worst of all Subdued at gun's point by Vasco da Gama on his second voyage in 1502, it was sacked and occupied by Almeida three years later. Its ties with India and the Persian Gulf were cut by the Portuguese. Its trade routes with the interior were severed by the main-

In the Wake of the Storm

land peoples, and its Swahili population dwindled. Some eighty years later its fate was finally sealed by catastrophic invasion from the mainland; the Zimba, marauding migrants from the south, came across the narrows which separate Kilwa Island from the mainland, stormed the town, and killed, it is said, some three thousand of its inhabitants.

But here, too, the subsequent history of the coast has its bearing on the course of European-African history. The comment that it makes may be pitched in a minor key, a chronicle of small events and marginal encounters; there is here, nonetheless, a valuable link between defiance of the Portuguese in the sixteenth century and subjection to imperial Europe in the nineteenth.

The English records pick up the story with James Prior and the cruise of the *Nisus* frigate in 1812. By now the Portuguese settlements were far gone in decay. That was understandable. Given the weakness of Portugal, the wonder is that these settlements should have survived at all. Landing at Mozambique Island, Prior visited a hospital but found "no specific disease, as far as I can learn . . . except *ennui*. Were I to remain here, I should die of it in three months."

Rejoicing in the name of Dom Antonio Manuel de Mello Castro e Mendoza, the governor had two residences. The visiting naval party found it hard to find the one he occupied. "It would be difficult to conjecture its existence without previous information, part of the exterior appearing more like an old storehouse than the mansion of the first personage in the settlement. We were led to it by the clashing of billiard balls, and the confused clamour of contending voices, so that we at first took it to be a tavern or gambling house."

Slaving was now the main business of the place, partly with Brazil and partly with the French islands of Mauritius and Bourbon, though there still remained a little trade in gold and ivory with the interior. Visiting the governor, Prior and Captain Beaver were poorly impressed by his qualities. He had apparently not visited any part of his government since coming to Mozambique. He affected "considerable state" but was neither communicative nor inquisitive upon points that his visitors thought interesting. "He has not once inquired, during the interviews with Captain Beaver, respecting the fate of his own country, the general state of Europe, or whether such places as Portugal and Spain yet existed or were blotted from the list of the independent nations." Perhaps his pride as a Portuguese nobleman took it for granted, in any case, that they were not. If so, this pride had evidently not prevented him from making a remarkably good thing out of his governorship. "With a very small official salary, it is said he has realised a fortune of £80,000." His attitude toward gubernatorial responsibilities, in short, was the same as that of his sixteenth century forerunners. He "farmed" his colonial "conquest" as a feudal vassal of his king. In this one may observe, once more, the fatal incapacity of the Portuguese social system to change with a changing world.

On Portuguese evidence, East Coast slaving from Mozambique to Brazil was now running at between 10,000 and 15,000 slaves a year. Compared with the West African trade, this was still a modest figure; and although it later rose to 25,000 a year (before finally dwindling to very few after 1850), it emphasizes the relatively small part that was played by European slaving from the East Coast as a whole. What caused the stagnation and decay of this seaboard region was not slaving, though slaving helped, but the reduction of all that vast network of maritime trade which had formerly linked these cities and settlements with the civilizations of the East.

One can see this from a slightly earlier French report on Kilwa. Though the French sailed eastward around the Cape long before the English and the Dutch, they made no impression on the coast itself. At the beginning of the second half of the eighteenth century, however, they began to tap the coast for slaves required by new plantations in their Indian Ocean islands of Bourbon and Mauritius. The pioneer in this commerce was a Frenchman called Morice. Wrecked on Zanzibar with a cargo of "many piastres" in a ship called the *St. Pierre*, Morice escaped to Kilwa, where, partly through being a surgeon (like Prior nearly fifty years later), he got on excellent terms with the sultan, who actually sold him a piece of Kilwa in exchange for four thousand piastres.

Exploiting this success, Morice negotiated a treaty with the sultan which gave him a monopoly privilege on the export of slaves. Signed in 1776, this Kilwa treaty was a distant echo of practice on the Guinea Coast. The sultan promised to deliver one thousand slaves a year at the price of twenty piastres apiece provided that he himself should have two piastres for each slave delivered. No other slaver was to be allowed at Kilwa — *"soit François, Anglois, Hollandois, Portugais, etc."* — until Morice had obtained his quota and declared himself satisfied.

The trade prospered in a small way. Another French report of the same period, a letter to the French Minister of Marine, Marshal de Castries, contains notes by a slaving captain called Joseph Crasson (or Crassous) de Medeuil, master of the *Créolle*. He was twice at Kilwa on slaving business, evidently in the 1770's. He found the place much as Prior would, a mere shadow of its former self, humbled and yet by no means starving. He says that Kilwa could supply millet, indigo, "excellent cotton," sugar cane, gums in abundance, and "second-class cowries" such as were used to make payments on the West Coast, and notably in Dahomey. Ivory was easily obtained. "And there are blacks who are excellent when selected with care."

EAST COAST FORTUNES

He selected some of these "excellent blacks," while the sultan, for his part, recalled the treaty with Morice and asked for French protection against his enemies, who at this time were partly his coastal neighbors and partly the Portuguese. Nothing came of this, and the trade remained small. Crasson says that French ships to his knowledge had taken 4,193 slaves from Kilwa in the previous three years, his own share being 387; they cost forty piastres each (double the price that Morice had agreed) and were carried mostly to Mauritius and Bourbon, though some to the French West Indies. Slaves were of course taken to the French islands from other East African ports as well; in 1799 Mauritius and Bourbon were said to have about 100,000 slaves between them.

Slaving and stagnation continued hand in hand. Later British naval visitors — Owen and Boteler in the years 1821-1826 — were repeatedly struck by the mournful appearance of these settlements and cities. Warmly hating the slave trade, they were inclined to make it guilty of all the evils they beheld.

"The riches of Quilimane consisted in a trifling degree of gold and silver, but principally of grain," reported Captain Owen, "which was produced in such quantities as to supply Mozambique. But the introduction of the slave trade stopped the pursuits of industry, and changed those places where peace and agriculture had formerly reigned into the seat of war and bloodshed. . . . The slave trade has been a blight on its prosperity; for at present Quilimane and the Portuguese possessions in the whole colony of the Rivers of Senna [the channels of the Lower Zambesi] do not supply themselves with sufficient corn for their own consumption." He found that between eleven and fourteen slave vessels came annually to Quelimane from Rio de Janeiro "and return with from four to five hundred slaves each on an average." Boteler, who sailed with Owen but whose book was posthumously published two years after Owen's, has the same description of Quelimane in slightly different words.

Manifestly the slave trade had played its degrading part here as elsewhere. It had grown much larger since the coming of the Portuguese. Yet it had remained relatively unimportant. Except from one or two ports at irregular intervals, this trade was too small to explain the failure of these settlements and cities on the southern segment of the coast to recover from Portuguese devastations in the sixteenth century. Prior had seen the truth more clearly. In addition to the slave trade, he wrote, "the true cause [of decay] must be sought, perhaps, in the decline of commerce and industry . . . and the only probable reason [for this decline] was the presence and superior power of Europeans in India." It was now exclusively to Europe that the wealth of the East was channeled. East Africa could have no further part in it.

5 *When You Pipe at Zanzibar . . .*

BUT EUROPEAN SLAVING FROM THE EAST COAST WAS NOT THE END of the story. Some of the seaboard cities were also in the business. One or two of them were making considerable profits from it; and none more than Zanzibar, by now a dependency of the Imam of the southern Arabian state of Muscat. One British naval visitor, Captain Smee, found in 1811 that the Governor of Zanzibar, an Arab called Yacout, was taking ten dollars a head in "premium" from every slave delivered to the French for their plantations on Mauritius and Bourbon. As well as selling to the French, Yacout

EAST COAST FORTUNES

was also supplying Muscat and other eastern markets — perhaps to a total of between 6,000 and 10,000 slaves a year.

Such exports, even so, were still on a relatively small scale; in the West, Brazil was taking more than five times as many. However evil the plight of the enslaved, East Coast peoples would not have suffered greatly from slaving, and nor would their neighbors in the interior. But the Arabs of Oman and Muscat were thrusting merchants who now pushed inland from the coast and mightily expanded the slave trade. By 1839, when Zanzibar had the lion's share of slaving, a British observer reckoned that between 40,000 and 45,000 slaves were being sold there every year. About half of these went northward to Arabia, the Persian Gulf, and Egypt. Most of the rest were smuggled southward to the Portuguese in Mozambique, who sent them to Brazil. American slave ships also drew cargoes from this source.

After 1840 the business of extracting slaves from East Africa became a major Arab enterprise. In that year the Sultan of Oman transferred his capital from Muscat to his dependency of Zanzibar. A man of great commercial talent, he set about reorganizing the trade of Zanzibar and of much of the coast on an entirely new basis. He stimulated exports of natural products from the mainland. He established clove plantations on Zanzibar. He sent envoys far and wide across the eastern world to win new markets or reactivate old ones. Arab merchants were again installed, as in early medieval times, at ports as far away as the southern coast of China. Here was a major effort to rebuild the former prosperity of the Indian Ocean trade between East Africa and its old partners. But now there was a difference; slaving had become a major part of the business, even a dominant part of it.

The years before and after 1840 — but especially after — were those of far-reaching Arab penetration of the East African interior. The Arabs and their Swahili agents went in along the old

When You Pipe at Zanzibar . . .

trade routes — from Bagamoyo, Kilwa, Tanga — and rapidly established trading stations on the Great Lakes and at suitable places in between. Armed with muskets, they overawed the weak and skillfully allied themselves with the strong. They pushed ever further into the interior. "It will be seen," the British explorer Speke could write in 1864, "that the Zanzibar Arabs have reached the uttermost limits of their tether; [they are] half-way across the continent, and in a few years they must unite their labours with the people who come from Luanda on the opposite coast." They had in fact already done so; in 1852 the Angolan archives speak for the first time of direct contact with Arab traders, six of whom had crossed the continent in that year.

It was this Arab penetration of the interior, having as its main object the provision of slaves for export and slaves for the new plantations of Zanzibar and its immediate mainland holdings, that led to the devastations which Livingstone and other explorers witnessed. The point here is that the devastations were recent; they were not characterisitic of East African history, whether in the interior or along the coast. After the coming of the Sultan of Oman and his traders, Coupland remarks, "the whole system of inland trade was extended and elaborated far beyond the more or less casual operations in which the Arabs of the coast have been engaged for ages past." In these years it was said with truth: "When you pipe at Zanzibar, they dance at the Lakes."

But the fact that the inland devastations were recent has often been forgotten. They understandably horrified the European explorers who were now pushing into the interior in the wake of the Arabs. But Livingstone himself was under no misapprehension about the order of events. He knew that he was witnessing the misery of a slave trade that was relatively new. Further to the south, in the Zambesi valley, he even found that the trails he had opened were being followed for the first time by slavers in

EAST COAST FORTUNES

Portuguese employ. Yet in Europe this slaving misery was increasingly believed endemic to the East and Central African interior, and as though in some way "natural" to the peoples of these regions.

From this situation, by routes that were indirect and yet connected, there came colonial enterprise and eventual conquest. This invasion of the African interior was repeatedly justified by the humanitarian aim of suppressing the Arab slave trade. Certainly, the task needed doing; and it was well done, especially by the British and the Belgians. But it was done in exchange for a new subjection — and one, moreover, which was intended to endure and under which Africans were to suffer new forms of servitude. Here, very clearly, one may see how the inability of African Iron Age institutions to resist slaving became a major cause of their overthrow. Traditional customs of domestic slavery were allowed to slide disastrously into competitive slaving for export; and the damage was all the greater in those regions, notably of East Africa, where other forms of trade had never flourished.

It is important to understand this process. The ideology of colonial conquest, now growing strong in Europe, would flourish on the notion that Africans were incapable of promoting and defending their own institutions. This was not true. But slaving made it seem true. Europeans were offered the picture of a continental interior that was unredeemedly savage, a pitiful victim of bloodlust and brutality powerless to help itself. Every evil tale (and there were many) seemed to strengthen this impression. There could, it appeared, be only one answer to the problem; and that was outright annexation.

This ideology persisted. One may find it in book after book of the colonial period, whether in the memoirs of those who carried the "white man's burden" or of those who justified his

When You Pipe at Zanzibar ...

carrying it. Scholars were as little exempt as colonial propagandists. The outstanding case is that of Coupland, author of standard British textbooks on East African history. A "new chapter in the history of Africa began with David Livingstone," Coupland was writing in 1928. "So far, it might be said, Africa proper had had no history. . . . The main body of Africans . . . had stayed, for untold centuries, sunk in barbarism. Such, it might almost seem, had been Nature's decree. . . . So they remained stagnant, neither going forward nor going back. . . . The heart of Africa was scarcely beating." In the same large-handed way Coupland wrote off the Swahili cities of the coast. They were, he said, Arab colonies from the earliest times and as such they had remained.

We can see now that Coupland was doubly mistaken. He was wrong about the coastal cities, for he ignored their Swahili nature. He was wrong about the peoples of the interior. They had not "stayed sunk in barbarism." They might be barbaric in a narrowly sociological sense, since they were nonliterate and generally nonurban; but they were certainly not barbaric in the sense that Coupland implied — of possessing no moral codes, laws, governments, or civilization of their own. Nor had they "remained stagnant"; on the contrary, they had moved through many phases of social growth that were common to other branches of the human race.

What an invading Europe found was not an age-old chaos and insecurity, as many imagined, but the disasters of a sudden social crisis. This was the crisis that opened the way to colonial occupation; and no doubt it is in this that the greatest effect of slaving in East Africa should be seen.

Such, in brief, is the story of East Africa's varying fortunes in connection with the outside world. Yet there were other regions where contact with Europe involved, in precolonial times, neither territorial encroachment as in the Congo, nor an outright destruction of existing cultures. And to see the European-African connection in all its astonishing and often baffling enterprise and vigor, it is to these other regions one must turn. They lie in the west among the peoples of the Gulf of Guinea.

six

Frontier of Opportunity

To be a king means to have plenty of slaves, without which you are nothing.

Emir of Bida in 1897

The coastland became the frontier of opportunity.
K. Onwuka Dike

Note: The western limits of the Gold Coast went, in fact, as far as Beyin and a little beyond.

1 Like Nothing Else . . .

THERE IS SURELY NO OTHER chapter in human experience like that of the Gulf of Guinea during these years. For sheer complexity of enterprise the records of the Guinea venture tend to make all other encounters between Europe and Africa seem pale, predictable, and sad.

Almost nothing in this story lacks drama or surprise. Little can be foreseen for long. Much death and sorrow there may be, sordid and chaotic; but all the same there persists a steady underlay of humor that goes ringing up and down the scale from the sly ironic to the swaggering absurd. Poker-faced ambition, solemn and socially respectable, is punctured by irreverent laughter. Deliberate brutality walks hand in hand with careful restraint. Furious rivalries and frantic *coups de main* are separated by slow periods of peaceful intercourse and dependable alliance. The common man suffers, often appallingly; but humanity, somehow or other, perseveres and fights doggedly back and survives.

It is a strange symphony of expedience that echoes from these years for those who care to listen; a harsh and highly fallible orchestration of forceful men and their wily strategems, the clash and clatter of cheating and chaffering and agreeing and disputing, the rattle of spears and muskets, the labored groan of hard-shifting sheets and yards on old ships cluttered with slaves and sick men,

FRONTIER OF OPPORTUNITY

slowed to a crawl by the barnacled scum of tropical seas and yet crazily bearing, somehow or other, humanity's past into humanity's future.

It seems to defy all reasonable explanation. Yet it has a pattern. And this pattern on the Guinea Coast, perhaps more clearly than any other aspect of the European-African connection, reveals a gradual transition of African society — the prelude both to subjection and regained independence.

Here, above all, there was great variety. The peoples of the Congo had never known a European connection that was not more or less confined to a single European power, and this a backward and relatively weak one, or to a single interest, the trade in slaves. Their experience of the non-African world was inevitably narrow, their scope for action and reaction necessarily small, their chances of playing off one competitor against another never more than minimal. But along the Guinea Coast there appeared the ships and traders of a dozen nations, and the trade passed through many hands and many phases.

There was also, on the Guinea Coast, a great innate strength of resistance. The peoples of the East African littoral had certainly known a long and varied connection with the outside world, yet they had known it only until the sixteenth century. By then they had built an urban civilization that proved softly vulnerable to the guns and ambition of the Portuguese, and the Portuguese went far to overwhelm it. But the peoples of the Guinea Coast offered no such easy target. They could defend themselves when attacked; and they did defend themselves.

At the beginning there was the same acceptance of equality among Europeans and Africans that occurred in the Congo, and in much the same circumstances. The Portuguese came to Benin as allies and missionaries. They encouraged Bini chiefs to visit Lisbon. They helped to build churches. They opened and

Like Nothing Else . . .

tried to monopolize an extensive trade in ivory and other goods, and soon in slaves. They established royal agents in the city of Benin. Sometimes their soldiers marched and fought in the armies of the Oba. As late as the early seventeenth century the king of neighboring Warri returned from Portugal with a white wife; his son, who became an important man in 1644, enjoyed the baptismal name of Dom Antonio de Mingo.

There were other such cases along the coast. But this early equality did not, as in the Congo, decline into servitude. On the contrary, it continued. It evolved. It developed new and unique forms. No matter through what conflicts and miseries the European connection might pass — and it passed through many — the two sides somehow held to each other. They might trust or mightily distrust each other, enrich or seek or ruin, respect the peace or break it; through thick and thin they were kept together by their common interest in trade. Year after year, to serve this trade, European crews and merchants underwent appalling risks in navigation and fearful months of sweat and fever on the coast; and nothing ever availed to hold them back. On their side the African partners in the business deployed patience and commercial cunning, persevered in gauging the manners of these newly discovered peoples from beyond the sea, and little by little took their measure. The history of the Guinea Coast between about 1550 and 1850 is increasingly and continuously the history of an international partnership in risk and profit.

So it is wrong to consider the Guinea experience as one that was simply ordered and imposed from outside, with the African part in it a purely negative and involuntary one. This view of the connection mirrors a familiar notion of African incapacity, and it has no place in the historical record. Those Africans who were involved in the trade were seldom the helpless victims of a commerce they did not understand; on the contrary, they understood

FRONTIER OF OPPORTUNITY

it as well as their European partners. They responded to its challenge. They exploited its opportunities. Their great misfortune — and this would be Africa's tragedy — was that Europe only wanted slaves.

The states and peoples that became involved in this connection, whether directly or indirectly, were themselves of great diversity of language and social structure. They were states and peoples of the Sudanese grasslands, of the forest belt, and of the seaside littoral. Not only were they various; they were also of great antiquity.

By the time of European arrival, late in the fifteenth century, many of these peoples had achieved an Iron Age maturity of social structure. Strong feudal states and empires had emerged.* And these possessed in their heritage, as modern research now suggests, some reason to regard themselves as occupying the heartland of Black Africa.

On this last point, which has a bearing on their self-confidence and stability, there are two kinds of evidence: archeological and linguistic. In Central Nigeria, at the confluence of the Niger and Benue over an area of several hundred square miles, archeologists have lately found the proofs of an Iron Age culture that is earlier than anything else of its kind so far known in Africa south of the Sahara. This Nok culture seems to have had vigorous life between about 500 B.C. and A.D. 200. It was undoubtedly transitional between stone and iron — a point which is neatly made by a smelting tuyère, or nozzle, that is now on show in the Nigerian Museum at Lagos; for inside this tuyère there lies, just as it was found, the butt of a stone axe.

There is no doubt that this Nok culture was ancestral to the development of the West African Iron Age. There is little doubt that the terra cotta figures and figurines of Nok were ancestral

---

* See pp. 8-11.

Like Nothing Else . . .

to the infinitely more sophisticated and masterly terra cotta and metal heads of Ife a thousand years later, themselves the ancestors of the brass and bronze work of Benin. Remotely from that early Iron Age culture and its allied cultures to the westward, there flowed a technological achievement which enabled the peoples of a later time to build the states and empires of the forest belt, Oyo and Benin, Adansi, Denkyira, Ashanti and their like.

To this one may now add some linguistic evidence. Hitherto it has been generally believed that the movement of Bantu-speaking peoples across central and southern Africa was largely from the northeast, from the region of the Great Lakes. But Greenberg, an American scholar who has lately done much to sweep African studies free of their clutter of racialist myth, has suggested that the heartland was not in the northeast but in the northwest, and specifically in this region of Nigeria and the Cameroons. There seems a good deal to support this view.

Traditions of Yoruba origin are one kind of evidence. These Yoruba of the powerful state of Oyo, with its spiritual capital at Ile Ife, have generally believed that their remote forerunners came from Arabia. And yet they have also held, by another tradition, that they live in the place where God created man. According to the Reverend Samuel Johnson, a Yoruba clergyman of the Church of England who made a profound study of what Yorubas believe, and whose book on the subject was published some sixty years ago, "All the various tribes of the Yoruba nation trace their origin from Oduduwa [their legendary hero-founder] and the city of Ile Ife. In fact Ile Ife is fabled as the spot where God created man, white and black, and from whence they dispersed all over the earth."

Now the forerunners of the Yoruba may possibly have reached southwestern Nigeria — coming originally, perhaps, from the old

FRONTIER OF OPPORTUNITY

civilization of Meroë on the Middle Nile — between A.D. 600 and 1,000. But these newcomers were not the only ancestors of Yoruba civilization, any more than William of Normandy's four thousand knights were the only ancestors of English civilization. They were a relatively small group of travelers, but hard tried and well armed; they conquered and settled and were then absorbed among the peoples whom they had found. For Yoruba civilization, as Willett has written, appears to be the result of "a fusion of a small intrusive ruling class, bringing ideas from outside, with a highly artistic indigenous population." And this fusion is reflected in surviving Yoruba tradition. Thus the Yoruba have remembered their own sagas of travel and settlement, though vaguely and dimly. But they have also remembered another and quite different line of tradition: a much older memory of those who fathered the "dispersal" from Yorubaland "all over the earth" — but actually, if Greenberg is right, into central and southern Africa.

The principal states of the Guinea Coast and its hinterland were therefore strongly established by the time of European coming. Although nonliterate, they had great inner coherence, social self-confidence, moral and customary and artistic vigor. Some of them had been heard of in Europe; most had not. But all of them, by the middle of the sixteenth century, were beginning to feel the tug of the new maritime trade along the coast.

Until now they had looked northward for commerce and contact with the non-African world. The states of the forest belt had looked to the savannah states to the north of them — to Ghana, Mali, Songhay, Kanem, the Hausa confederation — and these in turn had looked northward again across the Great Desert to the Arab and Berber states of North Africa. Now the position began to be reversed. The empires of the savannah land were losing their potency. And along the coast there appeared the ships and traders of Europe, pushing their way patiently eastward from one anchorage to the next.

And so, for the first time in history, this Guinea Coast became a frontier that could be used and crossed. It ceased to be the edge of nowhere and was henceforward a vital place of meeting with the foremost nations of the world.

The consequences of this great though gradual change of front were felt initially, of course, along the coast itself; and notably among the almost deserted creeks and channels of the sprawling delta of the Niger.

2 The People of the Salt Water

THE SWAMPLANDS OF THE NIGER DELTA WERE THINLY POPULATED or void of people before the coming of the sailing ships. Here in this back of beyond, along the profitless edge of an empty ocean, there lived only a few scattered refugees from the great states of the interior, odd families down on their luck, fragments of broken clans.

Yet within a hundred years there had emerged amid this maze of inland waterways — a Victorian traveler would fancifully call them "the Venice of West Africa" — a close-knit system of trading states; and within another hundred years these states had built themselves into a well-nigh impregnable position of commercial monopoly. They had become the indispensable middlemen between Europe and the densely populated lands behind the delta.

FRONTIER OF OPPORTUNITY

The history of these little states, Dike has said in his penetrating study of them, belongs both to the Atlantic and to Africa. They were almost as much the children of the Guinea trade — the slave trade — as were the plantation colonies of the Caribbean and North America. And yet they remained strongly African in accent and ideas. They were the West African equivalent of the somewhat earlier city-states of East Africa.

From the very beginning of their social growth, these peoples of the delta appear to have shown great ingenuity in getting the better of natural disadvantages — in soil, climate and excess of water — that were as daunting for them as for their European visitors. But they also displayed an outstanding political inventiveness. They evolved new ways of unifying people of diverse language and origin. They moved far towards a fully "political society." Their city-states are perhaps the most interesting of all the products of the European-African connection.

Early among the founders of this new society in the delta are thought to have been Ijaw people on the run from Benin's stiff-handed rule. Whether Ijaws or not, these settlers colonized riverbanks and chunks of land amid the water. They lived as fishermen, and they must have lived poorly.

Then came the Portuguese, passing them by at first. "There is no trade in this country," Pacheco was writing of the western delta in about 1505, "nor anything from which one can make a profit." One should go on up to Guato, port of Benin, and deal with the agents of the monarch of that empire.

Rapidly, this situation changed: partly by initiative of the delta peoples, who found ways of circumventing the royal prerogatives of Benin and tapping the rich trade of the Ibo country behind the eastern river mouths; and partly by insistence of the European captains and supercargoes, who sought new harbors in which to outwit their rivals and build temporary monopolies of their own.

The People of the Salt Water

In any event this combination of talent became centered on new settlements that were founded near the mouths of the Brass, Bonny, Opobo, and Cross rivers. These became the focal points of maritime trade for the lands that now are eastern Nigeria and the (ex-British) Cameroons.

New recruits joined these promising settlements. The delta became more than a refuge: it functioned now as a prime connecting point with Europe. Prominent among these migrants were families from Iboland, energetic people whose own customs were those of a "tribal democracy" that tolerated neither chiefs nor kings, human or divine, and for whom the theocratic oppression of Benin was perhaps especially odious. It was these Ibos who gave the delta system its turbulent individualism, famous among West Africans and Europeans alike, and who laid the social foundations on which ambitious men would raise kingdoms and republics in the years ahead.

Yet it would be wrong to consider the society of the delta as an Ibo importation. It became in fact something on its own, a compound of old ideas with new ideas, a mixture that was "neither Benin nor Efik, Ibo nor Ibibio," but, as Dike says, "a people apart, the product of the clashing cultures of the tribal hinterland and of the Atlantic community to both of which they belonged. The tribal [inland] Ibos called them *Ndu Mili Nnu* (People of the Salt Water), and so long as the frontier of trade was confined to the Atlantic seaboard so long did they remain the economic masters of these territories."

The frontier of trade was fixed along this seaboard for several hundred years. And with the rise of mass slaving in the seventeenth century the chances of gain became correspondingly enormous. It was on this that these settlements built their prosperity.

Like their new partners, the Africans who went into this business were people with a long commercial experience, gained partly

FRONTIER OF OPPORTUNITY

between themselves and partly by commerce with the northern states and empires of the Sudanese grasslands. What they needed, here in the delta, was not commercial know-how but effective social organization. They had to become strong enough both to obtain captives from their inland neighbors and, when occasion demanded, to present a common front against the Europeans. It was difficult for them to achieve this strength because the old and new dwellers in these islands and dry places on the banks of rivers were of many tribal loyalties.

Faced with such problems, the delta peoples found a solution in their characteristic city-state. These delta states — these nontribal trading corporations — showed themselves both skillful in weaving a common loyalty and flexible in absorbing new immigrants. Each developed its own exclusivist "citizenship" — to the point, indeed, that one may well see in these little states the first thoroughgoing application in West Africa of the ideas of modern nationalism. Like the nations of mercantile Europe they competed ruthlessly with one another for trade, profits, and even territory. And yet, over and above this rivalry, they undoubtedly felt themselves joined together by common interests and forms of government.

Some of the dozen or so leading states evolved into monarchies, others into republics, their choice depending largely on the influence of neighboring tradition. But within this broad framework there were new institutions, holding society together, that were peculiar to the delta. The "house system" was one of these. Dike defines this as "at once a co-operative trading unit and a local government institution." Each house was governed by a single powerful trader; and each state, whether monarchy or not, might have many houses. It was through the house system that a new rule of law was found that could be valid for immigrants of many tribes.

The People of the Salt Water

The basic idea behind this system was not invented in the delta. It was the characteristically African concept of "extended family," a group that includes every man, woman, and child with acknowledged blood relationship to one another. But the delta system carried this notion much further. Membership of a house included not only the ruling families and their relations, but their servants and slaves as well. "Master and servant, the bond and the free, all became members of one House, a veritable hierarchy, with numerous gradations, each ranks with its duties and responsibilities, its privileges and rewards."

Different origins were forgotten, different languages were discarded, different loyalties were broken; rapidly, all were welded into new customs and traditions. "The smaller houses numbered anything from three hundred to a thousand members; others, such as the royal Houses, numbered many thousands." The best slaves were retained to man the armed canoes that went on raid and search for captives needed by the European trade; and, as time went by, these slaves — who were not chattel slaves but men who were bound by special ties of loyalty to this or that master — became important traders in their own right, and sometimes kings.

Here and there the house rulers borrowed the old trappings and superstitions of divine monarchy in the interior. Like the god-king of Benin, the little house kings of the delta would expect slaves to be sacrificed whenever one of them should die. Elsewhere the house rulers became a governing oligarchy. They formed exclusive clubs and secret societies which held watch and ward over their states, settled disputes, regulated successions, and generally acted as judge, jury, and counterrevolutionary police. Later on, when the slaves they kept for their plantations had learned how to organize themselves, these oligarchies would

FRONTIER OF OPPORTUNITY

face situations they were no longer able to contain; and slave risings would put an end to slave massacres.

Throughout the years of the slave trade, even in times when slaving was past its worst, the delta rulers waxed in wealth and political strength. Dealing as equals with Europeans, jealously guarding their monopoly of contact with the hinterland, proud of their sovereignty, these chiefs and their people transformed this sterile belt of waste and swamp into one of the most prosperous regions of Africa. A European visitor in 1847 could find that King Eyo of Creek Town "had in his House many thousand slaves, and four hundred canoes with a captain and crew for every one. Besides his extensive trade . . . he employs his people reclaiming waste land, founding towns, and planting farms in well-selected positions which give him command of the rivers and channels of trade."

Another element that made for stability was the easy advancement of slaves. The system was socially mobile. Slaves could obtain their freedom by hard work or individual enterprise on behalf of their masters. "The wealth produced by a slave," according to Dike, "eventually set him free, for the master knew his slave intimately and the value of his work and rewarded him accordingly. It was this incentive, ever present in the House system, that made it in the nineteenth century an institution full of vitality, flexible and in a large measure beneficial to all."

3 *"Children of God"*

YET THE MASTERS WERE FEW, AND THE OVERSEA DEMAND FOR slaves was great. Through at least two centuries the demand was so great as to be practically insatiable. Countless thousands of slaves were obtained from the lands behind the delta. Given their numerical weakness, how could the delta states achieve this staggering rate of delivery? Here again their system revealed a peculiar compound of African and European influence.

On the African side the thing was done by another adaptation of tradition and belief. Like many of their neighbors, the Ibos of the highly populous lands behind the eastern delta possessed a supreme deity. This deity was accustomed to communicate with the Ibos through a famous oracle, Chukwu, which resided in the territory of an Ibo clan known as Aro. Other Ibo clans knew the Aros as Umu-Chukwu, the "Children of God."

Happy in their gift of fortune, this oracle of great authority, the Aros (the Umu-Chukwu) early fastened themselves into a special position of monopoly inside the general monopolist system that linked the hinterland with the coast. "This they did," Dike says, "by establishing Aro colonies along the trade routes of the interior." He compares them with the Greeks, "the course of whose colonising expeditions was largely directed by the priests of the Delphic Oracle."

In any case the Aros exploited their oracle with a realism and commercial ardor that would also have done them credit with medieval prince-bishops or tycoons of a later time; and they duly exercised the trade as part of their divine (and highly profitable) calling. They became the monopolist operators of the slave trade between much of Iboland and the busy ports of the eastern delta. In so doing they acquired political influence. This influence continued into colonial times: "Long Ju Ju," as Europeans called the Aro oracle, was destroyed by the British only in the year 1900.

Slaving was always a grim enough affair, and many captives were certainly taken in war or simply kidnaped. "Those sold by the Blacks," a French trader observed of Senegal in the 1680s, "are for the most part prisoners of war, taken either in fight or in

FRONTIER OF OPPORTUNITY

pursuit or in the incursions they [the raiders] make into their enemies' territories." But in the Niger delta the situation was different. "All that vast number of slaves which the Calabar Blacks sell to all European nations . . . are not their prisoners of war, the greatest part being bought by those people of their inland neighbours." Many, and perhaps most, delta slaves were in fact delivered by the Aro system.

It worked through the pressures of orthodox and socially respectable superstition among people for whom religion had an everyday compulsion, and for whom death was only the passage from one life to another. Any man who should offend the oracle — and the Aro priests saw to it that nothing was easier — was mulcted of a fine; but it was a fine that must be paid in slaves. Once paid, the "fine" was supposed to be eaten by the oracle; in truth, of course, the captives were simply handed along the Aro network to the traders of the coast who sold them to the Europeans. Perhaps this was one reason why the Ibos thought that Europeans were cannibals.

These priest-slavers had two powerful reasons for confidence in their system. In the first place, they and their oracle provided a valuable and even vital cement for the many factions, tribes, settlements, and "free cities" of this tumultuous delta society. The authority of the Aro oracle was the one imperative they were all prepared to recognize and respect. Through this the Aro priests fashioned among these disparate peoples a trading unity, useful though often broken, which they could not otherwise have had. Secondly, the Ibo god was a jealous god like others of his kind; and his word was law.

So harsh a law could scarcely have stood for long, one may think, without the sanctions of superior force. And sanctions, indeed, were soon found to be necessary. This was where the European connection made its vital contribution to the system. Slaving captains might be powerless beyond the decks of their ships. There was nonetheless one sovereign means whereby they could push their influence into the hinterland. "We sell them," a Dutch factor on the coast was writing home in 1700, "incredible quantities" of muskets and they, the Africans, "are wonderful dexterous" in using them.

Widespread use of firearms changed the course of history in the delta as surely as in other parts of Africa. It was their concentration of fire-power that enabled the delta chiefs to outface and overawe the numerically far stronger peoples of the interior. And muskets were almost certainly decisive in enabling the Aro trader-priests to maintain their monopoly — and keep their oracle respected — in face of mounting opposition from those who suffered from the system.

The Aro priests do not appear to have used the guns themselves. They hired others for that purpose. They called up mercenaries from the professional soldier-guilds of Iboland, the famous Abam, Abiriba, and their like, armed these with the muskets they had bought, and "conquered all the people who resisted their influence or killed their agents." Meanwhile lesser "Aro systems," presided over by lesser priests in the name of smaller deities and oracles, were engaged in the same business at other points behind the delta ports.

Thus the trade was organized by god and gun on one side as surely as by ship and plantation on the other. Here too, at any rate for the time being, equality held firm.

FRONTIER OF OPPORTUNITY

4 *Partners in Trade*

Bonny was the main port of sale for the Aro traders. It can never have been a promising or comfortable place. "Miles of rotting mud water," Mary Kingsley said of the Bonny River seventy years ago, "fringed with walls of rotting mud mangrove swamp." Here were the old hulks of the slave trade, the floating barracoons that were only a memory of the past in Mary Kingsley's day (although a fairly recent past), showing their "gaunt black ribs like the skeletons of great unclean beasts who have died because Bonny water was too strong even for them."

This was the "white man's grave" that Europeans justly feared, the killing seaboard of which the sailors sang:

> Beware and take care
>   Of the Bight of Benin:
> For one that comes out
>   There are forty go in.

Death by malaria was not so common by the end of the nineteenth century, thanks to quinine, but malaria was not the only killer. Yellow fever slew nine out of eleven Europeans resident at Bonny not long before Mary Kingsley's first visit. A fine show of callous humor was the accepted style among Europeans who were obliged to live in Bonny and its sister-ports; no doubt in self-defense, they felt it a duty to make their visitors' teeth rattle. "I went ashore to have tea with Captain Boler," says Miss Kingsley, "and was told more details about this particular epidemic, to say nothing of other epidemics. In one which the captain experienced, at the fourth funeral, two youngsters (junior clerks of the deceased) from drink brought on by fright, fell into the grave before the coffin, which got lowered on to them, and all

Partners in Trade

three had to be hauled out again. 'Barely necessary though, was it?' said another member of the party, 'for those two had to have a grave of their own before next sundown.' "

Yet at least it could be said of Bonny that its captives were delivered, decade after decade, with a minimum of violence and disorder. Elsewhere in the delta the organization was less peaceful. There was much armed raiding for captives, especially in the high days of "King Sugar" when slaves in the Caribbean were always in short supply. At Old Calabar, a little east of Bonny, Efik traders occasionally sold their own "criminals" — those found guilty of theft, adultery, or political awkwardness — but their regular practice was to put small cannon into large canoes and send parties upstream to press-gang any villagers they could find. Now and then they had the practical help of their European partners.

A typical joint enterprise appears in the memoir of an English sailor, Isaac Parker, who was five months in Old Calabar in 1765 and took part in one of these river expeditions.* A trader called Dick Ebro had invited him. They armed several canoes and went upstream into the maze of creeks behind the coast. There they landed and lay "under the bushes in the day when they came near a village," and took hold "of every one they could see." These unfortunates were handcuffed and loaded into the canoes, which then went on to another likely place.

This anarchy and terror in the hinterland (yet reaching, perhaps, no more than a few dozen miles from the ocean surf) was generally though not invariably in contrast with the peace and calm of trading operations at the point of delivery. By the eighteenth century, as we have seen earlier in this book, these operations rested on long years of familiar custom. Relations between

* Parker had sailed with the famous British explorer, Captain Cook, and is said to have had a "highly respectable" reputation.

FRONTIER OF OPPORTUNITY

the two sides were seldom intimate, but they were often marked by trust and a certain rough friendship. There was lavish hospitality on the African side. An eyewitness afterwards recalled of a characteristic banquet in the nineteenth century that the food was brought in by a "file of stout girls in native undress, each bearing on her head a large covered calabash . . . yams and fish, stewed together with palm oil, vegetables, and pepper . . . laughing and joking," and Eyamba, the house ruler, "helped them all himself, in succession . . . without asking anyone what he would choose. . . ."

There were feasts like this beyond number. After the feasting came the business. Many tales have survived of this tantalizing and often lengthy engagement.* Neither side could ever be quite sure of the other's good intentions because of the violence of the times, but even more because of the exceeding complication in weights and measures and currencies that were used. They watched each other warily. Yet most of these stories bear witness to a commercial stability that was strong enough to hold firm through many stiff meetings, hints of dark suspicion of betrayal, sudden outbursts of armed distrust, and all the other hazards and hesitations of a trade that had never proved easy.

Something of the complications on the delta coast can be seen from James Barbot's report on prices at New Calabar in 1699. He was buying ship's stores for a voyage to the Caribbean by way of the Congo, and needed 50,000 yams. These he eventually obtained at the price of one standard-sized bar for 60 "king's yams" — first quality — and one bar for 150 "slaves' yams." Butts of water cost two standard-sized iron rings each. "For the length of wood, seven bars, which is dear; but they were to deliver it ready cut into our boat. For a goat, one bar. A cow, ten or eight bars, according to its bigness. A hog, two bars. . . ."

* See pages 87-96.

Partners in Trade

Yet by far the best account of what the trade was really like in these delta city-states has come from an African source. It was discovered a few years ago in an Edinburgh library: the diary of an Old Calabar house ruler called Antera Duke that tells of the years 1785-1788, and vividly projects the African-Atlantic partnership from a delta viewpoint.

At Old Calabar there was neither a divine king nor an all-powerful oracle to help both government and trade. Here the "rich men and prime merchants" of the estuary — at their settlements of Duke Town, Old Town, Henshaw Town, Creek Town — managed their affairs, conducted their administration, and maintained their authority, not by ancient law or inherited custom, but by a new and exclusive society called *Egbo*, an Efik word meaning "leopard." Egbo was something between a wizard's gathering, a municipal executive, and an early African version of a businessman's club; and it possessed powerful religious and legal sanctions. It was not an aristocratic establishment, for anyone who became rich could always buy his way into it. Indeed, its essential function was to defend the interests of the rich and to safeguard their powers of government over lesser men and slaves. Egbo, in brief, was another instance of development towards a "political society" under the stimulus of new economic conditions and opportunities.

Egbo made the laws and also administered them. "Under the aegis of the chief and the important elders of the town," Simmons has written, "the Leopard Society promulgated and enforced laws, judged important cases, recovered debts, protected the property of members, and constituted the actual executive government." It punished crime and, whenever this was thought necessary, enforced trade boycotts against Europeans — to the point that some European traders also found it worth their while to buy themselves into membership of Egbo. The system was oligarchical,

FRONTIER OF OPPORTUNITY

but not necessarily antisocial in the circumstances of the time. "For it gave to all men of wealth," in Jones's words, "an overriding common interest in preserving the stability of the society and the social order of which it formed a part."

This was the society and social order that is portrayed in Antera Duke's diary. At first sight, even when changed into ordinary English from the trading "pidgin" of the coast, much of the diary seems incomprehensible. The entry for January 28, 1785, is clear enough:

> About 6 a.m. at Aqua Landing; a fine morning so I worked in my small yard. At 2 o'clock afternoon we two go aboard Captain Small's (ship) with three slaves. So he takes two and we came back.*

The original — to offer an example of Antera Duke's language — reads like this:

> about 6 am in aqua Landing with fine morning so I have work for my small yard after 2 oclock noon wee two go Bord Captin Smal with 3 slave so his tak two and wee come back.

Only two of the slaves were robust enough for Captain Small, so the third had to be brought back again. A small business that day, yet business as usual. Two days later Antera Duke is once again at Aqua Landing at six in the morning:

> a foggy morning, so I was going to work in my little yard, but at the same time we and Tom Aqua and John Aqua joined together to catch men.

A different business, but still as usual.

Next day another note is struck, and the obscurities begin.

---

* "Pidgin," according to Daryll Forde, was "a jargon which was mainly English in vocabulary although the constructions were often modelled on those of Ibibio." English renderings here are by Simmons.

Partners in Trade

Again the energetic merchant is up at six in the morning and walking the quayside. Since the morning is very foggy, he goes back to work in his yard, not expecting any ship's boats, but:

> after that Duke and all of us went to King Egbo to share Egbo money for 40 men.

What is one to make of this? The answer is that the club was sharing out its new members' entrance fees. Whenever a man was admitted to the Leopard Society he had to pay an initiation fee that was divided among all the members. In this case there were forty new members, and their fees were evidently worth a note.

Egbo and its operations are never long absent from the diary. They could not be, for they permeated every aspect of Efik life, an all-embracing system of laws and sanctions grafted skillfully to Efik beliefs in magic and the supernatural. On October 26, 1786, the diarist is not feeling well, so he starts by taking medicine. The day is to prove a busy one:

> Then heard that Egbo was run and when I heard I walked up to Egbo Young. We saw Egbo come down and the Egbo men said that Sam Ambo and George Cobham had blown on Captain Fairweather. So all our family were damn angry about that blow and we sent to call Captain Fairweather to come ashore and break trade first with our family for about 15 slaves and we fired three guns on shore. . . .

Here we have a dispute between a pair of African traders — Sam Ambo and George Cobham — and one of the slaving captains whose ship was anchored in the estuary. They had called out the police (the second grade of Egbo, known as "Brass Egbo" and responsible for law enforcement), and the police had "blown on Captain Fairweather." They had declared, that is, a suspension of trade between the disputing parties until an understanding should be reached. Antera Duke's family were "damn angry" because Captain Fairweather happened to be a client of theirs as well; so they sent aboard to ask him to come ashore notwithstanding, and fired three guns to clinch their offer. How Antera and his family arranged matters is not explained, but evidently all went off well because

> at 3 o'clock in the afternoon we saw Eyo and Ebetim come down with Esin Ambo, and they went to Sam and George Cobham to make them settle with Captain Fairweather.

A few days later the Leopard Society is conducting a religious duty peculiar to the Establishment of Old Calabar. Duke Ephraim, the leading man of Duke Town, has died; and at once there is the customary call for human sacrifice to accompany his funeral.

> About 4 a.m. I got up; there was great rain, so I walked to the palaver house and I found all the gentlemen here. So we got ready to cut off heads and at 5 o'clock in the morning we began to cut slaves' heads off, fifty heads off in that one day. I carried 29 cases of bottled brandy, and 15 calabashes of chop for everybody, and there was play in every yard in town.

Human sacrifice at the death of a leading man had long been inseparable from the traditional ritual and religious requirements of a number of Iron Age cultures. It was present in the delta just because it also existed in the cultures of the forest belt — notably at Benin and in other forest states such as Ashanti. There, of course, one should not imagine it as necessarily a matter of terror or dismay. Acceptance of death by royal wives and relatives and servants was a question of moral integrity and of quick passage to an honorable place among the "other half of humanity" — those who lived as spirits. What seems to have happened in some of the states that were profoundly affected by the coastal trade was that the custom of human sacrifice became increasingly distorted, both into a means of "conspicuous consumption" by

Partners in Trade

display of wealth in slaves and, as time went on, into an instrument of political repression.

Certainly this distortion grew worse. Its occasional terror reached a climax in the years of acute commercial insecurity that followed the abolition of the slave trade. Then, with the mainstay of these societies cut suddenly away, superstition sank to gruesome depths; it was into these that Benin would fall. A European missionary has left an eyewitness account of the greatest of the funeral holocausts of the delta states — that which accompanied the death of Eyamba V of Old Calabar in 1847. "Eyamba," he wrote, "had many wives, of the best families in the country, as also many slave concubines. . . . Of the former, thirty died the first day. How many by the poison ordeal, under imputation of witchcraft against his life, we never knew. Those who were honoured to accompany him into *Obio Ekpu*, or Ghost Land, were summoned in succession, by the message, once an honour, now a terror, 'King calls you.' The doomed one quickly adorned herself, drank off a mug of rum, and followed the messenger. Immediately she was in the hands of the executioners, who strangled her with a silk handkerchief. . . .

"Every night the work of death went on in the river, and screams of the victims were heard both in the ships and the mission-house. Some were sent out bound in canoes, and deliberately drowned. Others returning from distant markets, chanting their paddle songs and glad to get home, but ignorant of what had taken place, were waylaid, knocked on the head and tumbled into the river."

After Eyamba's funeral and its scenes of blood, European missionaries persuaded Egbo to pass a law forbidding human sacrifice. But the law was futile; an accretion from outside, it took no account of what the ruling oligarchy believed. Caught in its own trap of superstition, the lawmaking and law-enforcing Leopard

Society of rich men and prime merchants was powerless to control, much less to stop, these periodical though infrequent massacres. By now, moreover, sacrifice had also become a political weapon that was useful to powerful men as a means of destroying rivals. Eyamba had already used it in this way after the death of his predecessor. "Ordinary folk," Jones has written in his study of Calabar political organization, "might believe in the genuineness of these witchcraft accusations; the more knowledgeable recognised them as a deliberate method of removing dangerous rivals, weakening powerful houses, and settling old scores."

But where the law failed to stop human sacrifice, revolt succeeded. There now arose another society — a society, this time, of the slaves of the palm-oil plantations — that was vowed to self-protection. This society was called the Blood Men, and its object was not to shed blood but to save it. In the years after Eyamba's death the Blood Men gathered in the plantations around Old Calabar whenever an important man died, and marched to town in such force as to overawe any dignitary who should try to sacrifice a slave. The massacres were stopped.

Such was the highly specialized society that was called to life by the long years of coastal partnership. Nowhere in the delta — or, in different circumstances, along the whole of the Guinea Coast — was the product quite the same; and often the contrasts were many and vivid. Yet by and large, along wide reaches of the Gulf of Guinea, there arose a special network of economic and political conditions that would have remained unthinkable but for the oversea trade in general, and the slave trade in particular.

These societies became what they were through African tradition, native ingenuity, local eccentricities of soil and geography and population, but also through the nature of the commerce in which they were engaged. Throughout the whole record one can

Partners in Trade

see this last point repeatedly emphasized. It is clear in the delta. It is clear in the evolution of the small seaboard states of the Gold Coast littoral (the coast of modern Ghana), where no fewer than fourteen statelets were in existence by the seventeenth century. It is clear in the trading stations of the Slave Coast of modern Dahomey. The European connection, insisting on slaves, became an inseparable part of a close-woven scheme of cause and effect which brought new societies into being and which kept them alive and energetic, though at bitter cost to others. It is this that makes the underlying theme of Antera Duke's diary.

Week after week the entries recall each other.

> We settled comey [customs dues exacted by the towns of Old Calabar from all trading ships] on board Potter. . . .
> Captain Aspinall's ship goes away with 328 slaves. . . .
> Potter and his tender went away with 350 slaves. . . .
> At three o'clock after noon Captain Fairweather went away with 377 slaves. . . .
> We saw Combesboch tender go away with 280 slaves. . . .

The slavers pulled up their anchors and warped to the broad estuary, broke their sails and took their course for the Americas, the sultry coastal waters heaving in reluctant wake hour after hour, year after year, century after century. Such speed as they could make was the essence of their business. Too long on the coast would ruin their cargo and probably themselves; and they relied, as they had to rely, on a firm and efficient understanding with their friends ashore. By the end of the seventeenth century the partnership was known and valued and acknowledged. Its political effects were in full bloom.

5 Behind the Coast

THE HISTORY OF THE LANDS BEHIND THE GUINEA SEABOARD IS IN an altogether different situation from that of the hinterland of East Africa or the near-coastal regions of the Congo.

Here in the forest belt of Guinea there were powerful states and societies of which much is known and recorded. They had grown in strength and self-confidence from the early years of the present millennium, but their origins lay much further back in the obscure beginnings of the West African Iron Age. These forest states had seldom or never lost touch with the trading empires of the Sudanese grasslands and, through them, with the peoples of the Nile and North Africa. Many elements of their broad and varied culture, whether in the symbols of religion, the manners of government, or the techniques of art and industry, reveal an ancient and creative interweaving of ideas that were both native to their country and borrowed from northern neighbors.

It was from these forest states that Europe by way of Arab intermediaries drew the bulk of its supply of gold throughout medieval times. It was to them that grassland caravans took the copper of Darfur and Saharan Tegedda so that the master artists of Ife might cast their fine sculpture. For many centuries before European arrival on the coast, these countries were profoundly involved with the world to the north of them. But then, with that arrival, their horizon changed. So did the nature of their trade. And their history underwent a crucial change.

Even at today's early stage in historical research it would take several volumes to tell this story in any detail. All that I am going to attempt in these brief pages is to show where and how the oversea slave trade, exerting tremendous pressure, struck

Behind the Coast

along the lines of organizational weakness and finally if blindly split these forest states apart.

All the great states of the forest — Oyo, Benin, those of the Akan and Dahomey — became deeply involved in the slave trade; and each was influenced by its strains and pressures. More often than not, however, the consequences were in notable contrast with the political growth that occurred along the coast and most of all in the delta city-states. For whereas the peoples of the delta absorbed new tensions by evolving new forms of social organization, the states of the interior showed an increasing rigidity and resistance to political growth. Often enough, although with many local variations, their feudalism turned inward on itself, their elected rulers became tyrants, and the fabric of their social life grew dangerously stiff and insensitive. Though trading vastly with the coast, they traded increasingly to their own ruin. They grew powerful on this commerce, but their power proved mortal.

One can isolate three decisive aspects of this inland situation. The first is one of inner structure. These forest systems were based on ancient and elaborate ideologies of divine kingship and protonational exclusiveness, and each was powerfully cemented within itself by customary ties and religious loyalties. This idea of "belonging" was often a particular strength. But it proved a general weakness in face of the European demand for slaves. For it promoted among each of these peoples a conviction that "non-belongers" — that is, their territorial neighbors — were fair game for enslavement.

Every war became, as it were, a religious war in which a man fought not only for his own profit or in self-defense but also for a special and exclusive notion of "truth and survival beyond the grave." There is a broad sense in which these West African raiding and slaving wars were akin to the wars of religion between Christians and Muslims or Protestants and Catholics. It became

FRONTIER OF OPPORTUNITY

not only right and proper but even necessary to treat "nonbelievers" with much the same kind of indifference or active persecution that Europeans, for their part, had visited on "heretic and heathen." Salvation lay only within one's own group; the rest of humanity, no matter the color of its skin, was beyond the pale. Unions of related groups were successfully forged here and there in West Africa — notably among the Ashanti and among the Ibo of the eastern delta — but any general concept of West African unity over against an outside power such as that which could at times unite Christians in Europe or Muslims elsewhere was out of the question. With most of these groups the social mold was consciously and compulsively "separatist." It could not be reformed. It could only be broken.

And in the end it was the very strength of these forest systems that proved the crucial stumbling block to social change. Caught in their separate networks of belief about man and his future in the other world, these peoples were generally incapable of meeting a postfeudal economic challenge — the oversea trade in chattel slaves, in men as mere commodities — by developing a postfeudal political society. What some of them did develop instead was a different thing — an autocracy or militarized government that was new but also socially sterile. For this autocracy was not a dictatorship within a political system that could stimulate and yield to internal political opposition, and so move to newer forms of social organization; it was a personal rule that was based on the immutable sanctions of divine kingship and priesthood. Rebels there were; but the rebels, more often than not, were sold for export.

A second decisive aspect of the situation was inherent in the new rivalries of trade. Relations between the hinterland states were increasingly poisoned by a fight for monopolist privilege in the supply of slaves. Feudal wars widened into commercial

Behind the Coast

wars. Commercial wars, duly sanctioned by religion, degenerated into a free-for-all where any man might seize another — "panyar" him, in the doggerel of the slaving coast — if only his power sufficed. And at this point, precisely, a third aspect intervened: the advent of firearms in large quantity. With this, the feudal and commercial wars became wars for survival.

Such was the trinity of pressures — autocracy, monopoly, musket warfare — that was set in violent motion by the oversea slave trade and governed much of the subsequent history of those parts of West Africa most directly in contact with Europe.

Oyo, the old and venerable, greatest of the Yoruba states and the one which eventually included Ife, home of some of the world's finest sculpture, is a prime example of the process. Oyo began to achieve power and influence over wide regions at about the same time as the Portuguese sojourned in Benin, somewhat to the south and east. Oyo's standing armies assured loyalty to the Alafin, Oyo's ruler, and brought tribute to his government from vassal peoples as far afield as Borgu and Nupe in the northern grasslands, from the tribes of central Nigeria, from Dahomey in the west, and some from the small peoples of the coast itself. Even the distant states of the north, lying many hundreds of miles away, came to hear of Oyo as a wealthy partner in business and a useful ally in war.

Like its immediate neighbors, the Oyo governing system became entangled in the oversea slave trade by small degrees, from a little to a little more and finally to much. And here as elsewhere it was firearms that proved the irresistible bait. They offered the overwhelming weapon superiority — exercised by professional soldiers — that feudal rulers in West Africa had never before possessed over the mass of people. They were crucial in the shift of African feudalism from its "tribal and popular" form (as I have discussed it earlier in this book) into forms of autocracy that were

FRONTIER OF OPPORTUNITY

sometimes broadly comparable with those of European feudalism in high medieval times. For these rulers the road to more power and prestige lay directly through the purchase of firearms. If the price of firearms was slaving, they no doubt paid it with a light heart — at any rate, in the beginning. Afterwards, when it was too late for them to draw back, they came to see that muskets and slaving could also lead in quite another direction.

Soon enough, as matters turned, the Alafin found that his coastwise tributaries were intent on entering this lucrative business on their own; so were some of his own Yoruba vassals. Why should they continue paying tribute or fealty to Oyo when they were strong enough to defy the Alafin, or make a better profit through trading on their own account? By the second half of the seventeenth century there were enough guns in the coastal areas (bought in exchange for slaves delivered by the vassals of Oyo and Benin) to enable this new defiance to be made good. More and more of the Alafin's wealth and the effort of his armies were lost in sterile and ultimately fruitless wars of reassertion and reconquest.

Early in the nineteenth century these wars of attrition were capped by another disaster to Oyo. The northern regions of the empire were seized by new invaders from the grassland. These were the emirs of the Fulani, advancing southward under the furious banners of reforming Islam, pushing their conquests through Hausaland to the very frontiers of the forest belt. Once they had secured Ilorin, lying between Oyo and the Niger, they had severed the Alafin and his chiefs from their northerly source of captives for the coastal trade. The Fulani held firm; Oyo failed to dislodge them. And this befell the Alafin at a moment when the strongest of his southern vassals, the lord of Dahomey, had become powerful enough to declare his own independence of Oyo.

Although it fought hard, Oyo could not for long contain this double threat to its imperial system. Already weakened by the falling away of Yoruba vassals, the empire dwindled. The Alafin's high-handed authority failed or altogether disappeared. And so complete was this effacement that even the name of Oyo was forgotten or ignored in the outside world, although Oyo, more truly perhaps than any other West African state of the forest belt, had embodied in itself the flower of an ancient and memorable system of government. At the same time it ought to be remarked that Oyo, in spite of all its tribulations, vanished with a notable reputation in these countries, leaving behind it the savor of an age of considerable distinction. Benin, its neighbor and to some extent its successor, declined into a different fate.

6 Disaster at Benin

WHEN THE EARLY PORTUGUESE VOYAGERS REACHED BENIN, THEY found it the powerful capital of a considerable empire. In 1500 the city was a league long from gate to gate. A large moat, "very wide and deep," sufficed for defense. Its rule was said to be effective over an area that was about the size of southern England and Wales. All this is confirmed by Bini tradition. Egharevba, the historian of Benin, believes that the city entered its greatest period under Oba Ewerare the Great, who ruled in the years immediately preceding Portuguese arrival.

Though continuously in Benin throughout the sixteenth century, the Portuguese do not seem to have written much about it. They were well received as traders or missionaries, and on at least one occasion the king in Lisbon received an ambassador from the Oba of Benin; but their records, or at least those so far published, are disappointingly thin. With the coming of the Dutch at the beginning of the seventeenth century, the written sources greatly improve, for the Dutch were deeply interested in their trading partners. They wrote letters to their principals in Holland that are full of useful details of Benin.

"The Towne seemeth to be very great, when you enter it," says one of these Dutch accounts, evidently dating from 1602. "You goe into a great broad street, not paved, which seemeth to be seven or eight times broader than the Warmoes Street in Amsterdam; which goeth right out, and never crooketh, and where I was lodged with Mattheus Cornelison it was at least a quarter of an houres going from the gate, and yet I could not see to the end of the street. . . .

"At the gate where I entered on horsebacke, I saw a very high Bulwarke, very thick of earth, with a very deepe broad ditch, but it was drie, and full of high trees. . . . The gate is a reasonable good Gate, made of wood after their manner, which is to be shut, and there always there is watch holden. . . ."

But the rulers of Benin, though hospitable, were jealous of their authority and perhaps apprehensive for it, too. They would allow these traders from Europe no more than a limited freedom.

"When you are in the great Street aforesaid, you see many great streets on the sides thereof, which also goe right forth, but you cannot see the end of them, by reason of their great length. A man might write more of the situation of this Towne, if he might see it as you may see the Townes of Holland, which is not permitted there, by one that alwaies goes with you — some men say, that he goeth with you, because you should have no harme done unto you, but yet you goe no further than he will let you."

Benin was prosperous and comfortable in those early years of the seventeenth century. "The Houses in this Towne," continues this same Dutch report, "stand in good order, one close and even with the other, as the Houses in Holland stand." Steps led by to the entry of the houses of "men of qualitie," and here there were galleries "where a man may sit drie; which Gallerie every morning is made cleane by their Slaves, and in it there is a Mat spread for men to sit on . . . but they have other places besides, as Kitchins and other roomes. . . ."

The palace of the king, the Oba, was almost a "Forbidden City" within Benin. "The King's Court is very great, within it having many great four-square Plaines, which round about them have Galleries, wherein there is alwais watch kept; I was so far within the Court, that I passed over four such great Plaines, and wheresoever I looked, still I saw Gates upon Gates, to goe into other places, and in that sort I went as far as any Netherlander was, which was to the Stable where his best Horses stood. . . ."

When Olfert Dapper published his great collection of African reports some fifty years later, he was able to include an engraving which showed how Benin appeared to the Dutch travelers of the early seventeenth century. There, in that well-known picture, one may see the Oba riding in ceremonial procession with the city massed behind him in its dense urbanity and surmounted by the little turrets of the Oba's wooden Kremlin, each bearing "a copper bird with its wings spread." (Plate 14)

John Barbot, who was on the Guinea Coast between 1678 and 1682, says that "the inhabitants of this great city are for the generality very civil and good-natured people, easy to be dealt with, condescending to what Europeans require of them in a civil way, and very ready to return double the presents we make them. . . ." And although Barbot was writing at second hand or even third hand, borrowing from Dapper, who had borrowed from other Dutchmen, he was undoubtedly in a good position to know about the reputation of Benin among his fellow-traders and travelers.

These were impressed with the efficiency of Benin's government by a system of "king in council." Barbot remarks that "the king might be considered just and equitable, as desiring continually his officers to administer justice exactly, and to discharge their duties conscientiously. . . . He seldom passes one day, without holding a cabinet council with his chief ministers, for dispatching of the many affairs brought before him . . . appeals from inferior courts of judicature in all the parts of the kingdom, and audiences to strangers, or concerning the affairs of war and other emergencies. . . ." Though based on hearsay, these notes offer a fair enough picture of the main structure of government in Benin at least up to the middle of the seventeenth century.

There was extensive trade between Benin and vassal states or neighbors that were not vassals. Much of this trade, perhaps most of it, was a royal monopoly; but it was one that was much abused, as the Dutch soon found, by the Oba's chiefs and agents who were entrusted with the duty of bargaining with Europeans. No foreigner, according to Dapper, could bargain or buy except through the Oba's delegates or merchants whom he had empowered for the purpose (to whom, in other words, the Oba had "farmed out" the privilege of dealing with Europeans); and both sides thereafter were at the mercy of these agents and merchants. Sales could take months to complete.

Internal trade was more loosely organized. "They also have severall places in the Towne, where they keepe their Markets; in one place they have their great Market Day, called Dia de Ferro" — a witness to long Portuguese presence here — "and in another place they hold their little market, called Ferro. . . . They bring great store of Ironworke to sell there, and instruments to fish withall, others to plow and to till the land withall; and many weapons, as Assagaies and Knives. . . . This Market and Traffique is there very orderly holden." Barbot lists the exports of Benin as cotton cloths, jasper stones, skins, ivory, pepper, blue coral

Disaster at Benin

beads, and female slaves; no men slaves, he says, could be taken from Benin whether they were foreigners or not.

This "city-empire" had trouble with its neighbors like every other feudal state; sometimes it was successful, thanks to the valor of its kings, while at other times it failed. Like Oyo, Benin imported firearms to bolster the power of its armies and even, in the sixteenth century, made some use of European mercenaries by alliance with the Portuguese.

The Dutch accounts show that these feudal wars were generally to Benin's advantage up to the middle of the seventeenth century. But after that a steep decline set in. Earlier wars of conquest within a feudal pattern were now giving way to wars for slaves, and the fabric of Benin society seems to have suffered increasingly from this. In 1700 the well-informed Dutch agent at Elmina, William Bosman, was writing home to Holland that Benin no longer deserved the name of city. "Formerly this village was very thick and close-built," he told his employers in Amsterdam, "but now the Houses stand like poor men's corn, widely distant from each other." By this time, Fage adds, in a modern comment, "the continual warfare was destroying the prosperity and even the structure of the state. Large areas of the country had become depopulated and uncultivated. The armies returned with fewer and fewer slaves and sometimes destroyed each other in conflicts for what little booty there was to be found."

The decay continued and, with it, the failure to produce new solutions to new problems. Perhaps this Bini feudalism had already reached its point of maximum possible expansion and was in any case due for eclipse; and perhaps eclipse would have occurred without the intervention of new forms of war and trade. Even if that had been the case, though, decay could scarcely have taken the shape it did without the inescapable pressures of wholesale slaving and musket warfare.

FRONTIER OF OPPORTUNITY

Faced with an economic challenge which, if successful, could only depopulate the country and lead from one destructive conflict to another, the Bini Obas and their priests proved incapable of resisting it. Thus the government of Benin failed to escape from its Iron Age framework of divine kingship and theocratic rule; moreover, these institutions were reinforced and at the same time distorted. Through these years of impoverishment the royal monopoly apparently held firm and grew even stronger. Threatened by rivals, whether African or European, the Bini kingship fell back upon a theocratic tyranny that was operated in the name of the Oba by a priesthood of whom the Oba was increasingly a helpless tool.

Something of this may be traced in the decline of Benin's famous sculpture. Inherited from Ife, Benin metalwork was of high technical competence from at any rate the fifteenth century. Metal-casters in this city knew how to make heads and figures with great artistic skill and economy of metal, and their art in its best period — the fifteenth and sixteenth centuries — would have been outstanding in any continent. It was, one should note, specifically an art of the Oba's court, drawing on royal motifs, celebrating the Oba's power, portraying his soldiers and his allies, and always distinct from the popular work of the Edo peoples of whom the Bini were a part. This popular work, being a branch of the wide-ranging metal craftsmanship of the Lower Niger region, possessed a much more relaxed style and less formal choice of subject.

The courtly art of Benin grew notably coarser during the years of slaving warfare. After the end of the sixteenth century, in William Fagg's careful judgment, the heads and figures "became much more stereotyped and lacking in sensitivity, even though gaining a certain impressive quality." By now the emphatic humanism of the Ife heads was completely eclipsed; and one can draw a consistent and instructive parallel (without meaning to suggest that naturalism is necessarily "better" than abstraction) between the heavy styles of late Benin work, increasingly crude in conception and dense in weight of metal, and Benin's political decline after the middle of the eighteenth century. Moreover, this process of coarsening can be shown to have continued; the heads became clumsier and more gross in shape and feeling as the slaving years passed by and the old skills were overborne or set aside. (Plates 5 to 9)

By now, sharpening the anxiety of Benin's rulers, the delta states were in full bloom. They imported firearms of their own and defied the Oba as and when they would. Here the consequences were much the same as with Oyo: firearms could bolster the power of a central government, but they could also, in the hands of vassal states, lead to painful disintegration.

In defending their privilege and power, the priests of the Oba knew of only one final sanction, and that was ritual sacrifice. Once again one should be careful of the distinction between customary sacrifice and its distortion. "No person of rank or wealth," Dapper had recorded of mid-seventeenth century Benin, "dies there unaccompanied by bloodshed." Yet this, one may repeat, had been bloodshed of a special kind. "They let down the corpse into the pit," a Frenchman recorded of the 1670's (writing of what Europeans had reported about Benin at that time), "and then the most beloved domesticks of both sexes earnestly beg to be allow'd the favour of going into it, to wait and attend on their master in the other life; but this honour is granted only to the best qualified among them, and those the deceased king seemed most fond of, which often occasions great murmurings and discussions amongst them."

Some two centuries later, discussing the same point, Rattray would make the same explanation of sacrificial rites in old Ashanti.

There too the death of famous men was accompanied by bloodshed, but not, once again, for callous or bloodthirsty reasons. "In the first place, the persons killed on these occasions were supposed to resume after death their various duties under their royal master. . . . The ideas and beliefs of the men who acted as executioners on these occasions and of their 'victims' with regard to death were the same. Death was merely a transition, like birth, from one kind of life to another." Secondly, Rattray thought, the attitude towards death in those days was "one of comparative indifference," since people were not filled "with any vague, troublesome misgivings" about what would happen to them after death. Thirdly, most of those killed at funerals were "either prisoners of war, whose lives had only been spared for this purpose, or criminals who had been tried and sentenced to death, but like the former class had been preserved for such an occasion."

But most important of all, in Rattray's view, there was the positive wish for death among some of the highest in the land — "high court officials, relatives and wives of the dead monarch, who, no longer having any desire to live once 'the great tree had fallen,' compelled their relatives to slay them." And Rattray, who knew the failings of the Ashanti and yet loved them for their virtues, concluded: "The man or woman who, like some of these old Ashanti, was ready to die for an ideal, however misguided and mistaken it may have been, nevertheless is of the stuff which goes to the making of a virile and courageous nation, and is entitled to our respect and admiration."

Nothing like this can be said of the sacrificial habits of the Benin government during the last years of decline in the late nineteenth century, any more than similar explanations can be valid for the occasional massacres that the Blood Men stopped. These disasters were the measure of an institutional failure — a failure which should be attributed, not to a lack of natural capacity,

Disaster at Benin

but rather to the combination of circumstances that pushed steadily towards ruin. It is obviously true, of course, that this ruin was of limited extent. It was particular to Benin institutions, not general to the whole society. It left much of society intact, for these were strong and fertile peoples who have easily survived those bludgeoning years. Yet the old order and dignity of Benin were nonetheless destroyed.

This fatal combination of circumstance may be traced in the Bini system of royal trading monopoly, but even more decisively in the traditional sanctions of Bini religion. As early as the 1780's one may see how matters were trending. Already trade was less than in former times, and already the priesthood seems to have fallen back on its final sanction of human sacrifice in an effort to restore "the good old days." Every year, according to one British visitor, three or four people were sacrificed as "offerings to the sea, to direct vessels to bind their course to this horrid climate." As the coastal pressures grew stronger and Benin's trade continued to shrink, the priests redoubled their frenzy until Benin, towards the end of the nineteenth century, indeed became "a city of blood." The threat of European invasion was almost certainly the last and fatal incentive; and the Oba, by now, was powerless to stop the slaughter even when he had wished to do so. "The king," wrote Captain Gallwey in 1893, "struck me as being very willing to listen to reason, but he is tied down by fetish customs, and until the power of the fetish priests is done away with," there could be no peace. A couple of years later the British sent in a military force and made peace under a new power. And when the colonial period came to an end, sixty-five years later, the way was at last clear for full institutional adjustment to the needs and opportunities of the modern world.

FRONTIER OF OPPORTUNITY

7 One Gun: One Slave

IT IS ONE THING TO NOTE THE FAILURE OF AFRICAN CHIEFS AND governing institutions to parry the disintegrating and destructive pressure of the oversea slave trade. It is quite another to suggest that, given their circumstances and opportunities, they could ever have succeeded in doing so.

They were in any case never offered the chance of success. At no point were they presented with any choice except that of foregoing European trade altogether — to the almost certain profit of rivals and their own peril — or else of surrendering to the incessant demands of Europe. Cases were not lacking when African rulers struggled against this bitter choice and tried to limit or even to abolish the export of slaves; but these efforts were always — and, as one may think, necessarily — fruitless.

Affonso of Congo was not the only African ruler who attempted to free his country from the barbs of the slaving hook. A firsthand Swedish report of 1787 tells of an African king of Senegal in the far west of Africa who, "very much to his honour, enacted a law that no slave whatever should be marched through his territories."

This laudable measure could only remain a dead letter. For "at this time several French vessels lay at anchor in the Senegal [River], waiting for slaves. The route of the black traders in consequence of this edict of the king was stopped, and the slaves carried to other parts. The French, unable on this account to complete their cargoes, remonstrated with the king. He was, however, very unpropitious to their representations, for he returned the presents which had been sent him by the [French] Senegal Company, of which I myself was a witness, declaring at the same time that all the riches of that company should not divert him from

One Gun: One Slave

his design. In this situation of affairs, the French were obliged to have recourse to their old friends, the Moors. These, who had before shewn themselves so ready on such occasions, were no less ready and active in this. They set off in parties to surprise the unoffending negroes and to carry them all the calamities of war. . . ."

Sixty years earlier the rising power of Dahomey on the Slave Coast had prompted another effort of the same kind. In 1727, invading the towns of the Slave Coast, the king of Dahomey captured an Englishman called Captain Bullfinch Lamb and tried, through him, to reduce the local impact of the slave trade — a scourge from which his own people had suffered fearfully in the recent past. After holding him in honorable imprisonment at Abomey, the Dahomeyan capital some sixty miles from the sea, the king allowed Lamb to take ship for England, giving him a present of 320 ounces of gold and 80 slaves, and bidding him inform his masters (the phrasing, of course, is Lamb's) that "the Natives would sell themselves to us on condition of not being carried away."

This proposal met with no favor in London, needless to say, since no investor had any interest in buying slaves for use on the Guinea Coast; but the trading figures nonetheless show a remarkable decline after Dahomey had won control of the points of actual export.

Hitherto — that is, before 1727 — this fifty-mile segment of palm-fringed seaboard had earned its name in full measure, for its little city-states of Ardra and Ouidah (Whydah or Fida) and Jacquin were tremendous deliverers of slaves. Of Ouidah, important among these Slave Coast ports, Barbot could write in the 1680's that "they are so diligent in the slave trade that they are able to deliver a thousand every month." And a British naval surgeon some forty years later was still able to note that this was "the greatest trading

FRONTIER OF OPPORTUNITY

place in the coast of Guinea, selling off as many slaves, I believe, as all the rest together: forty or fifty sail (French, English, Portuguese and Dutch) freighting thence every year." Europeans had made regular establishments here, and in 1677 the Portuguese had even built themselves a little fort at Ouidah so as to manage the trade more efficiently. A curious fragment of the past, the Ouidah fort remains a Portuguese possession to this day, being officially part of the "oversea province of São Tomé and Principe Islands." *
(Plates 25 and 26)

Up to 1727, when Dahomey broke through successfully to the coast and achieved direct contact with the European traders who were there, annual exports from Ardra and Ouidah were running at about 20,000 captives a year. Thereafter they seem to have fallen sharply and never to have recovered their former scale. The governor of Britain's Slave Coast trading post, Archibald Dalzell, reported in 1789 that "the greatest number now sent off from this place [Ouidah] and the two great kingdoms of Ardra and Dahomey, together with several smaller ones united to them, is only 5,500." In a period when total delivery of slaves from Africa was touching levels that were higher than ever before, the Slave Coast seems no longer to have deserved its reputation.

For this reason and for several others, Dahomey was a state organization which remains of the highest interest in the study of African institutions. Here I want only to draw attention to one or two elements in its extraordinary condition. They show very clearly why the wounds of the slave trade had become really inescapable.

Like the city-states of the delta, and like those of the Slave Coast,

---

* The garrison of this fort of "St. John the Baptist" was officially doubled in 1960 — from one Portuguese officer to two. In July, 1961, the Government of the Dahomey Republic gave the Portuguese Government an ultimatum to quit Ouidah by the end of the month.

One Gun: One Slave

Dahomey was a child of the African-European connection. It seems to have emerged at the beginning of the seventeenth century, or about 1625, when the Fon people of the country behind the Slave Coast drew together in self-defense against the slave-raiding of their eastern neighbors, the Yoruba of Oyo. No doubt the Fon were interested in defending themselves from coastal raiders too; whenever the king of Ouidah was short of slaves for sale, declared a British report of 1721, "he marches an army, and depopulates. He, and the king of Ardra adjoining, commit great depredations inland."

But the new state of Dahomey could defend itself effectively only if it could lay hold on adequate supplies of firearms and ammunition. And these it could obtain only by trade with Ardra and Ouidah — and, of course, only in exchange for slaves.

Hence, Dahomey's power to resist Oyo (itself in turn subjected to the same pressure) depended on delivering slaves to the coast; the drastic but inescapable alternative was to enslave others — in order to buy firearms — or risk enslavement oneself. This indeed was the inner dynamic of the slaving connection with Europe; and it pushed Dahomey, as it pushed other states, into wholesale participation in slaving. No single state could safely or even possibly withstand this combination of guns and captives. Almost from the first, and in spite of the reluctance we have noted, Dahomey was caught in the slave trade's ruinous chain of cause and effect.

Even so, their new safety was precarious for the Fon as long as it rested on the will or whim of the coastal towns. Like other colleagues in the delta, these energetic middlemen of the Slave Coast were well aware of the strength of their monopoly, and they defended it and used it as vigorously and ruthlessly as they could. In the end Dahomey found their exactions intolerable. They refused to allow Dahomey to sell its slaves to the Europeans except through them, and this was the immediate reason why the fourth king of Dahomey, Agaja, waged successful war on them in 1727 and seized their towns. There on the coast itself, in Biobaku's words, Dahomey made contact with slave dealers of several European nations and Brazil, "and exchanged slaves captured in forays for rifles and cannon by means of which their forces became irresistible to their inadequately armed neighbours."

Huge quantities of firearms were poured into West Africa during the major period of the slave trade; and the state of Dahomey, increasingly a militarized autocracy, was among those that had the doubtful benefit. At the height of the eighteenth century commerce, gunsmiths in Birmingham alone were exporting muskets to Africa at the rate of between 100,000 and 150,000 a year, and it was common talk that one Birmingham gun rated one Negro slave. This last was Birmingham sales talk rather than a statement of fact, since African traders were seldom willing to sell a captive only for a gun and demanded other goods as well; yet the spirit of the saying was true enough. Firearms were indispensable to the Guinea trade.

European dealers on the coast might regret this flood of weapons, for it strengthened the bargaining power of their African partners; but there was nothing they could do about it. Like the Africans, they too were caught in the chain of cause and effect. They had to have slaves, and to get slaves they had to pay with guns.

Even if European traders wanted to refuse guns, they were far too distrustful of one another to operate any sort of common policy. As William Bosman observed at Elmina on the Gold Coast in 1700, the Europeans could never unite, and each European felt obliged to sell what the Africans would otherwise obtain, if he refused, from his rivals. And the Africans, on their side, were generally in the same case, although here and there, and

One Gun: One Slave

notably in the delta, they sometimes found enough unity among themselves to apply a boycott on their European partners.

Dahomey became famous — or infamous — in European eyes for the dictatorial power of its rulers. It departed from the general pattern of African state organization in being first and foremost a polity that was organized for war and built, almost directly, on superior weapon-power. It was seldom at peace with its neighbors in the east, who regularly invaded the Dahomeyans and whom the Dahomeyans invaded in return; and it fought a long battle for retention of its coastal base, where the maritime towns sometimes secured help from Europeans and sometimes from the Yoruba of Oyo. Its ruler even possessed a "Praetorian Guard" of several thousand fighting women-at-arms, devoted to his person and reputedly valorous in war. More or less continual warfare confirmed the king's autocratic power and seems to have encouraged these monarchs, whether for religious reasons or for motives of prestige, into something of the same bloody practices that occurred in Benin.

Late in the eighteenth century an English visitor, Robert Norris, described the royal establishment at Abomey. He took with him "a very handsome sedan chair and a chamber organ" and with these presents was well received at the palace. "On each side of it was a human head, recently cut off, lying on a flat stone with the face down, and the bloody end of its neck towards the entrance. In the guardhouse were about forty women, armed with a musket and a cutlass each" — these were the "Amazons" of Dahomey — "and twenty eunuchs with bright iron rods in their hands."

Entering an inner court with one of the king's ministers, Norris was received by two other ministers; all three Africans "knelt down and kissed the ground, pronouncing aloud some of the king's titles as we walked across this court, in which were ranged

FRONTIER OF OPPORTUNITY

six human heads." At last, in a third court, they were greeted by the king himself, "seated in a handsome chair of crimson velvet, ornamented with gold fringe and placed on a carpet in a spacious cool piazza . . . smoking tobacco and wearing a gold-laced hat with a plume of ostrich feathers." The king inquired of Norris "after the health of his brother, King George," and the visit concluded with Norris buying thirty-two slaves. (Plates 27 to 30)

Such visits to Abomey were rare because the policy of the Dahomeyan kings, no doubt fearing European penetration, was to forbid them. In their day-to-day dealings the traders on the coast were obliged to arrange their affairs with the king's "viceroy" there, the *Yavougou* (as Dalzell wrote the word), whose by no means empty title signified "captain of the white men." These traders understandably disliked Dahomey's power and generally regretted that the coastal towns had lost their independence, but they seem to have had a good deal of respect for the Dahomeyan achievement. And aside from their callous attitude to human life (in which, of course, they were scarcely peculiar in the world of the eighteenth century), the kings of Dahomey may well be thought to have done the best they could with the grim alternatives that were open to them. Their kingdom undoubtedly constituted to the outside world, as Biobaku says, "an odious stronghold of slavery and human sacrifice"; but then the outside world had a useful knack of overlooking its own destructive habits. More slaves were thrown alive into the Atlantic by slave-ship captains, sacrificing to their god of profitability, than were ever beheaded by the kings of Dahomey or the Obas of Benin.*

---

* Notorious but not unique was the master of the Liverpool slaver *Zong*, 1783, who caused 133 slaves to be flung overboard alive since they were "sick or weak, or not likely to live." He argued that if the slaves should die a

One Gun: One Slave

At least to their own peoples these rulers brought a new security. If they bolstered their prestige with a lavish display of human heads, they also boldly faced the implications of musket warfare and sheltered the Fon from the worst ravages of slaving. Out of the deepening chaos of the near-coastal regions they carved a state where law and order, if often summary and at steady cost in the enslavement of others, nonetheless largely prevailed. It was not glorious, but neither was the world they had to live in.

Just as this militarized kingdom was the product of the African-European connection as moved by the slaving-musket equation, so was its ultimate fate inseparable from the further development of European pressure. In the nineteenth century the Europeans shifted their policy. Hitherto they had been content with trading; now they desired conquest. Dahomey found itself faced with a new battle for monopolist control, no longer with Africans or with weakly manned trading posts at Ouidah and Ardra, but with the full might of industrialized Europe. In a sense this confrontation became inevitable once the fourth king of Dahomey had seized the coastal towns in 1727. Thereafter, though gradually and with many retreats, Europe saw Dahomey less and less as a trading partner but more and more as an enemy to be conquered and subdued.

Yet the new threat was slow in coming to a head. It was not until 1851 that France obtained a foothold on the coast in the shape of a "protectorate" over the trading town of Porto-Novo, and not until 1888 that Dahomey and France came to blows. Thereafter the process went swiftly: King Behanzin of Dahomey

---

natural death on board ship their loss would be borne by the owners, while the underwriters would have to pay if the slaves were thrown living into the sea. So he threw them overboard before they had time to die on his hands. In the event the owners did claim for these slaves, but the underwriters refused to pay the insurance. The owners then brought suit in the Court of King's Bench. They were awarded the verdict.

bought arms from the Germans, while the French landed two thousand men at Porto-Novo and invaded the country, defeating Behanzin's army in 1892 and declaring Dahomey a French colony two years later.

This transition from trading partnership to European conquest occurred elsewhere. As an integral phase in the European-African connection, it can be traced even more clearly — this time with the British — on the neighboring Gold Coast and in the forests of Ashanti. There too a strong new African state would exploit the slaving-musket equation in order to build a zone of security, only to find itself, as European policy shifted towards direct involvement, faced with a power that it could not in the end resist.

8 Ashanti: The New Battle for the Coast

IMAGINE, FOR A MOMENT, THAT THE SHIPS OF POWERFUL NATIONS had arrived in the Middle Ages, coming from an unknown continent, on the most remote shores of northern Europe. They would have found sparse and unsophisticated peoples, organized in small clans and family groups, who were accustomed to living on the ultimate frontiers of the world and for whom the power and prestige of civilization lay behind them in the hinterland. Such was the situation of the peoples of the Gold Coast seaboard — although the parallel, of course, is not exact — when the Portuguese and other Europeans reached them in the fifteenth and sixteenth centuries.

Some of these small peoples had lived here since times beyond

Ashanti: The New Battle for the Coast

memory; others had entered the coastal plains — a narrow land between the forest and the sea — during the great migrations of the Akan in the twelfth century or somewhat earlier. They were organized in little units and owed allegiance to more numerous and powerful peoples in the forest hills on their northern skyline. But they wore this allegiance loosely, since there was little tribute they could pay or service they could render.

The peoples of the forest were in a different situation. They too were a mingling of old inhabitants and immigrants from the north. But a complex process of state formation had long been in vigorous growth among them; and this process had culminated, many years before the first ships were signaled from the coast, in the early states of the Akan and their immediate neighbors. These drew their strength from the efficiency of their organization but also from a thriving trade in gold with the states of the Sudanese grasslands to their north. Ashanti and the lands nearby were famous as the source of gold.

It was with the southern outliers of this forest state-system that Europeans eventually made contact: with Akwamu and Akim, Denkyira and Adansi and others. But the contact was slow in the making, for the trade and preoccupations of these forest peoples all lay in the north, and they had never looked for any profit or peril in the south.

Meanwhile the Europeans landed and built castles with the good will — and also the advantage, since the newcomers paid rent — of the peoples of the coast itself. One can well imagine that the coastal chiefs were delighted with this unexpected source of new importance for themselves; they were now, after all, no longer "at the back of beyond." Thus the Portuguese captain who built Elmina Castle, Diogo d'Azambuja, had no difficulty in securing the agreement of Casamansa, the local chief, "a savage man . . . yet of good understanding and . . . clear judgment."

FRONTIER OF OPPORTUNITY

Azambuja ran into plenty of difficulties in the course of the work, and once it was done he lost no time in rubbing in the lesson of his new-built strength by burning down Casamansa's village. Quarrels, skirmishes, sieges, and reprisals were to be a regular part of the African-European record on this coast for several hundred years. More often than not, though, the mutual interest in trade was strong enough to overcome and always, in the end, to survive such brief affrays. Over the years a partnership evolved and led to the building of some forty European castles on this 250-mile reach of undulating cliff between Beyin in the west and Keta in the east — more or less the seaward boundaries of Ghana today. Yet it was invariably an instable partnership that was subject to sudden interruptions or outbursts of war.

There were two main reasons for this instability: rivalry between Europeans and rivalry between Africans, each fighting for monopoly control of their own side of the trade — the Dutch, for example, against the Portuguese, or Akwamu against Denkyira. This rivalry sharpened on either side as the profits of the gold and slave trade became increasingly apparent to Europeans, and the need for firearms and other European goods made itself increasingly felt among Africans; and in the end, as on the Slave Coast, this dual struggle for monopoly resolved itself into an outright battle between Europeans and Africans, the bloody prelude to colonial rule. But for the most part of the connection here, there was no thought of European conquest.

All the Europeans wished for on the coast was to defend themselves against each other and to dominate, so far as was convenient and possible, the little statelets on whose land the European castles were built. In the event it proved easier to dominate each other than to subdue the Africans. One can see this best in the Dutch experience. They were the strongest of the European

Ashanti: The New Battle for the Coast

maritime powers in the seventeenth century; as such, they took Elmina from the Portuguese, built forts of their own, and tried hard to keep out interlopers. They also tried to keep out the inland states who were now challenging, more and more openly, this new-found European power on the coast.

"The better to curb the blacks along the coast and to engross the whole trade," explains a French report of the late seventeenth century, certainly accurate for the general trend though competitive and therefore unfriendly, "the Dutch erected small forts at Butri, Shama, Cape Coast, Abomau, Kormantin and Accra, pretending to the blacks that they did it to protect and defend them against the outrages and insults of their neighbouring enemies of the inland country, who used often to attack them.

"Being thus grown powerful, the more to keep down the blacks and prevent their attempting anything against them, [the Dutch] laid duties on their fishery . . . forbade the coastal Africans under severe penalties to hold any correspondence or trade with other Europeans . . . and proceeded to lord it over them absolutely . . . though, on the other hand, they are obliged to pay yearly [taxes] to the native kings for the forts they have there."

This kind of bullying never worked for long. It offended against the partnership in trade that was fundamental to the whole arrangement. Besides, the inland states were too powerful to be pushed aside. At Accra in the 1680's, "the three European forts have little authority over the blacks, and serve only to secure the trade, the blacks here being of a temper not to suffer anything to be imposed on them by Europeans." At about this time the important state of Akwamu seized the Danish castle of Christiansborg and "forced the Danes' general to fly to the Dutch to save his life." Yet Akwamu needed the Danes just as much as the Danes needed Akwamu; and a little later the Danish Government

FRONTIER OF OPPORTUNITY

was allowed to buy back its castle for fifty marks of gold and an agreement to forgo any claim to reparations. And this was no isolated case.

This situation persisted along the Gold Coast for decades and even centuries, now with one system of alliances and rivalries in the ascendant, and now with another. Whatever disputes and squabbles might separate the partners for a time — and this often occurred — they always came together again and patched up their disagreements, so that some kind of peace among them generally held firm.

Other pressures were in play among the inland peoples. Between them there was always a natural tension, inevitably resolved in occasional bouts of conquest and absorption, because they suffered the instability of feudal and religious organizations in rivalry with one another. But the attractive power of European trade, and afterwards the absolute need for secure access to supplies of guns and ammunition, greatly sharpened these natural tensions until they broke increasingly into wars and invasions. And here too the slaving-musket equation led to a repetition, if in somewhat different terms, of experience on the Slave Coast. This took shape in the molding of the Ashanti Union.

Like Dahomey, this powerful and ambitious union was the product both of African political genius and of the curious pressures of the coastal trade. Unlike Dahomey, Ashanti was fashioned not into a militarized autocracy but into a militarized confederation under the acknowledged leadership of a single ruler, the Asantahene. It emerged at the end of the seventeenth century — at the time, that is, when scattered groups of Akan people in the Ashanti forest were subject to intensified slave raiding by their overlords, themselves responding to the increased demand for slaves from the European forts. The immediate overlords of the Akan who came together in the Ashanti Union were

Ashanti: The New Battle for the Coast

the rulers of Denkyira, then in close alliance with Europeans on the coast.

To assert their independence and meet the increasing threats to their security, the various branches of the Ashanti had to solve two problems: that of finding a common loyalty, and that of developing a military power. They were successful in solving both these problems thanks to two outstanding men, one a great military leader and the other a political initiator of remarkable quality, who must be reckoned among the most memorable figures in pre-colonial African history. Osei Tuto led the fight for independence; Okomfo Enokye forged a political alliance into an indissoluble union.

Hitherto the Akan clans and family groups of the Ashanti forest had recognized a loose relationship with one another, but stood apart, each in its own separateness, through the traditional worship of its own ancestors. They had plenty of reasons for standing together, but that was not their habit. Now, however, the habit of standing apart became painfully expensive. Already, in their divided weakness, they were obliged to pay tribute to Denkyira, and the prospect was of heavier tribute as the coastal trade developed. Besides, as long as they were divided, they would never be able to claim a profitable share in this growing business with the coast. They were in much the same position as the Fon of Dahomey: either they submitted to slave raiding by their more powerful neighbors, or they made themselves strong enough to repel raiders and take a hand in slaving on their own account.

They chose the second course. But first they had to cement their union. They had to find a sense of religious and national community. The traditions of Ashanti, as related tellingly by Ward, show how this was done.

"One Friday a great gathering was held at Kumasi; and there Enokye brought down from the sky, with darkness and thunder, and in a thick cloud of white dust, a wooden stool adorned with gold, which floated to earth and alighted gently on Osei Tutu's knees. This stool, Enokye announced, contained the spirit of the whole Ashanti nation, and all its strength and bravery depended on the safety of the stool. . . . This was the origin of the famous Sika Agua Kofi, 'Friday's Golden Stool' of Ashanti, which in spite of many vicissitudes still survives to-day with its unifying power unimpaired."

Okomfo Enokye, comments Ward, "was a statesman of genius. He succeeded where the Hellenes of old had failed: he brought his people triumphantly through their war of liberation and he held them together afterwards." By about 1700 Ashanti had utterly defeated Denkyira, thrown off its yoke of tribute, and broken through to the sea. From now on, if with many setbacks and interruptions, the armies and traders of Ashanti would scarcely ever lose their hold on the direct route to the coast. It was to their supreme ruler, the Asantahene, that the Dutch at Elmina now had to pay their rent after 1700 (the Dutch "note of agreement," held previously by Denkyira, having passed into Ashanti keeping); and throughout the eighteenth century this military nation continued its conquests and invasions both northward and eastward.

From self-defense, in short, the Ashanti passed to conquests which could give them hegemony of the lands behind the seaboard as well as control of the African side of the coastal trade. No doubt they had the ambition to make themselves feared as well as secure. Yet one can very well see in this national aggrandizement — as with Dahomey to the east — how the special dynamic of the slaving connection was already at work. For the safety of the Ashanti Union depended from the first on acquiring muskets; but muskets, as in Dahomey, could be obtained only in exchange for slaves. The fact that the gold trade persisted here scarcely alters this appreciation, since it was now of minor im-

Ashanti: The New Battle for the Coast

portance. And so the Ashanti, whether they wished it or not, were driven into the slaving business.

But slaving carried them inevitably towards conquest of their neighbors. They were seldom or never willing to sell their own people; hence they had to conquer foreign states and also, since other African nations were in the same game, control the trade routes to the coast. This in turn needed more firearms, and more firearms called for still more captives. Thus Ashanti grew into one of the strongest slaving nations of Africa, representing with Dahomey and the delta city-states the same leading part that Britain, France, and Holland represented on the European side. Ashanti became, Ward says, "deliberately a slave-dealing state. Many slaves were bought in the markets of the north . . . and were marched to the coast and there sold at a profit. . . . But many were obtained by raiding and warfare." Questions of power and wealth apart, slaving had become the price of Ashanti survival.

After 1700, accordingly, the Ashanti Union grew into an indispensable component in the network of commercial partnership that enabled Western Europe to accumulate wealth from transatlantic plantations. Indispensable — but also, in the end, indigestible. Looking southward from their forest domains, the Ashanti concluded that the power was theirs. Like Akwamu and Denkyira before them, they had subdued the little peoples of the seaboard and sworn them in as vassals. Thus the overlordship of the coast was theirs. They were the leading African power in this African country.

But along the coast the old alliances were not forgotten. Claimed as vassals by the proud Ashanti, the peoples of the trading settlements turned for help to their European partners in the castles. And although the consequences of this were not immediately apparent, the moment was to prove decisive. Hence-

FRONTIER OF OPPORTUNITY

forward, more and more consciously, Africa and Europe faced each other in a new relationship: one of rivalry, now, for sovereignty along the coast itself. As the power of Europe was concentrated increasingly into that of a single nation, Britain, and the power of Africa likewise into that of Ashanti, this new rivalry sharpened into war. Yet hostilities were long in coming. The first blows were not struck until 1806, when the British intervened on behalf of some of the coastal chiefs. Little harm was done on either side, and peace was rapidly restored since peace was still the major interest of both.

And so it might have remained but for the changing situation of Europe and the rise of European imperialism. But the British, like their European rivals, were ceasing to be content with a partnership in Africa in which they were the lesser power; they were no longer ready to hold their castles by the will of Africans. As the ideas of imperialism gained hold, the British began to claim the rights and powers that flow from conquest. The process was gradual and obscure, but it was also continuous. It evolved on the Gold Coast in somewhat the same manner as in India. There the British East India Company, partly to defend its commercial monopoly and partly to extend it, had pushed administrative power and military "protection" little by little into the interior. Then the British Government had taken over. For the British had found themselves faced with a clear alternative, as their penetration continued, between abandoning these advanced positions or confirming them by outright invasion.

Here on the Gold Coast the British had never possessed any advanced positions. Their power had not extended much beyond a rifleshot from their castle walls. Yet the new urge for "spheres of interest," for zones of monopoly that were barred to European rivals, for the "opening up" of a continent whose interior was still a mystery and perhaps a golden one — all this and the temper of the times pushed irresistibly towards the assertion of political control.

At first the British established diplomatic relations with the Asantahene at his capital of Kumasi in the Ashanti forest. Then, with the tide of imperialism at its flood, they invaded Ashanti. After bitter wars and many setbacks they conquered the country. Yet the last act in this transformation of the old slaving partnership into the colonial system was not enacted until 1902, when Ashanti was incorporated into the British Empire: only fifty-five years (though none could have foreseen it then) before the people of Ashanti regained their independence as part of the new state of Ghana.

9 The Partnership Cracks

MANY INFLUENCES WERE AT WORK IN REDUCING THE OLD CONnection between equals into one that Europeans would entirely dominate. Not the least among these, ironically enough, was the ending of the oversea slave trade.

The ending of the trade was of tremendous significance for Africans and Europeans on the Guinea Coast. It upset the trading habits of three full centuries, undermined systems of government, disrupted social customs, and opened the way for European intervention. But all this has to be seen as a process, a growth, a labor of many years. Britain's legislators might at one stroke declare the trade abolished in 1807, but that was only a beginning. Even if Britain had no longer any interest in slaves, others were differently placed; and these others continued to collect slaves as and when they could, and often in large numbers. Not

FRONTIER OF OPPORTUNITY

for seventy or eighty years after the British act of abolition would the last slavers creep from West African harbors and defy the risks of British naval arrest on their passage to the Americas. It was during these decades of the nineteenth century that the old equality degenerated, at first slowly and confusedly and then with gathering speed, until Europe had decisively the upper hand.

Two hundred years of slaving had produced along some parts of this littoral, as these pages have tried to show, a society that was specially adjusted to the trade. This society could survive an end to slaving only with great difficulty. Abolition did in fact produce a social crisis of more or less severity in all these states; and it was generally the case that European opinion — as in East Africa — mistook this crisis and its accompanying phenomena of insecurity and confusion for a natural inability of Africans to govern themselves in peace and tolerance. This misunderstanding, however easy in the circumstances, had violent results. Flying their banners of "trusteeship and civilization," European nations now began to interpret the particular effects of the old coastal partnership (on which, of course, they had built much of their prosperity) as the general and inevitable consequence of "leaving Africans to themselves." It seemed incumbent on Europeans — and it was certainly convenient — to intervene.

That is part of another story, of one that was to be a repetition of the old duality of motive which had governed Portugal's early relations with the Congo of King Affonso: Christianity, but also profit. King Leopold of the Belgians enshrined the modern version in characteristic words when launching his adventure in the Congo. "To pierce the darkness shrouding entire populations," he declared, "that is, if I may venture to say so, a crusade worthy of this century of progress." He and his soldiers "pierced the

The Partnership Cracks

darkness" soon enough; but almost their first action was to declare that all the land and all the products of the land belonged to them; and to this day the peoples of the Congo bear marks of their terrible impoverishment that followed. Elsewhere things went differently and better. But generally there arose in new and potent forms the myth of "savage Africa," now justifying colonialism as it had previously justified the slave trade: reinforced, moreover, by the complacent self-congratulation of bourgeois classes who were sure, in the lapped comfort of their joint-stock companies and their new suburban villas, that they were rightly and properly designed to rule the world.

In Africa the matter seemed otherwise. Astonished at Britain's sudden opposition to a trade she had done so much to call into being and extend, African chiefs and rulers at first tried to dissuade their partner from this momentous step. When they failed they had a great deal of trouble on their hands, for much of their trading network relied completely on the sale of slaves. But after a time, perceiving that the decision was final, they turned to other forms of trade. And it stands as striking proof of the vigor and resilience of these societies that they should so often have achieved the transition to legitimate trade — as non-slaving commerce now began to be called — with clear and rapid success.

They were helped in this by a new demand for soap and lubricating oil in Europe. There was pressing need for vegetable fat which could supplement the insufficient supplies of animal fat. This substitute was found in palm oil, long cultivated in the delta. Balked of human cargoes, a number of Liverpool merchants asked their captains to load with palm oil instead. Large consignments of delta oil were reaching Liverpool within a few years of the ending of the slave trade. By 1832 a former Liverpool slaving merchant, Tobin, was bringing in some four thou-

FRONTIER OF OPPORTUNITY

sand tons of oil every year; and two years later the whole export of the delta — of the "Oil Rivers" — was said to be worth half a million pounds sterling. All this oil was produced by the delta "house rulers" and their like.

Yet slaving continued from the "Oil Rivers," especially from the old Portuguese trading stronghold on the Brass estuary. Brazil, Cuba, and independent American operators all wanted slaves, and slaves were regularly smuggled out in large numbers despite every effort of the British Navy to prevent their transport.

And it was at this point that the changing nature of the trade became confounded with the rise of imperialism and led, here as elsewhere, to the assertion of political control and afterwards to conquest. One can detect three main steps in the process. First came naval intervention to prevent slaving and protect the interests of European traders, now increasingly turbulent, ambitious, and violently involved in conflict with Africans. Then followed the establishment of consuls with widening powers of political interference. Lastly, there came the proclamation of a "right to govern."

Each step led directly to the next. For if naval patrols succeeded in reducing slave exports, they also succeeded, by the same token, in promoting an economic crisis which palm oil would later, but only later, resolve. Yet economic crisis led quickly to political upheaval, and political upheaval called for consular arbitration. And consular arbitration could not be effective, in the end, unless it was backed by force. So in the end the troops were duly sent for.

There were other factors in play. Here in the delta, as on the Gold Coast, Europeans were now of a mind to win control of both sides of the trade; they began trying to dictate prices and credit rates by close combination with each other; and when they ran into African opposition that was too strong for them,

The Partnership Cracks

they regularly called in the British Navy. They were not always successful in getting naval support, but little by little, as the great imperial century moved on, the idea of military intervention in defense of British interests gained currency and even respectability, no matter how disreputable the interests in question might be.

Continued slaving, moreover, competed with oil production until it became a direct commercial interest of the British oil merchants in the delta (aside from humanitarian motives) to make a final end of the slave trade. Gradually it became clear to powerful and forward-looking merchants that the British Government must sooner or later intervene. And now a new and vital piece of knowledge came to light: in 1830 the Landers finally established that the Oil Rivers were the mouths of the mighty Niger and therefore the high road to the interior.

Expeditions began pushing inland. The European traders of the delta opposed this, as did many of their African partners, for they saw in European penetration of the hinterland a necessary end to their coastal monopoly. For a time it looked as though the old monopolists would prevail: the expeditions failed. Then came the next point of change. Europe discovered that quinine could defeat malaria, and this proved decisive. On Laird's first disastrous trading expedition up the Niger in 1832, malaria had taken such a fearful toll that only nine out of forty-eight Europeans had returned to tell the tale. Baikie's expedition twenty-two years later, making systematic use of quinine, lost not a single life although it went as far north as Fulani country. Three years after that the British Government subsidized the launching of steamers on the river; and in 1868, with the footfalls of history thundering on the scene, the first British consul in the interior broke out his flag at Lokoja two hundred and fifty miles from the sea. The colony of Nigeria was in the womb.

FRONTIER OF OPPORTUNITY

Any writer who should wish to explore the impact of colonial conquest on African society, and, at the same time, the intricate train of action and reaction which then led to the rise of African nationalism and regained independence, will find a rich and curious field in the history of the delta. Here the records of the transitional years — the second half of the nineteenth century, when the long partnership was ending — throw open an amazing gallery of old rogues and new humanitarians, brilliantly enterprising African merchants, desperate slaving captains moored away in forgotten creeks, true-blue British consuls and stubborn chiefs — all enmeshed in a densely fashioned net of much evil and great good, sober profit and fantastic speculation, wisdom and the wildest folly.

These men and their occupations were quintessentially the outcome of the European-African connection at one of its broadest and most interesting points, and I shall round off this narrative by offering one or two samples of their remarkable quality and experience.

10 *Men like Ja Ja: The Last Phase*

ONE CAN EASILY IGNORE THE POSITIVE SIDE OF ALL THIS COMMERcial enterprise, especially in the delta, by concentrating on the miseries it entailed; it was by doing so that nineteenth century Europeans came often to the most dismal conclusions about African society. This was rather like seeing the Industrial Revolution in England uniquely through the sufferings of little children in

Men like Ja Ja: The Last Phase

coal mines and women in basement workshops. The sufferings existed, and they undoubtedly condemned the system; but they were not the whole story. Humanity, somehow or other, survives and learns and corrects.

The process of surviving and learning and correcting was extremely difficult for the delta peoples because they were faced, all the while, with the mounting arrogance and pressure of Europeans who were no longer content to accept African equality. Yet the adjustment was attempted; and it was achieved, here and there, with outstanding skill. There is no better example of this than the life and work of King Ja Ja of Opobo.

A modern Nigerian historian says that the Ibo people of today regard Ja Ja "as the greatest man produced by their tribe in the last century," and surely they are right. Ja Ja would have been remarkable in any time and place.

He belonged to that period in the delta partnership when oil had largely displaced slaves, and European penetration had begun. Born into domestic slavery, he was nonetheless elected while still a young man to be the ruling chief of the Bonny house of Anna Pepple, an old-established trading unit that was famous throughout the African connection. This occurred in 1863 when Ja Ja was forty-two years old. Already a successful merchant, he soon proved his worth by restoring the dilapidated fortunes of the Pepple house. His predecessor in the headship, Alali, had died in great debt, owing European merchants a sum that was variously estimated as lying between ten and fifteen thousand pounds. Within two years of taking over command, Ja Ja had cleared off the whole of this debt and become, for the supercargoes who managed the European side of the business, the most popular of all the Bonny chiefs.

But Ja Ja's methods of enterprise, while arousing the admiration of his European clients, also excited the jealousy of his competitors. His thrusting commercial successes soon led him into trouble with the rival house of Manilla Pepple. Both houses armed for war, which duly came in 1869. Here again one may see the truly international nature of the delta system. For "while Africans did the fighting," comments Dike, "the opposing British interests supplied their respective allies with the weapons of war. This armaments race intensified the struggle and widened the area of conflict to the tribal interior. It was certainly the greatest war ever fought in the delta."

The results were not long in making themselves felt. Ja Ja found himself confronted not only with the armed competition of an African rival but also with the fact of European intervention. Here, as elsewhere, the point was reached where the partnership broke down before a determined British bid to extend their power from West African waters to West African land. Ja Ja met this challenge in his own way. With great foresight, seeing himself outmatched in Bonny itself, he moved in 1870 to Andoni country a few miles to the eastward and somewhat inland from Bonny; and there he founded a new state, Opobo, of which he became king.

At Opobo he flourished. This country, wrote an eyewitness, "became under King Ja Ja's firm rule one of the largest exporting centres of palm oil in the delta, and for years King Ja Ja enjoyed a not undeserved popularity amongst the white traders who visited his river." But it was too good to last. A time came when these traders combined together and cut the price they were willing to pay for Ja Ja's oil. To this monopolist gambit Ja Ja replied in short order with another of his own: he found means of shipping large quantities of oil to England on his own account, and forbade his people to sell more than a part of their produce to the whites.

The reply of the white traders to Ja Ja's independent shipping

Men like Ja Ja: The Last Phase

enterprise was to combine even more closely together. They drew up a plan whereby they would equally divide whatever produce came into the river, and thus eliminate competition among themselves, and, at the same time, kill Ja Ja's chance of finding a European who was willing to ship his produce.

But Ja Ja outmaneuvered them again. He had in any case found that the profit on sending his own oil to England was not so large as he liked, "owing to the length of time it took to get his returns back, namely about three months at the earliest, whilst selling in the river he could turn over his money three or four times during that period.

"He therefore tried several means to break the white men's combination, at last hitting upon the bright idea of offering the whole of the river's trade to one English house. . . . His bait took with one of the European traders: the latter could not resist the golden vision of the yellow grease thus displayed before him by the astute Ja Ja, who metaphorically dangled before his eyes hundreds of canoes laden with the coveted palm oil. A bargain was struck, and one fine morning the other white traders in the river woke up to the fact that their combination was at an end, for on taking their morning spy round the river through their binoculars . . . they saw a fleet of over a hundred canoes round the renegade's wharf, and for nearly two years this trader scooped all the trade."

Twenty or thirty years earlier Ja Ja would have met with no more than verbal protests for this sovereign act of restriction in his own country; the European supercargoes would have denounced the measure, but thereafter they would have tried to restore peace on the best terms they could. The case was common enough. But now a different spirit reigned among them. They could and did call in the power of their own government. They carried their complaints to Consul Livingstone — the great explorer's not-so-great brother — and Consul Livingstone was more than sympathetic. This marked the beginning of a bitter struggle between the British and Ja Ja that the African was bound, as things now stood, to lose.

For what Ja Ja was really doing was to lay it down that he, and he alone, should decide how the oil trade was to be conducted. He claimed and exercised the right to prevent African and European competitors from entering the oil markets under his control, and these were the best in the delta. He barred the way, in Dike's words, "not only to the Bonny middlemen but also to the invading Europeans . . . [who] found him the greatest impediment to their occupation of eastern Nigeria." A trial of strength became inevitable. In 1887 the British moved in. Backed by the navy, Consul Johnston (a great imperial thruster) had Ja Ja seized and taken to Accra on the Gold Coast. There he was tried before Admiral Hunt Grubbe on various charges connected with treaty-breaking but arising, in truth, from Ja Ja's dogged insistence on African sovereignty, and condemned to five years' exile in the West Indies, where he died.

Trial or no trial, Ja Ja was clearly a victim of imperialism. Had he not faced foreign invasion, he might have realized still wider triumphs and ambitions and carried the whole of the delta into a new system of law and commerce, social and economic structure, which could have validly confronted the problems of the early twentieth century. For Ja Ja was at home in the widening world of his time. He used techniques of commerce that were no different from those of his clients. He understood the capitalist system at its most intimate heart, there where the ticktock of money interest is at work and the crucial factors of marketing are felt and registered; and there is no reason why he should not have developed an economy of cash production in eastern Nigeria. It can

Men like Ja Ja: The Last Phase

be said of men like Ja Ja (and Ja Ja was by no means unique, among the people of the delta, for energy of mind and enterprise) that they made the very best they could of a relationship with Europe in which Europe had yet to offer anything that history can record with even modest satisfaction, let alone with pride. For these reasons, men like Ja Ja and the new techniques for which they stood were often, in a real sense, the forerunners and the foundation of modern nationalism in West Africa.

Yet the success and free-ranging scope of men like these, rapidly and skillfully transforming the old slave markets into palm-oil markets, must be weighed against the social disintegration that was directly linked with so much of the connection. Great energies went to waste. Much wealth was squandered. Talented men were obliged to work within a framework of possibilities that was ultimately void of any chance of constructive expansion. As European pressure intensified, this society was shaken to its roots. There spread across it a sense of fatal insecurity. And it was this neurotic condition (felt, as the abundant records show, by almost every man of substance in the delta and in its neighboring country) that led to the extravagance of autocracy and the gross futility of superstition into which many of these governments fell and which, in turn, did so much to invite British occupation.

One could illustrate this trend with a mass of evidence. It was this same feeling of hopeless doom that ultimately drove the priests and the divine king of Benin out of their wits. It was this that caused the Oba in 1897 to refuse a meeting with Consul General Phillips, replying to Phillips's messenger that "he had heard of the white men going all over the country and taking the chiefs prisoner, saying, 'Now, my friend, we have got you and will keep you.'" Indeed, he must have heard of such things, for the British had already deported King Pepple and King Ja Ja. Why not the Oba too? When Phillips persisted in coming up to Benin, he and his party were ambushed and killed. A few months later Benin was occupied by the British Army.

Another case makes the point even more clearly. In 1895 certain chiefs of the Brass city-state were accused of tolerating or encouraging human sacrifice — known generally, to Europeans of the day, as cannibalism. A useful statement by the Brass chiefs, taken down by Sir Claude Macdonald, then consul general in the delta, notes the pressure exerted by the priests for chiefs to "offer up prisoners" to sacrifice. The statement points out that the Christian chiefs resist this pressure, but they are now in a minority. "Some years ago the Christian party was much stronger and more powerful than their opponents. Many chiefs who were brought up as Christians have now gone back to fetichism . . . the reason for this being that they had lost faith in the white man's God, who had allowed them to be oppressed, and their trade, their only means of livelihood, to be taken from them without just cause or reason."

How well grounded were these complaints of European monopoly may be guessed from a report by Sir John Kirk a year later. "The rules in force," he declared, referring to the sharply monopolist regulations of the newly formed Royal Niger Company, "are practically prohibiting to native trade, and the Brass men are right in saying that this is so."

Having broken the power of the African merchants, the European merchants were now determined to exercise all power themselves. And their natural ambition was to force down the buying price of oil, cut out all independent operators on either side, and sell their own goods as dearly as they could. To these African chiefs and traders of the delta it must have seemed that God had indeed turned his back on them and could now be attracted to their side again only by the most desperate measures.

Men like Ja Ja: The Last Phase

Even so, the Royal Niger Company found it no easy matter to rule the delta; nor did the British Government itself. The delta chiefs fought back, and they fought hard. How and why they fought, and what manner of men they were, may be glimpsed from the case of Ja Ja of Opobo. Or, to offer a contrast, from that of Nanna of Brohemie Town.

The story of Chief Nanna of Brohemie, a delta settlement not far from the city of Benin, has many aspects that are worthy of note. It makes in fact no bad epitaph to the closing years of the precolonial relationship of Africa and Europe. Nanna was another of those hard-driving merchants of the delta who had learned how to live with the changing needs of the nineteenth century. He enjoyed good relations with the British in a cautious sort of way, and in 1887 a British vice-consul even went so far as to "nominate" Nanna as the governor of Benin. However void of real meaning this nomination may have been, Nanna undoubtedly considered himself a sovereign in his own land. What he could not achieve by cunning or persuasion he would certainly, he thought, be justified in carrying through by force. He was a great supporter of trade with Europeans — after all, he depended on it — but a great opposer of European political intervention. He put down powerful barriers to British penetration; and these sooner or later were bound to prove intolerable. The test of power came in 1894.

Nanna won the first round. A British "punitive expedition" (for such, by now, were the imperialist terms of European presence on the coast) failed to reach him in his stronghold at Brohemie. Consul General Moor, writing to the Foreign Office from Old Calabar on the last day of August, 1894, told the disagreeable news. Pushing up through dense and tangled swampland, the British force had come at last to the outskirts of Brohemie only to find themselves confronted with a "most powerful"

FRONTIER OF OPPORTUNITY

stockade about three hundred yards long, constructed of hardwood logs stuck firmly in the ground in rows two or three deep and about eight feet high. The British took this stockade and found inside it twenty-three cannon (Moor calls them heavy cannon), "loaded, trained and primed"; luckily for these much-tried British soldiers, the gunners of Chief Nanna had deserted him. "The charges consisted of 3 lb. balls and tubular bamboo frames filled with broken iron pots."

Having carried this potentially nasty obstacle, the British then got into a maze of creeks that were difficult to cross. They persevered until they came to Brohemie. But at Brohemie they were met with fire from "at least thirty or forty cannon . . . in addition to plenty of rifles." Some of these cannon, they observed, were "trained directly down the creek so as to render the approach by boats most hazardous, if not impossible." This was discouraging; what was worse, and finally decisive, was that the British could then find no way of bringing their two 7-pounder field guns to bear. They had dragged these guns to Brohemie with tremendous difficulty, and now they lacked strength to drag them back again. So they spiked them and retired.

But these were high imperial times. This kind of setback could not be overlooked. A few months later Rear Admiral Bedford led a naval force up the Benin River and seized Brohemie by sheer weight of metal. And what Bedford discovered inside Brohemie is of no small interest to the general history of the delta, if only because it throws a clear light on the kind of capital accumulation that was made by the leading chiefs and prime merchants of the country.

Reporting to the Admiralty, Bedford said that the defenses of Brohemie showed months if not years of preparation, "and a considerable amount of intelligence . . . in all the arrangements. For instance, the guns were admirably placed to meet any attack from the direction expected . . . and were well and strongly mounted. . . ."

"Below Alluma's house was found the magazine, containing 1,500 kegs of powder, which was protected by first double iron-sheeting, then logs of timber three deep, and outside corrugated iron sheets again three deep. . . . Nanna's house was next visited, where large stores containing munitions of war and trading materials in very large quantities were found. . . . Scattered about all over the town, and in large quantities, in the stores, were leg and neck irons, also handcuffs, evidently for use in keeping the large number of slaves owned by Chief Nanna in order by most severe means. . . ."

There were, Bedford continued, a total of 106 cannon from 3-pounder to 32-pounder in size, including "a large number of 9-pounders, very good-looking cast-iron guns," and stores of powder made up in neat muslin bags and cylinders of split bamboo with iron balls and pieces of scrap iron, permitting rapid fire.

That was one form of capital accumulation. Nanna had also contrived another. Bedford found an astonishing quantity of gin. Altogether, he reported, Nanna had collected no fewer than 8,300 cases of twelve bottles apiece — a grand total of 99,600 bottles of hooch.

Guns and gin — these, at the end of all this stubborn effort, remain as pathetic witness to the kind of blessings that delta Africans had managed, abundantly through the years, to extract from oversea civilization. There were other and better things in the European connection — notably the beginnings of modern education — but these other things were marginal and insignificant as yet. Not until later, in the wake of the colonial hurricane, would the channels of intercourse become wide enough here for the civilization of Europe, in any worthwhile meaning of the term, to have anything to say or give

seven

Four Centuries:
A Summing-Up

Minha Mãe
  (as mães negras cujos filhos partiram)
tu me ensinaste a esperar
como esperaste paciente nas horas defíceis

Mas em mim
a vida matou essa mística esperança

Eu não espero
sou aquele por quem se espera

A Esperança somos nós
os teus filhos . . .
a esperança em busca de vida.

              Agostinho Neto, poet of **Angola**

My Mother
  (black mothers whose sons depart)
you taught me to wait and hope
as you had learnt in bitter days

But in me
life killed that mystic hope

I am not the one who waits
But the one who is awaited

And we are Hope
your sons . . .
Searching for life.

An End and a Beginning

WITH COLONIAL INVASION, THE AFRICAN-EUROPEAN CONNECTION entered upon a decisively new phase. Thereafter action and reaction occurred with increasing speed. The first declarations of modern nationalism were heard in West Africa no more than twenty years after European conquest, and the main colonial period on the Guinea Coast has lasted little longer than half a century, and not much more elsewhere.

These colonial years were always humiliating, often harsh, sometimes terribly wasteful. But they were relatively few: less than a third of the duration of the major period of the slave trade. They barely spanned two lifetimes. And they led with growing awareness to a new social consciousness, to a political awakening, to a rebirth of African culture and inner confidence. This, in the light of imperialist aims, was their supreme irony; but for this reason, as well as for the lesser but necessary purpose of ending my book, I exclude them from "the years of trial."

I have called the precolonial period "the years of trial" because it was then, through those long centuries, that Africa grievously and continuously suffered from a connection with Europe that was neither one thing nor the other: neither the equality that could open wide channels to the outside world nor the sharp subjection that could provoke and stimulate, however blindly or unintentionally, the rise of African reassertion, political change, and economic growth. The years of trial were years of isolation and paralysis wherever the trade with Europe, essentially a trade in slaves, could plant its sterilizing hand.

This is a broad statement, but I think it is broadly true. Of

A SUMMING-UP

course there were exceptions. A handful of Africans did succeed in reaching the outside world as free men. Yet all but one or two of them were chiefs and the sons of chiefs — men who were in any case committed to the slaving system and without an interest in changing it. Indeed, it was familiar British and French practice to win the friendship of local rulers on the coast by entertaining their sons in Europe. This was part of the slaving network of alliance, and it often worked exceedingly well.

Sometime in the summer of 1750 the British Admiralty received a letter of thanks from the king of Annamaboe on the Gold Coast, together with an offer of the labor of twenty thousand men to help the British build a fort on his land. The old man had double cause to be grateful. He had sent one of his sons to England, together with a companion, on a slaving ship whose captain had seized and sold them in the West Indies. But when the story became known in England, the youths were released by order of the British Government, which duly paid their ransom. They were brought to England and "put under the care of the Earl of Halifax, then at the head of the Board of Trade, who had them clothed and educated in a suitable manner"; and they became the talk of the town.

"There are two black princes of Annamaboe here," Walpole wrote in his London diary for March 23, 1749, "who are in fashion at all assemblies, of whom I scarce know any particulars [of their story] . . . though all the women know it and ten times more than belongs to it." Before returning to Africa, the two young men were received by the king and visited Covent Garden where they were greeted by "a loud clap of applause." In an aristocratic society it seemed quite logical to applaud a black man who was also a prince, while enslaving his "subjects" in a manner fit only for beasts. Established attitudes toward white men were not, after all, much different.

An End and a Beginning

Such visitors to Europe could have no more effect on the situation in Africa than the enterprise and exploits of the slaves and ex-slaves in the Americas. It is notable that until the middle of the ninenteenth century the only successful relationship between free Africans in Brazil and their old homeland lay within the slaving circuit. Typical was that "free Negro, born in Brazil" of whom Governor Abson of the British fort at Ouidah was writing in about 1790: Antonio Vaz Coelho, who made several voyages to Ardra on the Slave Coast, where he at last settled and became "a very respectable trader" — and introduced the idea of mounting swivel guns on war canoes.

All roads, in those gray years, led to slaving. In a strict sense the European connection was a tragic one for Africa: not, that is, excluding humor and decent hope, love of life or the will to survive — but denying, whenever it came to the matter of choice, any alternative to the death and damnation of the slave trade. This must be one's starting point in trying to assess the consequences of these four centuries.

How much did Africa suffer from depopulation? Slaving struck other coastal and near-coastal regions than those considered here; yet what was true of the Congo, the East Coast, and the eastern Gulf of Guinea was also true of these other regions. And generally it would seem that depopulation was the least important consequence of the oversea slave trade. Here and there it may even have done something to alleviate the problem of overpopulation.

There was a great loss of people and staggering waste in their use; and at certain times and places this loss and wastage undoubtedly crippled society. Present-day population densities offer some hints. Today in West Africa there is comparatively great density along the coast itself — more than fifty inhabitants

A SUMMING-UP

to a square mile in many regions — and considerable density in the forest belt. Yet most of the intermediate zone between the forest belt and the Niger grasslands is sparsely peopled; here the density is seldom more than ten to a square mile and is often less than one or two.

Soil and other natural factors go far to explain this variation. But if it is also true that a great number of West African slaves was drawn from this intermediate zone — precisely where peoples lacked strong states of their own — then this relative scarcity of population may well have some connection with the slave trade. Color is lent this by the fact that the lands of the Mossi in modern Upper Volta are unusually rich in people; there, in the realm of the still surviving Moro Naba of the Mossi, population density once again approaches the level of the coastal regions. And the Mossi were one of the rare peoples of the intermediate zone who successfully defended themselves against slaving.

Yet the evidence for serious depopulation through the trade is far from conclusive. Very large numbers of captives were shipped from the forest lands of Nigeria over a very long period; yet these are still among the most densely peopled regions of all Africa. "If we may judge from nineteenth century records," Dike comments, "over-population was the rule in all sections of the [Ibo] tribe." Here, at any rate, slaving seems to have had no adverse effect on the birth-and-survival rate. This should not be taken to mean that slaving helped the birthrate but rather that the birthrate in these fertile and favored areas helped the slave trade, just as, in much earlier times, the same high population density in southern Nigeria may have set in motion some of the great Negro migrations that populated central and southern Africa.

Several peoples of the intermediate zone were raided both from the south and the north and must have come near extinction. Others suffered less and were able to refill their ranks; from the

An End and a Beginning

purely demographic point of view, they probably suffered no more than the populations of Italy and Scotland in recent times, when annual average emigration has about equaled or even exceeded the birthrate. This is not to palliate the slaving loss, but merely to conclude that depopulation was seldom a primary social factor of the oversea trade, and even less of the overland trade.

One must look elsewhere for the main impact of this "new colonial system of slavery which," to quote the *Encyclopaedia Britannica*, "instead of being the spontaneous outgrowth of social necessities and subserving a temporary need of human development, was politically as well as morally a monstrous aberration." Whether the slave trade, on which Western Europe founded so much of its prosperity, was really an aberration — or whether in fact it merely epitomized the nature of progress in that day and age when, as Marx observed in the face of child labor and factory enslavement, progress resembled "that hideous pagan idol, who would not drink the nectar but from the skulls of the slain" — is beside the point of this present inquiry. Viewed as a factor in African history, the precolonial connection with Europe — essentially, the slave trade — had powerfully degrading consequences for the structure of society. But far-reaching depopulation was seldom prominent among them.

The economic evidence is more severe. It cannot yet be absolutely proved that the European connection between 1450 and 1850 was a cause of economic stagnation, or that this stagnation grew worse after slaving became dominant around 1650. For even after the trade got into its stride, Africans continued to weave textiles, smelt and forge metals, practice agriculture, and carry on the manifold techniques of their daily life. With agriculture, moreover, there was even a gain from European contact, for the ships from South America introduced new and useful crops that

A SUMMING-UP

became of great importance to Africa: here were the African origins of maize, manioc, pineapples, and several other valuable foods.

Yet in spite of an undoubted improvement in food supplies (for the new crops were soon in cultivation by many African peoples), there can be no doubt that on balance the economic effects of European contact worked steady and decisive damage.

After about 1650, with diminishing exceptions, African production-for-export became a monoculture in human beings. This can be seen to have suffocated economic growth in coastal and near-coastal Africa as surely as the extension of European production-for-export of consumer goods gave the maritime nations of Europe, at the same time, their long lead in economic development.

The reasons for this suffocation were various. It was obviously an impoverishment to send away the very men and women who would otherwise produce wealth at home. In exporting slaves, African states exported their own capital without any possible return in interest or in the enlargement of their economic system. Slave exports differed radically in this respect from the more or less forced emigration of impoverished men and women from nineteenth century Europe. Thus the millions who left Britain in those years were able to enter the mainstream of capitalist expansion, and thereby benefit the mother-country in many indirect ways. But the African slaves could contribute nothing except to the wealth of their masters — a wealth that never returned to Africa. Dealers in Africa undoubtedly received payment for the slaves they sold; but the nature of the payment was strictly nonproductive. The very conditions of the exchange prevented the kind of capital accumulation that could have led to a more advanced economy. Such "capital" as the kings and prime merchants could accumulate was in mere baubles or the weapons of war. From an economic standpoint, in short, European slaving may be rightly

An End and a Beginning

regarded as a primitive and particularly destructive form of colonialism: the sale of consumer goods for the raw material of slave labor.

Wherever towns grew strong there was, true enough, a shift to cash economies and capitalist savings and investment. This happened in the great market centers of the Western Sudan, trading across the Sahara, and perhaps still more in the cities of the medieval East Coast that enjoyed contact with India and Arabia. But these developments occurred only where slaving did not dominate the trade. With the partial exception of the delta partnership, the European connection was powerless to reproduce such results — precisely because it was above all a slaving connection.

In face of an ever more pervasive demand for slaves, local industries dwindled or collapsed. Where the only produce that was readily marketable was the producer himself (or herself), handicrafts and cottage industries could barely survive, let alone expand. Cheap European textiles drove out the excellent cloths of the Guinea Coast. Pereira had spoken of these as early as 1506, noting that the Portuguese purchased these cloths and carried them to Europe. Benin was especially famous for its textiles. Yet by 1850 these had fallen to minor importance, although the textile output of Kano in northern Nigeria (produced in an economic system that was far beyond any direct influence of the oversea slave trade, and where the overland slave trade never dominated commerce) flourished and grew at the same time. Dahomey textiles met the same fate as those of Benin, even though Governor Dalzell could write as late as 1789 that Dahomey still manufactured "very pretty and durable cloths of cotton. . . . Their dyes stand washing very well, especially the blues, which are inferior to none." It speaks much for the quality of this manufacture that it could survive at all in face of massive European sale of cheap Lancashire and Indian cottons.

A SUMMING-UP

These local industries declined while chiefs and merchants fattened on the slave trade. Yet here too there was no real expansion of the economic system. For this new trading wealth became increasingly a matter of individual prestige and display. Consider how the king of Bonny responded in 1826 to the offer of a bride by the king of Warri.

"King Pepple having repeatedly sent presents by his canoes to the King of Warri, with whose nation he carries on an immense trade . . . [and] the latter hearing of his amazing wealth and extensive connexions with the Europeans, offered him his eldest daughter in marriage. . . . So great and unexpected an offer was received by Pepple with the greatest exaltation, and to convince his intended ally how deeply he appreciated the distinguished favour he had conferred upon him, he loaded canoe after canoe with rare and most valuable treasures: English, French, Spanish and Portuguese merchandise were extracted from his warehouses — gold and silver plate — costly silks and exquisitely fine cloths — with embroidered laces and other articles too numerous to mention."

A glittering display of Pepple's wealth awaited the king of Warri when he eventually brought his daughter for the marriage ceremony. Pepple himself described the scene to a visiting European in graphic "pidgin" that loses nothing by being left in the original:

"That time I first hear, Warri's canoe come for creek, I fire one gun from my house — then all Bonny fire — plenty powder blow away you no can hear one man speak. I stand for my house — all my house have fine cloth. Roof, walls, all round, he hung with proper fine silks. No possible to look one stick, one mat: all be covered.

"My Queen Father stand for beach. His foot no touch ground. He stand on cloth. All way he walk, he walk for cloth. . . . I give

Wine, Brandy, plenty puncheon — pass twenty. I give for my people and Warri's. All Bonny glad too much. . . . Every man, every woman, for my town, I give cloth — pass one thousand piece I give that day. Pass twenty barrel powder I fire that day."

There in a nutshell lay the truth about "capital accumulation" during the high days of the delta trade. Merchants who were also monarchs spent their wealth as traditional rulers must: to glorify their name and reputation and enlarge their power by winning allies from among their peers. The system was stable within its limits, but its limits stopped short of the economic growth that could have led to systematic investment. And the slave trade continually fortified those limits by enhancing the power of kings and prime merchants, while siphoning off those pressures of population or political dissent which had pressed, elsewhere, towards economic change and expansion.

After the ending of the slave trade, the powerful men of the delta went in for palm-oil production on a large plantation scale; Pepple, like Ja Ja, owed his wealth to oil exports rather than to slaving. Would this new form of production have developed rapidly into a West African capitalism? Perhaps. But it was never given the chance. Pressing on its heels, there followed colonial conquest; and the circumstances of invasion proved even more depressing to economic growth than the slave trade. These circumstances changed, yet even as late as the 1950's one may note that the many thriving merchants of West Africa had seldom developed into full-blown capitalists; more often than not, they remained trading middlemen who were content to sell African raw materials in exchange for non-African consumer imports. This was partly the reflection of subsistence economics persisting into modern times, but there is ground for thinking that it was also a consequence of the special trading systems of the past.

On the economic side, then, the slave trade exercised a serious

A SUMMING-UP

and continuous effect in retarding and reducing African production. For this reason the European relationship generally failed to induce the social and cultural expansion that occurred among the trading cities of the "Saharan seaboard" or among those of the Indian Ocean littoral in pre-European times. The scale of this failure greatly varied. It was practically complete in the Congo and in East Africa. It was far from complete in some parts of Guinea. Yet even in Guinea the more favored areas paid a heavy price for their middleman prosperity in the social troubles that engulfed the lands behind them — and eventually themselves as well.

It is on the political side that the full damage may be found — and, at this stage of historical research, most clearly of all in the lands of Guinea.

Four great phases of political relationship can be traced. Each had profound formative influence. In the beginning, contact was a mere accumulation of points of intercourse, sometimes peaceful though often warlike. The early mariners did little more than burgle or bang on West Africa's back door. Yet even this gave the coastland a new importance to its peoples.

This enhanced importance of the coast had its effect in the sixteenth century. The inhabitants of this new "frontier of opportunity" quickly adjusted themselves to the business of defending and promoting their interests in oversea trade. This was the second phase, the phase of widening commerce and political alliance.

With the seventeenth century there came the forging of a close-knit partnership between the Europeans and the peoples of the coast. This was no rapid or smoothly worked achievement. It involved a bitter fight for monopolist privilege: between Euro-

An End and a Beginning

peans for monopoly by sea, and between Africans for monopoly on land — and occasionally between allied groups of Europeans and Africans together. Yet in this third phase they evolved with one another a balance of power based on slaving that held good until the nineteenth century. Europeans accepted their restriction to trading from shipboard or from occasional footholds on shore; and Africans settled into a distribution of powers and rights that gave primacy to each strong coastal people in its own region.

There were interruptions. The balance of power kept breaking down on land and by sea. The British fought the French; the Ardras fought the Dahomeyans. Yet the wars were not so frequent as to become a general rule. As often as not there was peace among the partners. The first decisive break occurred in the eighteenth century when inland peoples lost patience with the coastal middlemen and struck through them to direct contact with Europeans. Thus Europeans on the Guinea Coast were now faced with expanding African powers for the first time. Hostilities threatened. Wars broke out. But the Africans were too strong to be overawed, much less overthrown. Besides, once their rights were accepted, they were ready to enter the partnership themselves. Provided that Europe was content with equality of rights and respect, slaving could continue.

Then in the nineteenth century, with the fourth phase, the balance shifted again. British and French abolition of the slave trade went hand in hand with the rise of a new imperialism. Europeans were no longer content with equality of rights. They wanted domination. Soon they became involved in African politics, intervening by way of alliance with the statelets of the coast against the new powers of the hinterland. Inevitably, industrial Europe triumphed over nonindustrial Africa.

Now a review of this changing relationship will show that

A SUMMING-UP

each of these phases was linked organically to the next. The slave trade, the crisis of its abolition, colonial invasion: all were aspects of a continuous process. Thus the old coastal partnership — the unique and extraordinary slaving relationship that bound the servitudes and freedoms of Europe and Africa so curiously and inextricably together — paved the way for the colonial system. The one beckoned the other.

This can best be seen in the consequences of slaving on African forms of government. The European connection repeatedly confirmed the conservative element in African feudalism and, at the same time, distorted the influence and power which this element could wield. Generally, the relationship tended to petrify African institutions within traditional forms that grew ever more brittle and inflexible. It played into the hands of those who had most to gain from obstructing social change. It paralyzed the will to evolve new and more effective — more modern — political institutions. There were exceptions, but the exceptions prove the rule.

Aside from bolstering the power of chiefs, slaving also provided a ready means for ridding chiefs of their critics. It was easy to remove the spokesmen of those who suffered most from the system, and who therefore wished to change it. In this respect the powerful men of West Africa behaved no differently from those of Europe: they transported their "malcontents" and "troublemakers" to lands that were safely beyond the sea.

No one can be sure how often this was done. Yet it is not speculation to say that the inland theocracies regularly called in religious sanctions to denounce critics as criminals and thereby turn them into captives for disposal. Nor is it speculation to say that political opponents in the delta states — where a political society was in budding growth — were given the same treatment. This may be taken as one reason why African revolts against the slaving system seldom occurred at home but frequently on shipboard and across the seas.

In this elimination of rebels or potential rebels, the chiefs invariably had the backing of their European partners. When the Blood Men of the Old Calabar plantations invaded the town in 1850, records Waddell (and he was there), the apparition of these armed bands from the bush "so alarmed the ship captains, for their property ashore, that they sent off hastily to Fernando Po, for the consul and a man-of-war." Like other observers of the African scene, before and since, these captains had misunderstood the evidence of their own eyes. They feared for their property, yet the Blood Men wanted only to protect the lives of slaves. The European traders on the spot were even more upset. "Talking of these things at King Eyo's table, one of them said: 'I would like nothing better than to see the heads of a hundred of these fellows cut off.' To that humane sentiment another old trader added: 'They ought to be shot down like dogs.' "

When nothing happened, because the Blood Men found that there were to be no human sacrifices and accordingly went back the way they had come, "those who wanted to shoot them and behead them off-hand were ashamed of their panic when the consul and the man-of-war came, and had nothing to do." Consul Beecroft, backed by his warship, lost no time in arranging matters so as to confirm and defend the *status quo:* "farm slaves" — that is, the Blood Men — were to be "forbidden to invade Duke Town armed, combinations for unlawful purposes prohibited, and runaways delivered up on demand."

Then Waddell adds his most revealing passage. "Though King Eyo kept silence during the discussion at his table [of the above arrangement between himself and Consul Beecroft] he was not insensible to the danger that might result from a spirit of combination among the slaves; and he sought to prevent its spreading

A SUMMING-UP

by the old methods of denunciation and terror. . . ." In other words, since Eyo could no longer rid himself of inconvenient critics, as his predecessors had done, by handing them over to Europeans who regarded not their opinions but only their muscular development, he threatened them with death if they should dare to organize an opposition. And in doing this he could still rely on the backing of a man-of-war and the approval of a British consul. For although Consul Beecroft had obtained from the rulers of Old Calabar the confirmation of an earlier agreement against human sacrifice, the truth was that the Blood Men were the only force that could and did make an end to that practice. Yet Consul Beecroft pledged himself to help King Eyo to frustrate the Blood Men. Once again the built-in defenses of the coastal partnership were at work in favor of a conservation that could only, in the long tale of history, cramp and stultify.

African chiefly rule had been — often still was — an efficient and representative form of government. But it suffered increasing perversion. Continued wars and raids on the mainland, Alfred Moloney was writing to the British lieutenant governor of Lagos colony in 1881, were "to the personal advantage of a few influential Chiefs on either side who fan the flame to their own benefit, but to the detriment of their country and countrymen." Later on, when colonial rule had engulfed the whole of this country and imposed a *Pax Britannica*, chiefs would continue to seek their personal advantage by accommodations with imperial government, and would thereby prepare their eventual downfall. Apart from some who fought and were defeated, and a few who retired in dignity and said no more, most of the traditional rulers of West Africa accepted imperial Europe as a master who would at least perpetuate their own special positions of privilege, if at the cost of their actual power; the emirs of northern Nigeria, thanks to

An End and a Beginning

the British doctrine of "indirect rule," were even successful in conserving both their privilege and their power.

The reasons for European progress between the fifteenth century and the nineteenth are common knowledge. I have tried in this book to examine the reasons for a comparative African stagnation and decay and thus explain, from an African standpoint, why the "cultural gap" between leading states in Africa and Europe widened across this period from a narrow step to a gulf; why colonial conquest followed swiftly and completely; and why it became easy for Europeans to regard Africans as "primitive," "without culture," "incapable of civilization on their own," and the rest.

Through these four centuries the balance of gain was all one way. In any effective sense there was no creative marriage of cultures, no passage of ideas, no sharing of wealth or achievement. To Europe the trade with Africa was always an enrichment, and this enrichment could and did lead Europe into new and more productive forms of society and government. But to Africans the relationship was incapable of carrying through the social and economic changes which were now required; on the contrary, it steered all those societies that it touched into economic or political frustration. The whole connection may be seen, indeed, as another demonstration of the appallingly wasteful nature of capital accumulation during the Industrial Revolution in Europe.

The connection worked another evil. Among Europeans it produced the mentality of race superiority which helped to hasten colonial conquest and still lingers like a poison in our midst. They came to believe that the slave trade was none of their contriving but a "natural" outcome of Africa's indifference to human life. In 1832 the British Government agreed to send an expedition up the Niger "with Commissioners charged . . . to make treaties with the native chiefs for the suppression of this horrible traffic [the slave trade]; and to point out to them the advantages they will derive, if, instead of the wars and aggressions to which it gives rise, they will substitute an innocent and legitimate commerce." A worthy object, no doubt, but perhaps a trifle hypocritical in view of all that had gone before? Yet we may be fairly sure that it never occurred to those excellent commissioners, bent on their errand of mercy, to reflect that this horrible traffic was a direct and deliberate consequence of centuries of European insistence. Europe, not Africa, had fathered the oversea slave trade; but Europe had ceased to recognize its child.

On Africans the mentality of the slaving years has tended to produce a contrary effect: it has tended to indoctrinate Africans with a sense of inferiority and even, here and there, of guilt and shame; and this too, in one or another devious form, still persists. "We, the Europeans," it was afterwards said, "were certainly wrong to enslave Africans but at least we stopped the trade: while you, the Africans, not only persisted in the trade but perversely enslaved your own people. Can you really believe you are fit to run your own affairs?" This was said regardless of the fact that Europeans had also, in their own time and place, enslaved "their own people"; and that Africans had in any case no sense of continental unity, while African religion made the concept of "one's own people" a purely local one. The truth was that Africans had almost never "enslaved their own people"; they had handed over other people who happened to live in Africa. In this they were no less "moral" than the Europeans who had instigated the trade and bought the captives.

Both the one and the other — the pride and the shame, the sense of superiority and the sense of inferiority — are survivals of a past that needs now to be resolutely buried. But it will not be

An End and a Beginning

buried unless the true character and course of the slaving enterprise are understood; and it is the effort to promote this understanding, even within the narrow limits of present historical knowledge, that may, I hope, finally justify these many pages.

For all this, now, should be over and done with. Humanity is too much cluttered and dismayed by the memory of past errors and botches. It is time to learn from them whatever can be learned and then forget them. People remain. People in Africa, no matter how the habit of those old years might ruin and ravage, held on nonetheless to their belief in life and in themselves. Thanks to this firm hold, the slave trade passed over them without permanent damage. Today they reassert their equality and unity with the rest of mankind. At last the slaving chain of cause and effect, terminating in colonial subjection, is broken.

One should be careful not to overstress the accent on "stagnation" in these years. There was repeated individual effort to meet new situations in new ways. Reassertion took shape time and again in the skill and vigor with which Africans evolved new techniques, matched their wits against foreign partners and eventual enemies, and tried to forge new structures of society. It was made by all those men in Africa who fought against capture and exile, the overweening power of chiefs, or invasion from abroad.

And clear evidence of this same reassertion of African humanity can be found elsewhere as well. For it was made by all those countless slaves who refused to accept their fate and rose in revolt against their masters, founded free republics in the Americas, or died in the attempt. It was proclaimed by the "mutineers" on board ship, by the nameless heroes of Palmares, by the revolutionaries of Haiti, and the Negro soldiers of Bolívar. Equality; but also, even though they did not know it, unity as well. For these brave men were the natural allies and companions of Sharp and Clarkson, Reynal and Grégoire, the Anti-Slavery Society and

A SUMMING-UP

the Société des Amis des Noirs — not to speak of a later time and the pioneers of Negro liberation in the United States.

Now in our own day the same liberating unity is once more forged across the world, and all those men and women in Europe and elsewhere who have seen or now see the cause of their own human enlargement in the renaissance of Africa are welcomed by the lifting voices of resurgent life in Africa itself: inexhaustible, ever-quickened, keen with hope.

Acknowledgments

No BOOK OF THIS KIND COULD BE ATTEMPTED WITHOUT GOOD ADvice. Among the scholars who have generously helped me, I should like especially to thank Professor K. O. Dike for encouragement and for guidance regarding the delta states; Dr. G. S. P. Freeman-Grenville for indispensable help regarding Swahili history; and, generally over the months and years, Dr. Gervase Mathew, Dr. Raymond Mauny, Professor Théodore Monod (to whom I am also grateful for the quotation from Jean Temporal), Dr. George Shepperson, Mr. Thomas Hodgkin, and Dr. Eric Williams. Responsibility for what I have written is entirely mine.

I am most grateful to Mr. Lucio de Miranda for invaluable help in translating letters from King Affonso of Congo to the kings of Portugal; to the Curator of Rhodes House for allowing me to consult the Morice manuscript and the microfilm of other French manuscripts photographed by the University of Chicago Library from documents in their possession; to Commander T. Fox Pitt and the Anti-Slavery Society for permission to consult papers; and to M. Mario de Andrade and his publishers for permission to quote the lines by Agostinho Neto, printed in *Antologia de Poesia Negra de Expressão Portuguesa* (Oswald, Paris, 1958)

Bibliography

THE FOLLOWING IS A GUIDE TO AUTHORS AND BOOKS QUOTED OR otherwise mentioned in the text, together with a short list of other relevant works. A fuller background bibliography may be found in my book entitled *The Lost Cities of Africa*.

The reader should bear in mind that any such lists can at this stage be no more than a guide to knowledge that is still greatly deficient. What Dr. Freeman-Grenville has lately said of East African history is true of almost all precolonial history in Africa: that "we are only at the beginning of its serious study, and there is a vast field for research in the collection of oral traditions and of documents in private hands, as well as for the classification and study of documents in libraries scattered all over the globe."

I hope that these two books of mine will play some part in stimulating and inspiring other writers to go further and do better.

INTRODUCTION

BLACK MOTHER

Anonymous (slave trade)	*Fugitive Thoughts on the African Slave Trade* (Liverpool pamphlet), 1792
Beltran, G. A.	"Tribal Origins of Slaves in Mexico," *Jnl. of Negro Hist.* 42, 1957
Carlyle, T.	*The Nigger Question*, 1849
Eschwege, W. E. von	*Journal von Brasilien*, Vol. 1, 1818

Bibliography

Ewbank, T.	*Life in Brazil*, 1856
Freyre, G.	*The Masters and the Slaves* (trans. S. Putnam), 1946
	Problemas Brasilieros de Antropologia, 1959
Gardner, G.	*Travels in the Interior of Brazil*, 1846
King, J. F.	"Negro History in Continental Spanish America," *Jnl. of Negro Hist.* 29, 1944
Mawe, J.	*Travels in the Interior of Brazil*, 1812
Pi-Sunyer, O.	"Historical Background of the Negro in Brazil," *Jnl. of Negro Hist.* 42, 1957
Ramos, A.	*O Negro Brasiliero*, 1934
	"Acculturation among the Brazilian Negroes," *Jnl. of Negro Hist.* 26, 1941
	Die Negerkulturen in der Neuen Welt, 1946
Simonsen, R. C.	*História Economica do Brasil* (2 vols.), 1937
Walsh, R.	*Notices of Brazil* (2 vols.), 1830
Williams, E.	"The Golden Age of the Slave System in Britain," *Jnl. of Negro Hist.* 25, 1940
Zelinsky, W.	"Negro Population in Latin America," *Jnl. of Negro Hist.* 34, 1949

ONE
FACT AND FABLE

Ba, A.-H., and Daget, J.	*L'Empire Peul du Macina*, 1955
Baildon, H. B.	*Poems of William Dunbar*, 1907
Barros, J. de	*Da Asia* (24 vols.), 1777 [first three *decadas* only, 1552-1553]
Barrow, G. W. S.	*Feudal Britain*, 1956
Beattie, J.	*Bunyoro: An African Kingdom*, 1960
Bloch, M.	*La Société Féodale:* (Vol. 1), *La Formation des Liens de Dépendance*, 1939; (Vol. 2), *Les Classes et le Gouvernement des Hommes*, 1949
Chilver, E. M.	"Feudalism in the Inter-Lacustrine Kingdoms," in *East African Chiefs*, ed. A. I. Richards, 1960

Davidson, B.	*The Lost Cities of Africa*, 1959
Dunbar, W.	See Baildon, Paterson
Forde, D. (ed.)	*African Worlds*, 1954
George, K.	"The West Looks at Primitive Africa, 1400-1800," *Isis*, March, 1958
Handlin, O.	*Race and Nationality in American Life*, reprinted 1957
Hennig, R.	*Terrae Incognitae* (Vols. 3, 4), 1953, 1956
Maitland, F. W.	*Domesday Book and After*, reprinted 1960
Maquet, J. J.	"The Kingdom of Ruanda," in *African Worlds* (ed. D. Forde), 1954
Mauny, R.	"Evocation de l'Empire du Mali," *Notes Africaines*, Inst. Français de l'Afrique Noire, April, 1959
Oberg, K.	"The Kingdom of Ankole in Uganda," in *African Political Systems*, M. Fortes, and E. E. Evans-Pritchard, reprinted 1958
Olderogge, D.	*Zapadni Sudan v. XV-XIX vv.*, 1960
Paterson, J.	*Life and Poems of William Dunbar*, 1860
Potekhin, I. I.	*On Feudalism of the Ashanti* (paper read to the Twentieth International Congress of Orientalists), 1960
Rattray, R. S.	*Ashanti*, 1923
Sidibé, M.	"Soundiata Kéita, Héro Historique et Légendaire," *Notes Africaines*, Inst. Français de l'Afrique Noire, April, 1959
Tannenbaum, F.	*Slave and Citizen*, 1947
Williams, E.	*The Historical Background of Race Relations in the Caribbean*, Trinidad, 1955

TWO

THE YEARS OF TRIAL

Atkins, J.	*A Voyage to Guinea, Brasil and the West Indies*, 1737
Azurara (Zurara), G. E. de	*Crónica dos Feitos da Guiné*. See Beazley.

Bibliography

Beazley, C. R., and Prestage, E. (eds.)	*The Chronicle of the Discovery and Conquest of Guinea*, by G. E. de Azurara (Zurara), (2 vols.), 1896
Bernal, J. D.	*Science in History*, 1954
Blake, J. W.	*Europeans in West Africa* (2 vols.), 1942
Botsford, J. B.	*English Society in the 18th Century as Influenced from Oversea*, 1924
Ca' da Mosto (Cadamosto)	See Crone.
Clarkson, T.	*Essay on the Slavery and Commerce of the Human Species*, 1788
	History of the Rise, Progress and Accomplishment of the Abolition of the African Slave Trade (2 vols.), 1808
Commons, House of	*Abridgement of the Minutes of the Evidence* (on the slave trade), 1789
Crone, G. R.	*The Voyages of Cadamosto*, 1937
Donnan, E.	*Documents Illustrative of the History of the Slave Trade to America*: (Vol. 1, 1441-1700), 1930; (Vol. 2, the 18th century), 1931; (Vol. 3), 1932; (Vol. 4), 1935
Falconbridge, A.	*An Account of the Slave Trade on the Coast of Africa*, 1788
Fernandes, V.	See Monod.
Fox-Bourne, H. R.	*English Merchants* (2 vols.), 1866
Gaston-Martin	*Histoire de l'Esclavage dans les Colonies Françaises*, 1948
Gomes, D.	See Monod.
Hakluyt, R.	*Principal Voyages of the English Nation* (Vol. 4), reprinted 1926
Huntley, H.	*Seven Years' Service on the Slave Coast of Western Africa* (2 vols.), 1850
James, C. L. R.	*Black Jacobins*, 1938
Kimble, G. H. T. (trans.)	*Esmeraldo de Situ Orbis*, by Duarte Pacheco Pereira, 1937
Laird, MacGregor	*State of the Interior of Africa* (notes included), Anti-Slavery Society Papers, p. 37, Jan., 1838

Bibliography

Lilley, S.	*Men, Machines and History*, 1948
Lowe, J., Jr.	*Liberty or Death* (pamphlet), 1789
Ly, A.	*La Compagnie du Sénégal*, 1958
Mackenzie-Grieve, A.	*The Last Years of the English Slave Trade*, 1941
Mauny, R. (trans.)	*Esmeraldo de Situ Orbis*, by Duarte Pacheco Pereira (Centro de Estudos da Guiné Portuguesa), 1956
	Les Navigations Mediévales sur les Côtes Sahariennes Antérieures à la Découverte Portugaise (1434) (Centro de Estudos Históricos Ultramarinos), 1960
Monod, T., with Texeira de Moto, A., and Mauny, R.	*Déscription de la Côte Occidentale d'Afrique* (1506-1510) (Centro Estudos Guiné Portuguesa), 1951
Monod, T., with Mauny, R., and Duval, G.	*De la Première Découverte de la Guinée* (Centro Estudos Guiné Portuguesa), 1959
Namier, L. B.	*The Structure of English Politics at the Accession of George III* (2 vols.), 1929
Newton, J.	*Thoughts Upon the African Slave Trade* (pamphlet), 1788
Pereira, Duarte Pacheco	*Esmeraldo de Situ Orbis*. See Kimble and Mauny.
Plumb, J. H.	*England in the Eighteenth Century*, 1950
Ragatz, L. J.	*The Fall of the Planter Class in the British Caribbean 1763-1833*, 1928
Scelle, G.	*La Traite Négrière aux Indes de Castille* (2 vols.), 1906
Schoelcher, V.	*Esclavage et Colonisation* (with preface by C.-A. Julien, introduction by A. Césaire, edited by E. Tersen), 1948
Scott, W. R.	*The Constitution and Finance of English, Scottish and Irish Joint-Stock Companies to 1720* (3 vols.), 1912
Société des Amis des Noirs	*Addresse à l'Assemblée Nationale pour l'Abolition de la Traite des Noirs*, 1790
Wadstrom, C. B.	*Letters, etc.*, 1788

Bibliography

	Observations on the Slave Trade (Anti-Slavery Society Papers: Binns Collection), 1789
Williams, E.	*Capitalism and Slavery*, 1945
Williamson, J. A.	*Sir John Hawkins*, 1927
Winterbottom, T.	*An Account of the Native Africans in the Neighbourhood of Sierra Leone* (2 vols.), 1803

THREE

MANNER OF THE TRADE

(See also Introduction and Parts One and Two)

Bandinel, J.	*Some Account of the Trade in Slaves from Africa*, 1842
Barbot, James	See Barbot, John.
Barbot, John	*A Description of the Coasts of North and South Guinea; and of Ethiopia Interior, vulgarly called Angola*, 1746
Bosman, W.	*A New and Accurate Account of the Coast of Guinea, etc.* (English edition), 1721
Equiano, O.	*The Interesting Narrative of the Life of Olaudah Equiano or Gustavus Vassa the African*, 1793
Herskovits, M. J.	"Anthropology and Cultural Change in Africa" (Communication of the University of South Africa), 1957
	The Myth of the Negro Past, reprinted 1958
Jobson, R.	*The Golden Trade*, reprinted 1954
Johnston, H. H.	*The Negroes in the New World*, 1900
Kuczynski, R. R.	*Population Movements*, 1936
Shepperson, G., and Price, T.	*Independent African*, 1958
Smith, W.	*Voyage to Guinea*, 1726
Stedman, J. G.	*Narrative of a Five Years' Expedition against the Revolted Negroes of Surinam, 1772-7* (2 vols.), 1796

Bibliography

FOUR
MANI-CONGO

Angelo and Carli, Fathers	See Pinkerton (Vol. 16), p. 157.
Battell, A.	See Ravenstein.
Boxer, C. R.	"The Old Kingdom of Congo," in *The Dawn of African History* (ed. Ronald Oliver), 1961
Burton, R. P.	*Lacerda's Journey to Cazembe*, including *Journey of the Pombeiros* (trans. R. A. Beadle and C. T. Beke), 1873
Cadbury, W. A.	*Labour in Portuguese West Africa*, 1910
Cadornega, O.	See Jordão.
Cavazzi, G. A. da Montecuccolo	*Istorica Descrizione de' Tre Regni Congo, Matamba et Angola*, 1687
Childs, G. M.	*Umbundu Kinship and Character*, 1949
Clark, J. D.	*The Prehistory of South Africa*, 1959
Cuvelier, J.	*L'Ancien Royaume de Congo*, 1946
Duffy, J.	*Portuguese Africa*, 1959
Felner, A. de A.	*Angola, apontamentos sobre a ocupação e inicio do estabelecimento dos Portugeses no Congo, Angola e Benguela*, 1933
Ihle, A.	*Das Alte Königreich Kongo*, 1929
Jadin, L.	Report into researches in the archives of Luanda, *Bull. of Inst. Royale Coloniale Belge*, 1, 1953
	"Relation sur le royaume du Congo du P. Raimondo da Dicomano," *Bull. of Académie royale des Sciences coloniales*, Brussels No. 2, 1957
Jordão, Levi Maria (Visconde de Paiva Manso)	*História do Congo (Documentos)*, 1877
Merolla, J. M. da Sorrento	See Donnan, (Vol. 1), p. 319.
Montesarchio, G. de S.	See Cuvelier, p. 279.

Bibliography

Paiva, Manso	See Jordão.
Pigafetta, F., and Lopez, D.	*Relação do reino do Congo e das terras circunvezinhas* (Port. edn.), 1949-1951
Pinkerton, J.	*A General Collection of the Best and Most Interesting Voyages and Travels, etc.* (espec. Vol. 16), 1814
Pombeiros	See Burton.
Proyart	See Pinkerton (Vol. 16), pp. 548-597, and Donnan (Vol. 2), p. 549.
Ravenstein, E. G.	*The Strange Adventures of Andrew Battell of Leigh, in Angola and the adjoining Regions*, reprinted 1901
Robinson, K. R.	*Khami Ruins*, 1959

FIVE
EAST COAST FORTUNES

Allen, J. W. T.	"The Collection of Swahili Literature and Its Relation to Oral Tradition and History" (unpublished)
Axelson, E.	*South-East Africa*, 1940
Boteler, T.	*Narrative of a Voyage of Discovery . . . from 1821 to 1826* (2 vols.), 1835
Boxer, C. R., and Azevedo, C. de	*Fort Jesus and the Portuguese in Mombasa 1593-1727*, 1960
Coupland, R.	*Kirk on the Zambesi*, 1928
	East Africa and Its Invaders, reprinted 1956
Crasson, J. de M.	Rhodes House MS Afr. vol. 6, du Curt Reports 29.1. 1791
Dames, M. L.	*The Book of Duarte Barbosa* (2 vols.), 1918
Freeman-Grenville, G. S. P.	"The Tanganyika Coast (in Medieval Times, etc.)" (paper read to the London Conference on African History and Archaeology), 1953
	"Coinage in East Africa Before Portuguese Times," *Numismatic Chronicle*, 1957

Bibliography

	"Swahili Literature and the History and Archaeology of the East African Coast," *Jnl. of the East African Swahili Committee*, July, 1958
	"Medieval Evidences for Swahili," *Jnl. of the East African Swahili Committee*, Jan., 1959
	"East African Coin Finds and their Historical Significance," *Jnl. of African Hist.* 1, 1960
	"Islam and Christianity in East Africa," *African Ecclesiastical Review*, July, 1960
	"Historiography of the East African Coast," *Tanganyika Notes and Records*, Sept., 1960
	"The (East African) Coast 1498-1840," *Oxford History of East Africa* [Vol. 1, to be published]
Hichens, W.	*The Soul's Awakening* (al-Inkishafi: Sayyid 'Abdallah bin 'Ali bin Nasir), 1939
Lanning, E. C.	"The Earthworks at Kibengo," *Uganda Jnl.* Sept., 1960
Livingstone, D.	*Missionary Travels and Researches in South Africa*, 1857
	Narrative of an Expedition to the Zambesi (with C. Livingstone), 1865
Morice	Rhodes House MS. Afr., vol. 6
Oliver, R.	"A Question about the Bachwezi," *Uganda Jnl.*, Sept., 1953
	"Ancient Capital Sites in Ankole," *Uganda Jnl.*, March, 1959
Owen, W. F. W.	*Narrative of Voyages to Explore the Shores of Africa, Arabia and Madagascar* (2 vols.), 1833
Prins, A. H. J.	"On Swahili Historiography," *Jnl. of the East Africa Swahili Committee*, July, 1958
Prior, J.	*Voyage Along the Eastern Coast of Africa to Mosambique, Johanna and Quiloa etc. in the Nisus Frigate*, 1819
Velten, C.	*Märchen und Erzählungen der Suaheli*, 1898

Bibliography

SIX
FRONTIER OF OPPORTUNITY

Bedford, Rear Admiral	*Correspondence Respecting the Disturbances in Benin, etc.*, Acting Consul-General Moor to Foreign Office C/7638, 1895
Biobaku, S. O.	Lugard Lectures, 1955
	The Egba and Their Neighbours, 1957
Bowdich, T. E.	*Mission from Cape Coast to Ashanti*, 1819
Bradbury, R. E.	*The Benin Kingdom and the Edo-Speaking Peoples*, 1957
Cardi, C. N. de	See Kingsley (2), Appendix.
Cornevin, R.	*Histoire des Peuples de l'Afrique Noire*, 1960
Dalzell, A.	*History of Dahomey*, 1793
Dapper, O.	*Déscription de l'Afrique*, 1686
Dark, P.	*Benin Art*, 1960
Dike, K. O.	*Trade and Politics in the Niger Delta 1830-1885*, 1956
	"Trade and the Opening Up of the Niger," *Nigeria Magazine*, Oct., 1960
Egharevba, J. U.	*Short History of Benin*, 1953
Elisofon, E.	*The Sculpture of Africa*, 1959
Fage, J. D.	*Introduction to the History of West Africa*, reprinted 1959
	An Atlas of African History, 1958
	Ghana, A Historical Interpretation, 1959
Fagg, B. E. B.	"The Nok Culture in Prehistory" (paper read to the Historical Society of Nigeria, Dec. Congress), 1958
	"The Nok Terracottas in West African Art History" (paper read to the Pan-African Congress on Prehistory), 1959
Fagg, W.	*The Sculpture of Africa*, 1959
Forde, D. (ed.)	*Efik Traders of Old Calabar*, 1956
Forman, W. and B.	*Benin Art*, 1960
Gallwey, Capt.	*Affairs of the West Coast of Africa*, H.M. Stationery Office, Africa 11 of 1893

Bibliography

Goldie, Sir G. W.	*Report on the Niger-Sudan Campaign*, 1897
Greenberg, J. H.	*Studies in African Linguistic Classification*, 1955
Haut Commissariat de la République Française en A.O.F.	*AOF 1957: Tableaux Economiques*
Hodgkin, T.	*Nigerian Perspectives*, 1960
Jahn, J.	*Muntu*, 1958 [Eng. edition, 1961]
Johnson, S.	*History of the Yorubas*, 1921
Jones, G. I.	See Forde.
Kingsley, M. H.	*Travels in West Africa*, 1897
	West African Studies, 1899
Kirk, Sir J.	*Report on the Disturbances at Brass*, HMSO Africa 3, 1896
Lugard, F. D.	*On Nigerian Amalgamation*, Cmd. 468, 1920
Martin, E. C.	*The British West African Settlements 1796-1821*, 1927
Moloney, A.	*Correspondence on the War between Native Tribes in the Interior*, Lagos Cmd. 4987, 1887
Norris, R.	See Dalzell.
Phillips, Acting Consul-General	*Papers Relating to the Massacre of British Officials near Benin and the Consequent Punitive Expedition*, C/8440, 1897
Priestley, M., and Wilks, I.	"The Ashanti Kings in the 18th Century: A revised chronology," *Jnl. of African Hist.* 1, 1960
Roth, H. L.	*Great Benin, Its Customs and Horrors*, 1903
Simmons, J.	See Forde.
Spitz, G.	*L'Ouest Africain Français*, 1947
Suret-Canale, J.	*Afrique Noire Occidentale et Centrale* (Vol. 1), 1958
Talbot, P. A.	*Tribes of the Niger Delta*, 1932
Trimingham, J. S.	*Islam in West Africa*, 1959
Waddell, H. M.	*Twenty Nine Years in the West Indies and Central Africa*, 1863
Ward, W. E. F.	*A History of Ghana*, 1958

Bibliography

Willett, F.	"Ife and its Archaeology," *Jnl. of African Hist.* 2, 1960
Wolfson, F.	*Pageant of Ghana*, reprinted 1959

SEVEN

FOUR CENTURIES: A SUMMING-UP

Allen, W.	*Picturesque Views of the River Niger*, 1840

Index

ABOMEY (DAHOMEY), 239, 243-245
Affonso, Dom (Mani-Congo): partnership with King Manuel, 121-128; his aims for Congo, 144; troubled by São Tomé, 145-146; attempts to reduce slave trade, 146-148
Africa, Africans: pre-discovery legends, 3-4; European and American views, 5-7; stability, compared with Europe states, 7; self-confidence and resistance to invasion, 10-11; revised estimate of, 98-102; reassertion of humanity, 289-290
Amirou Mangal (great chief), 12
Angola, 130, 132
Ankole, social order in, 18
Annamaboe, princes of, 274
Antera Duke, diary on slave trade, 217 ff.
Aro oracle, 98, 211-213
Aros, slave trading by, 211-213
Ashanti Union, 250-255; conquered by British, 255
Assientos for Guinea slaves, 49
Atkins, John, quoted, 57, 94-95
Azambuja, Diogo d', 247-248
Azurara, G. E. de. *See* Zurara

BACHWEZI, 176-177
Baptista, Pedro João, 155
Barbados, occupied by English, 58
Barbot, James, quoted, 106, 154
Barbot, John, quoted, 57, 86-93, 106, 231
Beecroft, Consul, 285-286
Benin, 214, 220, 225, 227-228; story of downfall, 229-237
Bermudas, occupied by English, 58
Bird, Captain Japhet, quoted, 93
Black lady of Africa, 4

Blake, Captain John, quoted, 84
Blood Men, 222, 236, 285-286
Bonny, slave trading at, 214-215
Bornu, social classes in, 16
Bosman, William, on Benin, 233
Brett, Mr., quoted, 56
Brohemie, seized by British, 267-268. *See also* Nanna, Chief of Brohemie

CABRAL, PEDRO ALVARES, 44
Cadornega, Oliveira, quoted, 131-132, 150
Calabar, slave trading at, 215-217
Cannibalism: imputed to Africans and Europeans, 57, 96-98; Aro oracle on, 98
Cão, Diogo, 117; discovers Congo River, 118; visits Mani-Congo, 119
Carloff, Captain, 55
Cavazzi, Father, quoted, 10; on cannibalism myth, 97
Chang Hsieh, quoted, 170-171
Chattel slaves, disappearance of, 26
Clarkson, Thomas (abolitionist), 70-71, 95
Clement IV (Pope), 22
Colonial invasion, effects of, 273 ff.
Columbus, Christopher, 25, 33, 44
Commercial exchange, emergence of, 53
Company of Adventurers of London Trading into Parts of Africa, 55
Congo: governmental and legal system, 136-140; Christian enlightenment, 140-141; trade and currency, 141-143; shortage of transport, 149; Portuguese invasion and undermining, 150-151; slave trade in, 154-162; impoverishment, 158; resurgence, 162. *See also* Mani-Congo
Congo River, discovery of, 118

INDEX

Coupland, R., quoted, 195
Curaçao, occupied by Dutch, 58

DAHOMEY, and slave trade, 239-246
Danes, occupy St. Thomas, 58
Dapper, Olfert, on Benin, 231-232, 235
Delany, Martin, quoted, 19
Denmark, trades with Guinea Coast, 55
Depopulation of Africa, 275-277; and slave trade, 276
Dike, K. O.: on Niger delta, 206, 210; on depopulation of Africa, 276
Dondo, Ngola of, 150-151
Dutch, invasion of Gold Coast by, 54 ff., settlements by, 58

EANNES, GIL (GONSALO), 9, 37
East Coast: civilization and culture, 166-175; early trade, 169; history of city-states, 171; Arab influences, 171-172; Swahili language, 174-175, 185-186; Iron Age states, 175-179; slaves and slaving, 180-196; Portuguese penetration, 183-185
Egbo. See Leopard Society
Elizabeth, Queen, 51; engages in Guinea trade, 42
Elmina (fort), 41; built by Portuguese, 9; captured by Dutch, 54, 249
English: settlements by, 58; speculation in West Indies, 60-63
Equiano, Olaudah, on cannibalism, 97-98

FAGG, WILLIAM, on Benin, 234
Ferreira, Gonçalo, 39
Feudalism: in Africa's Iron Age, 11 ff.; in Europe and Africa, compared, 25-30; unification in African societies, 28; tribal equality in, 29; effect of migrations on, 29-30

Fort Nassau, built by Dutch, 54
Freeman-Grenville, G. S. P., on Indian Ocean trade, 179-180
French, settlements by, 58
Fulani, invade Hausa states, 14

GALLWEY, CAPTAIN, on Oba of Benin, 237
Gama, Vascoda, 25, 186
Gold: from Elmina, 9; from slave sales by Portuguese, 41; trade in, preferred to that in slaves, 41-42; in East Coast city-states, 177-178
Gold Coast: Dutch invasion of, 54; European-American battle for monopoly, 248 ff.
Gonçalvez, Antam, capture of Africans by, 33-36
Great Circuit trade, 51, 62, 85
Greenberg, J. H., on Nigeria and Cameroons, 203
Guadeloupe, occupied by French, 58
Guinea, English investment in, 54
Guinea Coast: states and empires, 18; slaves from, by Spanish decree, 48-49; English and French voyages to, 49-51; international partnership, 201; Nok culture, 202-203; meeting place of nations, 205; forest states in slave trade, 224-227; significance for, of ending of overseas slave trade, 255 ff.; effects of colonial invasion, 273

HAMMADI, AMADOU, 12
Hausa states of Nigeria: invaded by Fulani, 14; sultans, 14-15
Hawkins, John, trades with Canaries, 50-51
Hawkins, William, brings gold from West Africa, 41
Henry of Congo, 126
Henry, Prince of Portugal, 33, 35; capture of Africans for, 33-36
Hollden, Captain Edward, quoted, 93-94

INDEX

Ibos, 206-207, 211
Industrial Revolution, from trade expansion in Indies, 62-68
Ivory, in East Coast city-states, 177-178

Ja Ja, King of Opobo, oil enterprise of, 261-267
Jefferson, Thomas, on Africans, 5
John III, King of Portugal, 128-129, 144-148
Johnston, Sir Harry, on effect of slave trade, 101
José, Amaro, 155

Kerimba Islands, 183-184
Kilwa, 165-167, 173-174, 180, 185, 188-190
Kingsley, Mary, on Bonny River, 214-215
Kirk, Sir John, quoted, 266

Lançarote, 37
Leeward Islands, occupied by English, 58
Leopard Society (Egbo), 217-220
Leopold, King, on Congo adventure, 256
Lisbon, first slave-capture expedition from, 36-37
Liverpool, West Indies speculation by merchants from, 61-63
Lords of Congo. *See* Mani-Congo
Lok, 41-43

Malfante, Antonio, 3
Mandingos, 103
Mani-Congo (lords of Congo), 119-162; dominions of, 130; description and origin, 131-132; royal palaces, 132-134; powers of, 135; dissension with Portuguese, 142
Manuel, King of Portugal: partnership with Mani-Congo, 121-128; partnership with John III, 128-129
Martin V (Pope), 22

Martinique, occupied by French, 58
Matamba, 130
Mello, Fernam de (vassal of São Tomé), 146
Merolla, Father, 140-141
Mexico, African labor in, 102-104
Miles, William, 60-61
Mingo, Dom Antonio de, 201
Morice, Kilwa exploit of, 189-190

Namier, L. B., quoted, 61
Nanna, Chief of Brohemie, struggles against British penetration, 266-272
Needham, Joseph, quoted, 27
Niger delta: city-states of, 206 ff.; as connecting point with Europe, 207; house system of trade, 208-210; slave trade, 210-213
Nigeria: Iron Age culture in, 202; birth of colony, 259
"Noble savage," 98
Noli, Antonio da, 39
Norris, Robert, on Abomey, 243-244
North America: settlement and occupation of coastlands, 58; colonies and British trade, 72-74

Oba of Benin, 231-232, 234-235, 237, 265-266
Oil trade, as non-slaving commerce, 257; King Ja Ja's enterprise, 261-267
Oil Rivers, 258-259
Oliver, R., quoted, 177
Opobo, state of. *See* Ja Ja, King of Opobo
Osiat, Thomas, 95-96
Ovando, Governor, of Hispaniola, 45-46
Oyo (Yoruba state), 227-229

Pepple, King, 280
Pereira, Duarte Pacheco, quoted, 21-22, 39-40

INDEX

Pizzaro, Fernando, 46
Portugal: sends mission to African chiefs, 8-9; first slave captured by, 33-37; breaks Muslim monopoly of African slave trade, 38. *See also* Mani-Congo
Prio, James, 167, 187
Proyart, quoted, 138

QUILIMANE, 189-190

RATTRAY, R.S., on ritual sacrifice, 236
Regimento of 1512, 122-126
Revolts of Negro slaves, 47
Ritual sacrifice, 220-222, 234-237
Ruanda, kingdom of, 16-17

ST. CHRISTOPHER, occupied by English, 58
St. Eustatius, occupied by Dutch, 58
St. Thomas, occupied by Danes, 58
Sanhaja Berbers, 38
São Tomé (island), 145-146, 148-149
Silva, Guzman de, 51-52
Slave trade: European arguments for, 18-20; by European merchants, 22-24; accepted by Europe and Africa, 24; effect on African-European balance of power, 30; Lisbon captives as beginning of, 37; from Portuguese seizures, 38; begun by Saharan chieftains, 38-39; trebles in fifty years, 40; condemned by France, 42; spreads to England, Europe, and United States, 44; rapid growth after fifteenth century, 44-45; spurred by labor demand in West Indies and Central America, 45, 48; in Christian slaves, 45-46; cruelty and waste of, 46, 92-95; essential to Spanish-American adventure, 48; extension through settlement, 58-59; opened to all French, 60; for British and French colonies, 67; swollen by industrial expansion, 67-68; figures on, 67-68, 79-81; engulfs maritime effort of Europe, 68; abolition, 68-75; by Britain, 69; work of humanitarians, 69-72; influence in America, 75; stages of installation, 81-87; through chiefly rule, 85-86; methods of bargaining, 87-89, 109; manner of payment, 89-90; reactionary views on, 101-102; African origins, 102-107; African-European relationship, 108-112; in Congo (*q.v.*), 154-162; on East Coast, 180-196; as Arab enterprise, 192-193; suppression of, 194; ideology of colonial conquest, 194-195; significance of, for Guinea Coast, 225; change with rise of imperialism, 258; competition with oil trade, 259 ff.; degrading consequences, 277; economic results, 277-282; political damage by, 282 ff.; inferior mentality from, 288
Smith, William, quoted, 95
Songhay Kingdom, slaves in, 13
Stokes, Captain, quoted, 56
Sugar growing: by slaves in West Indies, 48; expansion of slave trade from, 58; introduced in French West Indies, 59; Britain loses market, 74
Summing-up, 273-290
Swedish African Company, 55

TOBACCO PLANTING, extension of slave trade from, 59
Tobago, occupied by Dutch, 58
Towerson, gold voyages by, 42; quoted, 52-53
Tribal names, 103-104
Tristão, Nuño, 36; capture of Africans by, 35-36
Tuat (oasis), 3

USMAN DAN FODIO (FULANI CHIEF), 14-15

INDEX

VASSALISM, compared with slavery in United States, 20-21. *See also* Feudalism

WARD, W.E.F., on Ashanti, 251-252
Warri, King of, 280
West India Company, 55
West Indies: penetrated by Europeans, 58; English speculation in, 60-63
Western Sudan, status of "slaves" in, 13

Wheeler, Charles, on African society, 98-99
Williamson, J.A., quoted, 43
Windham, Thomas, 41
Winterbottom, Thomas, on slave trade, 70-71

YORUBAS, 103-105, 203-204

ZANZIBAR, slave trading in, 191 ff.
Zhinga, Queen of Matamba, 151-152
Zurara (Azurara), G. E. de, quoted, 33, 35